"Writing my story with the Ignite team was so smooth. I love the editors and the process. I learned a ton from it. And it's a lot of fun. So get in there, before all spots are taken. You won't regret it."

~ Toma Molerov, Marketer & Coach, Malaysia

"My lifelong dream to write a book came true when I joined the Ignite community! Being part of the Ignite writing process was not only easy and fun, it was transformational in helping to awaken the story within me. It has catapulted me in creating a life that I love based some of the foundational Ignite Steps I've distinguished in my story. The Ignite books are cleverly designed for the author AND reader to awaken to a new perspective, gain insights on what's possible and choose actions that can create their reality. Being part of the Ignite community is truly a dream come true.

-Natalie Syrmopoulos, Canada

"My illustration was born from the purest of LOVE for all beings. It resembles my emotional journey I went through in reaching my Ignite moment for this book. This is my humble gift of LOVE and gratitude to my beautiful mum who I miss every day, the amazing IGNITE community and you dear reader…"

~ Gordana Hay, Belgrade

Contents

FOREWORD BY
NICOLE GIBSON

CEO & Founder, Love Out Loud

"Love isn't finding perfection, it's the unconditional permission to explore imperfection." The first line of my book, and a realization that changed my life forever. How would it be if humans remembered that we were given this life to embrace everything that makes us... us? If we met each other's flaws with adoration, compassion, and curiosity? If we began to feel into just how natural it is for us to choose love and acceptance?

I spent the first two years of my career traveling through the Australian desert, working with communities. Every day, my focus was to serve others and hold space for their stories to emerge. I noticed that the less I interfered with the space, the less I held onto judgments or opinions, the deeper others would share. It was profound. I started to recognize, through the diversity of individuals I met, that fundamentally we are all walking each other home. There is far more of what makes us the same than what separates us. When we learn to meet each other in love, anything becomes possible. We transcend the need for power, control, manipulation, and force. We become unified in a moment, and it is here that humanity meets its true power.

Here's the thing; love is not a damsel in distress or a knight in shining armor. Love is the raw, messy, and uncharted areas of one's mind, heart, and soul. Love is the entry point into infinite possibility; the earthquake that shakes the grounds of everything you once thought was real in order to give you the profound opportunity to meet the truth of who you are.

Love is an accumulation of perfectly sequenced imperfections that allows you to see the world as an interconnected cosmos and permits you to receive the miracles available to us in each moment.

Love's poetry aside, there's one important thing to consolidate here: love is a verb. The action of love is required so immensely in the world right now as we awaken to a new way of being and are invited to create a more unified and connected planet. Choosing love is a practice present in every moment, every day. And it is especially important to choose love when met with challenges and resistance internally or externally.

How did I awaken to this? I wish I could say that I just arose one day and declared that I was going to be a messenger of love. It wasn't so simple. I went through years of suffering and immense battles with control and perfectionism, only to realize that my mind was futile in the face of love. That although we can spend our lives attempting to control a force — one that is inevitably going to conquer — we can't. In surrendering my pain, in allowing myself to be communicated to and guided by a power much greater than me, I realized that we have the potential to experience a true kind of heaven on Earth when we open the gates of our heart and choose to devote ourselves to trusting in the arms of love. This is a path designed for warriors.

After recovering from a lived experience with anorexia nervosa through my teenage years, I had many realizations about the path I wanted to pursue in life and how I saw priorities. Living within a self-created prison for so many years, I began to see how fragile life truly was. One very profound thing I learned through this experience was that a life lived within self-orientation creates suffering, isolation, and misery. Every thought I had around how others perceived me took me away from being available to the present moment and its gifts. Being given a second chance at life, I recognized the importance of transcending our ideas of self. I began to recognize the power of love and it's capacity to support us in finding meaning, purpose, and connection to the world beyond us.

When I was 16, my health was in a critical place. I felt so alone and invisible in my experience; on the one hand, so needing love and support, yet so ready to dismiss and reject it. In the midst of this, it was one of the most unlikely characters who left the most indelible mark on my life and evolution.

My school principal approached me one day during a school lunch hour — at best, a very tense time for me. He asked if I could speak to him in his office.

Immediately I was overcome by shame, panic, and an incredibly immense desire to run. Following him back to his office, I could feel my heart beating out of my chest. I felt a strong apprehension that he was going to, in fact, confront me about my health. When I arrived at his office, he sat down at his desk and invited me to sit in the seat opposite with a wave of his hand.

I was terrified. The tension I could feel in our physical space felt like a suffocation, creating a sense of physical disablement. In my fragile state, I was unable to fight the resistance in my body and couldn't bring myself to sit in proximity with him. I walked to the corner of the room and sat down to try and give myself some oxygen. I braced myself, feeling my whole body tense and contract. What he said next was one of the most powerful and unexpected things I have ever heard:

"Nicole, I'm not here to cause you to feel afraid or tell you that there's something wrong with you... I just want you to know that you're not alone in going through what you're going through."

I began to sob. Then cry, uncontrollably.

For the first time, amidst all the pain, I had a space where it was safe to come as I was. I felt a mix of relief and deep grief, finally coming to terms with the fact that I needed help. I felt exposed and raw.

After a while, my principal asked me a question.

"Do you know what my favorite thing to do after school has always been?"

I shook my head.

"It's to have a beer. A cold beer. Every single day for 30 years."

I frowned, feeling confused by his question and his answer, and wondered if this was his suggestion for what might alleviate some of my pain.

He opened the drawer to his desk and got out a piece of paper and pen. He began to write, then signed the piece of paper as though it was a contract and stuck it on his wall with sticky tape.

It read, "I will not have a beer until you hit your weight target."

I realized that I had been avoiding his eye contact this whole time, so I brought myself to lock eyes with him. It was uncomfortable and almost painful to be present with his kindness and generosity of spirit. He had such warmth in his blue eyes. Struggling to comprehend this gesture, I allowed myself to receive him. How could someone care so much about my situation as to invest through their own sacrifice?

I asked him, "Why would you do this for me?"

"Nicole, I will never understand what it's like to be a 16-year-old girl going through what you're going through; however, I do understand what it feels like to be climbing a mountain that feels impossible to get to the top of… and to be doing that alone."

He paused.

"I just don't want you to feel alone in this."

This moment changed the trajectory of my life. It taught me something that became extremely defining to my whole journey. It taught me the power of love.

It taught me that love has the power to shift someone's entire timeline. That to love is to lead. That to love is to powerfully transform the status quo. Although my recovery was not immediate, through the space I was offered in love, I was given a torch to see the light I felt so estranged from. I realized that we *all* have the power to turn the light on for others; that it is, in fact, our *responsibility* to do so. To elevate each other and walk each other home.

In life, we are only ever making two choices: love or fear. You're either saying yes to the moment, or you're saying no. You're either stepping toward expansion or you're contracting. When we're in contraction, when we're rigid, fixed, and afraid, we are rejected. We're creating a separation between ourselves, others, and life. We're allowing hesitation to build a self-made prison of doubt and self-orientation. We're failing to understand the gifts that are ever present.

What I've also come to realize is that, for the most part, our world, as well as the societies and cultures that exist within it, has operated predominantly from a place of fear. Building systems with symptoms like oppression, limitation in thinking, prejudice, and mental illness. Feeding the perceptions of separation and difference. We've forgotten that our strength can only lie in our solidarity and our unification.

After working in the field of mental health both as a Commonwealth Commissioner and CEO of a Non-Profit based in Australia, I realized something very important and profound. I realized that these challenges we're facing as a human species are not the problem, they are the *symptom*. They are the symptom of an imbalanced and unnatural system. Every system is perfectly designed to create the outcomes it creates. When we have systems built on fear and scarcity, we in turn create more fear and scarcity in the world.

Having worked within 'the system' for many years, I recognized that we can change all the policy in the world, yet it won't necessarily translate to changing the way you and I show up every day. Changing policy doesn't always change human hearts. There are many things that are considered illegal, yet there are still criminals. There are many laws set to protect human rights, yet human rights still remain in violation globally. The only way to truly create change in a lasting, sustainable, and powerful way is when we learn to show up differently. It's when we learn our individual responsibility to serve the greater good.

It is when we begin to see through the lens of love that we're able to properly progress and find solutions that create true impact. It's not until we see with love that we are then able to create systems from love. We will never be able to create progressive solutions in our world with the same thinking that created them.

It's not until you and I have found the source of love within us that we're able to give and receive it freely. Just as the tree takes water through its roots from the ground so it can produce oxygen for life, or how the waves in the ocean travel thousands of miles to gracefully crash with no resistance on the shoreline, we too must learn the harmony and ease that love invites us into. Love provides us with a strategy to endure life difficulties with a strong sense of directionality and grace. It provides us with a purpose beyond ourselves and an ability to transcend the limitations of time and space.

This is my call to you as you journey through the stories of love throughout this book: open your own heart to new possibilities and a new way, for heaven on Earth is simply a choice that hasn't been chosen yet. Compassion is the true key to our evolution as a species, as it leads us down the path of unity. One family, one planet, one choice. So, choose love.

Introduction by
JB Owen

Founder and CEO of Ignite

Love: The Inside Scoop

When W. S. Gilbert first said, "It's love that makes the world go round," he was absolutely correct. From the fierce and powerful love of a mother cuddling her child to the passionate love of two intertwined bodies; from the bowing reverence of loving one's God to the gleeful love one feels for their job, craft, or sport; love fills the heart and moves the soul.

Love IS the one language we universally understand and desire. If you asked a million people from every corner of the globe what is the one thing they treasure the most… they would probably say love. Love from a spouse, a friend, a partner, a child, and a parent are just a few of the many forms of love we, as humans, seek. In fact, our need for love is so strong that we will climb mountains, travel through perils, give up everything, and do almost anything to experience it.

From the moment of our birth, we are often dipped like chocolate strawberries into the adoring love of our parents, grandparents, and family members. We learn immediately how glorious love feels. We learn that our world is wonderful as we receive love. Over time, love comes and goes in waves of elation and bliss followed by storms of sadness and separation. We endure the crests and falls of love because it feels so grand both in the pursuit of it and the high of obtaining it.

There is no surprise that love touches us all in many different ways. Friendly love. Neighborly love. The love of a sibling, a co-worker, a congregation member, or a devoted mate. Yet the deep desire for the 'love of self' trumps them all. The peace and contentment that comes with loving self is the highest form of all love; the bliss in obtaining self-love is the biggest, greatest, and most satisfying love of them all.

This may seem cliche to some. In fact, many will attest to love being spurred on by a multitude of sources; a romance, a success, a religion. Outside factors have often triggered love in different ways. Yet it is the love from within that truly uplifts the soul and changes the heart to not just feel love but gift it to others.

We have been told that one cannot truly love another until one loves themselves. This is a common belief for many, and it is in this quest for ultimate love that we seek it elsewhere so we can, in turn, find it within ourselves. Self-love is the truest form of love; when we have it, we tend to give it to others more often. Love from within is the flame that grows more love in other areas, like love for your country, for humanity, and for the infinite Universe. Inner love is like an engine on full output and enables unconditional love to flow freely outward in a multitude of ways. The birth of love is the birth of peace and harmony for all human beings. It is that love that we wish to create more of so that all the people of the world may enjoy it.

The Collective of Love

This book is a collection of stories fostering, creating, and basking in love of every ilk. In these pages, you will find a plethora of tales that orbit love from every angle. These are the true, raw, and real stories of individuals who have forged the trail to find love, feel love, embrace love, and accept love in all its many forms. These are deeply personal accounts of all the many facets of love. Like the sparks of light emanating from a diamond sitting boldly on a velvet pouch, these stories are the glimmering reflections of how love touches our lives completely and shines brightly in our hearts.

Of course, just as a diamond needs pressure, conflict, and time to fuse, these stories are the same. Like the rare beauty of the precious stone, these accounts lay bare the elements of fusion, form, and fascination. They come in all the kaleidoscopic colors of a diamond's shard, and they hold the same extravagant worth and priceless value that the rarest diamond ever held.

The best thing is that each of the stories transverses the path to love uniquely. They show how feeling love is not a one-way ticket nor straight like an arrow. The blossoming of love is more like a vine than a rose, as it takes many twists and turns to reach its destination. These stories show how awakening to love can happen like a whisper or converge like a tsunami, yet the deep inner knowing of it always leads back to self. While the true essence of love is often sparked by another individual or another source, the absolute feeling of its wholeness comes from within.

Like our authors, you, too, may be on your own journey of finding love. It may have eluded you until now. You may have had it then lost it, or it may be brimming in your heart currently and happily filling your cup. Or it may be like mist in the wind and the notes of a song; close but not within your grasp. However love is showing up (or not showing up) in your life will most likely be reflected in one, if not more, of the stories in this book.

We know that love is a tender subject. Some days it is brimming forth; others, it is pained and waning. Wherever you are on your love endeavor, we wanted to make our stories match your moods. To make this book even more enjoyable to read, we created a legend to help guide you to the perfect story to support your needs. In the top right-hand corner of each chapter, you will see a row of symbols indicating the tone and type of story the author has written.

Some of the stories are all about *new* love swirling in romance. Others are about a love that brought *healing* and new awareness. You'll find stories that center around self-acceptance and *self-worth*, while others push the boundaries and touch on the newer, *expanded* love paradigms. The symbols adorning each story are simply a guide, should you want a story to warm your heart or awaken your senses. You might be wanting something sentimental, or feel open to something a tad bit controversial. The legend is there to help you select the story that will fit your mood.

We are proud that this book has within it many stories from many different sources. Like its multi-colored cover, it reflects the many faces of all people. Color, creed, gender, preference, desire, and devotion are all represented within the pages of this book. Conventional is present, yet so is unconventional. Love does not discern but instead welcomes all, embraces everyone, and allows many forms to exist. Ignite is proud to be a microcosm of the world and the stories here represent each and every walk of life with pride.

New
Love

Conscious
Love

Expanded
Love

Healing
Love

Self
Love

Transformative
Love

Light Up and Love Up the World

Now more than ever, love is the cure the world needs. Each one of the individuals in this book stepped forth to write their story knowing that, on this planet, what we need more of is love. Love heals. Love changes people. Love opens up ideas, welcomes collaboration, and fosters friendships. Love is the medicine we can all take to heal the hurts of our past, and it becomes the fuel to push us forward into a better future. Love is a healer, a beacon, a catalyst, and an igniter.

This book was written on the premise that we need more love in the hearts of all. That, with love, we can overcome any challenges and erase any differences. Love is the universal common denominator in us all. With more of it, we can do more, be more, and unite more. We can fill our hearts and nurture our souls in a positive way so that we all feel filled in our own lives. We believe that if each of us is bountiful in love, then love will bring forth both positive change and benical connections to the world as a whole.

Our wish as a community of authors is that when you read these stories, you will be deeply transformed by the individuals who opened their hearts and shared their deep and honest truths. We hope that you are Ignited by the loving and intimate stories of people who are fanning the flames of love in all its aspects. We want our desires to kindle a desire in you: the desire to bring forth more love in your life and, in turn, to the people around you.

Our authors wrote their stories so that you can learn from their profound relationship with love. Each author eloquently shared how love snuck into their life and blossomed like a blue-ribbon winner at the state fair. Every word they shared was lovingly written with the intention of inspiring a personal, heart-felt transformation in *your* life. They wanted to be the ones to hug you tightly and guide you supportively as you embark on a life-changing journey into your own self-love. They know that love isn't easy; it's not always clearcut and it is sometimes elusive. However, they also know that discovering love can also be glorious, powerful, and healing. They each offer their kindred connection and support you in your quest for love however it unfolds.

As you read the upcoming pages, you will find every story starts with a *Power Quote*. It is a self-affirming, self-empowering statement that inspires. It is what you would want to hear to pick you up and, at the same time, lift you up. Power quotes are phrases that you can use when you need a little encouragement. They are statements meant to create thought, insight ideas, spark action, and evoke change. Every power quote is designed to remind you of what you have within you, what you know you can accomplish, and how your life is yours to make amazing.

Below the power quote, you will see each author's personal *Intention*. These are the genuine insights and powerful wishes the author wants to share to inspire you. They are their heartfelt messages filled with purpose and meaning. Each author wants to IGNITE more love in you and they share in their intentions how they hope their story will do just that for you.

Their *Story* follows as an honest account of how they found love and made the most of it. Through their stories, they explore and explain how love changed them and helped them become a better version of themselves. They share their vulnerable feelings and authentic emotions of consciously awakening to the *Ignite* moment that resulted in a magnificent understanding of love. We all have *Ignite* moments that change us, define us, and set us on a beautiful new path or exploration. These stories are those moments told in the most honest and heartfelt way. They show that *life-altering* moments not only impact us but ultimately inspire us to love ourselves and those around us more completely.

Once you have read their stories, you will find a list of *Ignite Action Steps*. These are doable actions our authors took to overcome the obstacles and push past the hardships that come with aspiring to love. Each author shares the most effective ideas, processes, and practices that worked in their lives for you to implement into your life to envelop yourself in more love. Each Ignite Action step is different and unique, just like you are, and each has proven to have lustrous results when done consistently.

The goal of an action step is to inspire you to close the book and go try it. Or, to wake up the next day and implement it into your life so as to bring forth more love. Be it outside love, inside love, immense love, or all-encompassing love, love is the richest comedy there is and these action steps are designed to harvest more of it in your life, every single day.

As you begin reading the book, know that many readers flip to a page at random and read from there, trusting that the page they land on holds the exact story they need to hear. Others read the table of contents, searching for the title that best resonates with them. Traditional readers start at the beginning, while others will go directly to a story recommended by a friend. However you decide to devour this book, we believe it will be perfect and right for you. We know that you may read it cover to cover in one single sitting or pick it up and put it down a dozen times over a long period of time. The way you enjoy an Ignite book is as personal as every story in it, and we give you complete permission to read it your way and in your style.

What we do ask is, if a story touches you or in some way inspires you, that you reach out and tell the author. Your words would mean the world to them. Since this book is all about love, we want to grow more of that among us. Feel free to share your sentiments with the authors by using their contact info at the end of their chapter. Every author would love to hear from you and know how their story impacted your life.

If writing your own story is percolating to the surface, please reach out to Ignite. If you have a story to share (which we all do) and feel compelled to begin writing yours, we want to hear from you. We believe every person has a story and everyone deserves to be seen, heard, and acknowledged for their story. If your words are longing to come forth, we want to support you in making that happen. Our desire is to ignite a billion lives through a billion words, and we can only do that together.

As you dive into the upcoming pages, Love is about to fill your heart. We embrace you right from the start, from the beginning, saying, welcome. Join us. You are loved. We want this to be the book that awakens and blesses your life forever. May you be loved and adored completely from this page onward.

Much love,
JB

IGNITE
LOVE

PETER GIESIN (PG)
AND JB OWEN (JB)

"Be Legendary in Love."

Our intention is for the reader to discover that love is their destiny. Love is an adventure. It takes courage and fortitude to find the love you have always desired. Your experience of love will be different only when YOU are different. Love takes a willingness to step into the unknowingness; loving yourself and awakening to what matters within you.

LEGENDARY IN LOVE

PREFACE

*The story you are about to read is a modern-day fairy tale;
it is our adventure of finding true love.*

Once upon a time…

(This is how all fairy tales start: two people looking for love, one lost, the other searching; one in a tower, the other fighting a dragon.)

(PG) At the age of 45, I found myself in a unique and unexpected situation; one that I knew would change my life forever. I was proud of myself for attacking the situation head on with the courage only a devoted and loving father could have. At the same time, I was shaking in my boots at the responsibilities that stood before me: my 8-year-old daughter and my 14-year-old son. I had just become a single father, provider, and sole caretaker of two precious human beings.

This was a foreign concept to me. It was my belief that marriage and love, which I naively (and maybe a bit foolishly) considered to be one and the same, would last forever. To me, when two people committed themselves to each other and started a family, this became an eternal vow not to be broken. Why would I think that? My parents had been married for over 45 years, weathering whatever hardships were thrown at them with grace, and showed no signs of ending. This new broken paradigm of mine shattered my vision of love like a car windshield struck by a rock. My wife had left me and I couldn't fathom that could have happened to me.

Understanding why, assessing the damage, and especially finding love, all had to take a back seat as my priorities shifted away from me and toward my two kids. I no longer mattered. My only responsibility was to ensure that they were safe and supported: physically, mentally, and emotionally. My number one concern was that they didn't become a statistic of divorce; that they continued to thrive and prosper, and felt unconditional love.

Over the next four years, I closed my heart and body to love and slowly receded into the dark caverns of my soul. I told myself it was because my kids needed my undivided attention. In reality, I was lying to myself. I didn't want to put myself out there again just to be hurt. In fact, I had resolved to be the old man sitting watching TV in my white t-shirt, a TV dinner in front of me, all alone. That seemed way easier than experiencing the heart-shattering pain of losing love, so I simply soldiered on, day after day, letting love become a fairy tale and allowing myself to die inside.

The part of me that didn't dwindle, however, was my need for adventure. In fact, that desire to experience the world began to grow into an obsession. I took every opportunity I could to travel to new and exciting destinations, try new foods, and expand my horizons. I found this new enthusiasm the perfect way to educate my kids while exploring what I wanted from life. That little old man sitting in front of the TV was no longer appealing.

(JB) At 45 years old, I lay in bed staring up at the ceiling, unable to sleep and listening for even the slightest sound. It had been close to a year of sleepless nights and troubled thoughts with my senses on high alert, hypervigilant should he come stumbling back, rattling my door handles, tapping on my window, sitting on my porch and pleading to come home. I had finally cut the cord on my tumultuous and unhealthy rebound relationship. Three years with a relapsing alcoholic had taken its toll on every fiber of my body, mind, and broken-down spirit.

Amid the endless exhaustion, frazzled nerves, and constant feelings of being off balance, my self-worth was at an all-time low. The father of my children was disgusted with my frivolous (and stupid) decision to hook up with my old high school sweetheart despite knowing he had been a drug addict and alcoholic in previous years. Naively I thought eight years sober meant he was sober going forward. Little did I know that the next drink and the next relapse was only mere fingertips away. My in-laws abhorred my situation and scornfully gave me their opinions each time they came to pick up or drop off their grandkids. My own parents were beyond compassion. They knew him from our younger years. They had seen the screaming matches between us, the endless break ups, his excessive partying and drinking for someone under age. They knew he had a temper and had seen first-hand the marks on me that proved it. My reconnecting with him fell far outside any sympathy or understanding they could muster.

I, of course, forgot all the drama of our high school years and leaped head first into a renewed love affair after my marriage ended. Although he was charming and sweet in the beginning, his alcoholic insanity showed up within months and led me down a disastrous trail — far worse than facing any ogres or dragons. I was the fish that jumped from one burning frying pan into the other, only to find the second one worse than the first. Love had taken its toll on me and I had sworn off men, romance, and anything to do with relationships.

I needed a reprieve. A reset. A renewed sense of self. I wanted to escape the town where he knew all my movements — what time I practiced yoga, what grocery store I shopped at, where and when my son had hockey practice. I deeply desired to take my two kids, ages 8 and 11, away from it all; removing them out of the hell they had been exposed to.

I dreamed of playing on the beach, seeing new sights, and breathing fresh air into our hearts — hearts that had been hardened by abuse and manipulation. Despite the concerned faces of my friends and frowns of disapproval from the school. I withdrew my children from their classes to set out on a year of uncharted travel to reclaim the happiness that had been lost.

This brings our adventurers to the ADVENTURE that would change their lives forever.

The Red Thread

(PG) It is 2 AM. I have been up for over 24 hours and now I am supposed to welcome my roommate and her two children (none of whom I have met, other than via a 15-minute phone conversation and trolling her Facebook™ page) into the apartment that we would be sharing for the next 30 days.

Before they arrive, let me quickly share how this strange meeting came to be. We were both attending this new personal growth immersion experience where 400 people move to a new city for 30 days and teach/learn/explore cutting-edge personal growth techniques.

I had rented a small, quaint 3-bed apartment in central Barcelona, Spain. Several months before the event was to take place, I received a message from the owner that he had to cancel my booking. Oh crap! In perfect Peter fashion, I sprang into action. The options were limited, but I finally located a 6-bed apartment for double the cost. Having no other choice, I booked it, resigned to the notion of eating the extra cost.

I woke up with buyer's remorse and almost cancelled the entire trip. I recalled reading on the event's Facebook page that other people were seeking roommates. My introverted self, shaking, with knots in my stomach, posted the following message:

Hi Gang!! I managed to find a cute little apartment in downtown Barcelona about 1 kilometer from the event location. It has one double bed and 4 single beds spread across 4 different rooms. I only need 3 beds for myself, my 17-year-old son, and 12-year-old daughter. We will be arriving May 26 and heading back to the US on June 20. I would be happy to share the extra three beds. PM if you are interested.

In less than an hour, I received a response from JB Owen. It turns out that JB had been traveling the world with her two children for the past nine months doing charity work. She sounded extremely nice. Her kids were of a similar age to mine. She was attending the same seminar as we were and she seemed normal enough, according to her Facebook page. I told myself, "What could possibly go wrong?" With a bit of trepidation dipped in optimism, we chatted via Messenger and agreed to be roommates.

My insides started to rumble a bit at the idea of meeting a new woman, especially one as beautiful and worldly as JB seemed to be. It had been three years since I had any feelings for a woman. I longed for the idea of being connected to someone both emotionally and physically. Exploring life by myself was boring and many times heart-wrenching, and I often missed those feelings of being committed to another person. But I did not want a relationship of any sorts. I didn't want the pain that I associated with love, so I immediately and emphatically shut those feelings down.

Buzz!!… Buzz!!… The loud ringer from the entrance signaled that JB and her kids were here. Given the late and ungodly hour, I leaned over and looked down from the balcony. I saw this beautiful woman with bleach blonde hair clad in shimmering rhinestones as if she just walked out of a nightclub. Beside her stood at least a dozen suitcases. I thought to myself…*They only have two small bedrooms. Where were they going to put all of that stuff?* I made my way groggily down the 4 flights of stairs to greet them. Having been traveling all year, they seemed to have developed a system. I stood there quietly and left them to it. Not very gentlemanly, I know, but I was a bit overwhelmed with the intensity… especially at 2 AM.

I did not in that moment actually see the red thread winding itself around me as JB walked into the apartment. I did feel a strange tingling sensation flow through my body as she brushed against me while heading to her room. Every part of me asked myself what the hell was happening. I wanted to immediately yank the door open and run. In fact, the next morning, I left with my two kids before anyone else was out of bed. I didn't want to see JB; more importantly, I didn't want to explore those feelings that had unexpectedly arisen in me.

(JB) "Be on your best behavior," I told my kids as we pulled up to a charming stone building deposited in the center of a walled-in row of apartments, smack dab in the coolest and most eclectic part of Barcelona.

Despite our 2 AM arrival, the street lights were bright and the headlight from the Uber dramatically illuminated decorative facades.

My kids and I had taken a late-night flight from the island of Ibiza directly into the large and historic city filled with modern Gaudí architecture. Despite being after midnight, the three of us were eager to meet the single dad from New Jersey and his two teenagers whom we would be sharing an apartment with for the next 30 days. A few months back, while world-schooling with my children, I decided to attend an alternative program devoted to people advancing their personal growth. I had been part of this self-help community for many years and this was the first time we would all be getting together and living in one city for a month. Since leaving Canada nine months before, I had been seeking new ways of living off the beaten path. My kids and I had been spending a month at a time in a new country doing charity work. This month was Spain and a chance to meet other families committed to advancing their education and self-development.

Originally I had rented a flat for just the three of us, but a water leak in the apartment left us scrambling to find a place on short notice. Desperate for suggestions, I went to the Facebook group for the event and saw on the rooming board a dad with his two kids who had a large apartment with three extra beds. Having spent the last nine months in casitas, on couches, in Airbnbs™, and even spending weeks in a treehouse, where we slept mattered little to us. Our year-long adventure was designed to break down our old life and go with the flow, jump at possibilities and welcome something new.

A few times, I joked with friends in emails that I was going to Spain to live with my new boyfriend, I just hadn't met him yet. I teased that I had agreed to cohabitate with a single dad and anything could happen. I made light of it; but deep inside, I knew nothing would come of it. I was going on two years of self-imposed celibacy and had made a private commitment that I would not let any man derail my precious time with my kids. Our trip was for us to heal, reconnect, and find laughter in our hearts again. I did not want them distrusting me or being put aside for a budding new romance. I owed them my undivided attention and devotion. Saying yes to sharing an apartment was mostly about reducing my rent costs and minimizing the potential of other guys hitting on me.

When Peter came to open the door sleepy-eyed and shy, I felt a wave of relief that the red thread had remained untangled and he would not be a distraction to my 'staying single' plan. He was quiet and a bit sheepish compared to the loud outspokenness of both me and my kids. He stood a bit shell-shocked as my son and I rattled our numerous suitcases across the cobblestone street, oblivious to the sound reverberating through the stillness of the night. We clanged open the steel gate to the tiny elevator and noisily stacked our suitcases inside, three high. We laughed loudly as we manoeuvred them on top of each other, then bickered as my 9 year old complained about.walking.up.the.four.flights of stairs because the elevator was too small. It took my son four tries to slam closed the elevator door and ascend upward. Anyone trying to sleep would have found it difficult. With Peter out of hearing distance, my son turned to me in the tiny lift and said... "Sorry, Mom. I don't think he's your guy."

The Moment

(PG) One would think that might have been my Ignite Moment when Cupid shot his arrow and I fell madly in love with JB. It is partially right. I think Cupid did fire the arrow, shooting straight and true; however, with over three years of a closed heart, the arrow simply grazed the surface. Little did I know that even that tiny knick was enough; I just needed time to find the love I was looking for.

The next 30 days were full of new people, new experiences, and new dreams. JB and I lived as roommates, friends, and fellow attendees; co-parenting our kids and interacting socially when the opportunity arose. I have to be clear that there was no romantic relationship, nor even an emotional attachment. She gracefully did her thing and I happily did mine. We walked together to the event, shared groceries, and took turns watching the kids. We'd visit over tea in the morning or chat while doing the dishes at night, but she had her circle and I was enjoying forming mine.

JB had been part of this community for over five years. She was a social butterfly and the bell of the ball... she knew everyone and wasn't afraid to show it. As a newbie, and with the limiting belief that I was an introvert, I kept to myself and rarely interacted with more than one or two people per day — JB being one of those people due to our living arrangements.

Even though I felt that she was well out of my league, I used our situation as an opportunity to learn and explore this new world of personal transformation.

Unbeknownst to me, this was Cupid's magic working from the inside out. Over the month in Barcelona, JB became the role model that I wanted to follow in my life. She was positive when I was negative; she was fun where I was boring; she was inspirational compared to my pessimism. I began to learn from her and see possibilities where they hadn't existed before.

When the event was almost over, JB suggested that I extend our trip by eight days and go to Rome with her. I jumped at the opportunity. Some one-on-one time with her to process everything I had heard and experienced was exactly what I needed. It was like going to the mountain with Mohammed. I knew I would leave this experience a changed man and I was not wrong. Every day, we talked about life, past experiences we had (mainly hers), our dreams and aspirations, and the changes one needs to make so that we can manifest our reality. I was enamoured with her presence and the confidence she had to be her own person and live outside of the norm.

A week later, with a bit of longing, we parted ways. I didn't want the learning to end, nor did I want to think about not seeing JB every day. Our time together had become special; something I looked forward to and deeply enjoyed. We spent every waking moment together exploring Rome, talking non-stop about business, travel, life, and even past love. Looking back, I realize that our connection was moving beyond that of just roommates; but at the time, I was clueless and simply let it slide by. With quaint goodbyes and a small peck on the cheek, I returned back to the world from which I had taken this fairytale adventure. I never expected to see or hear from her again. I only hoped that I had learned enough to continue the transformation on my own.

Much to my surprise, JB and I continued to talk every day. The conversations easily shifted from business, meditation, and personal fitness to what each of us was doing, how the kids were, and how we missed each other. It shouldn't have been a surprise that, shortly after JB returned home, I found myself on an airplane headed to 'help her unpack,' as she had just moved back home into a new house.

I laugh now when remembering how little unpacking happened during my stay. This was the first time since we had met that it was just JB and I. We cycled, we juiced, we talked. And for the first time, romance entered the picture. Cupid's magic was in full bloom.

The Universe unfortunately had a different idea. Sensing my trepidation, it decided to put me to the test. The day after JB and I were intimate for the first time, I timidly walked into her office to share that I needed to leave immediately due to a death in my family. I took the bait the Universe had laid out, not even considering JB's feelings, and I had her drop me off at the airport a couple of hours later.

My heart slid shut with a clang as the voice in my head said, *"This wouldn't work. We live 3000 miles apart. I don't want a long-distance relationship. I don't want to be on an airplane every couple of weeks. I don't want to hurt her. I don't want to be hurt again."*

With those feelings pounding in my chest, I departed with no hope of pursuing what might have been. I spent the next three days with my family, grieving… not over the loss of my aunt but once again over the loss of love, short lived as it was.

The red thread was frayed and near breaking. I didn't have the courage to even call JB. It was much easier to let the scab heal over and just go back to my old existence. The good news, however, was that JB, in true form and connected to the Universe much more than I was, decided not to give up so easily.

A few days later, she boldly picked up the phone. She shared her condolences, we exchanged some niceties, and then she let go with her full power.

"Not sure why you don't trust the Universe? I think that there is more in play than just a long-distance romance. We don't know what is in store for us, but shouldn't we at least give it a try? It is up to us to make this work. What do you truly want, Peter?"

I knew at that moment that this was the woman, the connection, and the commitment to love that I had dreamt of my whole life. This was the devotion and conviction I had witnessed between my parents for the past 50 years. I said, "I've been a fool. I will do whatever it takes to make this work. I want us to do more than just love one another; I want us to be Legendary In Love."

(JB) I am not sure why I said it; it just felt normal and right. A few nights before our month together was about to end, I asked Peter, "Why don't you extend your trip and come with us to Rome?" I was continuing my year of travel with a few more months left before the kids and I would go back to Canada and live closer to my mother. Peter nonchalantly said yes, and while the others at the event said good-bye, the six of us playfully whisked off to continue our adventure.

Eating the world's best pizza, taking pictures at the Trevi Fountain, and standing extra close while in line at the Vatican sparked a few feelings in me that I tried to push down. Life was becoming calmer with Peter. His gentle demeanor, loving support, and wit with directions brought an ease to our travels and more fun to our exploring. Our kids got along famously, freeing Peter and I for long bouts of conversation and lingering time to philosophize. And for some wonderful reason, he just loved it when I talked and he always listened intently.

I admit that I started to have feelings one night over *carrapicho* and wine. The kids were in the hotel room, tuckered from a long day of cannonballs in the pool, and for a brief delightful dinner, Peter made me feel like a woman, not a mom. We eventually parted and he returned to the United States, yet our communication continued. We spoke almost every day and debates about theories and ideas shifted to sharing family events, what the kids were up to, and plans for the future.

When I returned to Canada after 12 months of traveling, I found it challenging to reintegrate. Even though I moved back to my hometown to be close to my mom, I didn't know anyone. Conversing with Peter became my lifeline as I picked away at unpacking boxes. I felt bored and lonely, as my kids had gone to spend the last bit of summer with their father. Peter and my constant chats were the best part of my day.

To my surprise, Peter offered to fly to Canada and 'help me unpack my boxes.' I was thrilled he was coming, elated for the help, yet nervous he would see me in my home, somewhat more vulnerable than I had been before. It felt intimate and personal, something we had not had to deal with in our cute little apartment or Airbnbs. His arrival was wonderful and without skipping a beat, we fell into a domesticated rhythm of running, cooking, taking long walks, and sitting side by side while working on our computers. Peter is the kindest and most adoring person I had ever known and when I found him snoozing on the couch one night, my heart melted to his presence in my life. I knew he had become my best friend and everything we did was a fit. For the first time in years, I wanted to be held, loved, and honored — by him.

After spending so much time with Peter, falling into the depths of his arms came easily. Letting down my walls and shedding my hard coating was both magical and amazing. The next day, with the butterflies of intimacy still fluttering in my stomach, Peter announced he had to leave. There was a death in his family and he had to fly home immediately. Graciously I agreed, but once he walked away to go pack his suitcase, the tears poured down my cheeks. How cruel of a joke the Universe had played on me. I had resisted feeling any emotions for so long and the day after I gave in, he had to leave and our private time together was over.

But the red thread of connection had been intertwined between us and, despite his lack of communication after he returned to the US, my mind and heart were invested. I knew it was no coincidence that he had rented that big apartment, that I had lost mine, that of all the people on Facebook, we saw each other's post. The chances of him traveling alone with his kids and me traveling with mine to the same event, extending our vacations, staying connected, and finding our way back to one another across two countries proved it was something extraordinary.

Days later, when we finally spoke, his demeanor had changed. His energy was different. Sadly, his reality, practicality, and sensibility had crept in.

"I think we should just be friends. I respect you too much to hurt you. Our kids' feelings are a factor and I don't want a casual connection. I am not willing to hurt one another over long distance. You live 3000 miles away. I'm sorry, I can't see it working out. "

My kids like to say that Peter 'friend zoned' me that day. I like to say he put me in the box reserved for other people; not us. Not the two amazing people who found each other halfway around the world and spent a blissful time getting to know one another void of pretenses and artificial behavior. Compassionate to his fears, I told Peter that we are the lucky ones and we needed to trust the *Masters* had masterfully conspired to bring us together, against all odds, and we are foolish to believe that they will not provide a perfect solution for our future. Despite both of our inability at the time to see the 'how' behind fostering our love, I simply asked him, "Why would you want to be just friends when you could have so much more?"

Happily Ever After...

(PG) Three weeks later, I locked the door of my house and unlocked my heart. I headed to the airport with my two kids and our six suitcases for a 'tester semester' in Canada. JB and I had decided to listen to our intuition and trust that WE were both worth it. I stepped off my porch with nothing but courage and the confidence that this was the woman of my destiny. I felt her feminine power from across the continent awakening my masculine from it's deep slumber. I was ready for TRUE LOVE and willing to do whatever it required to honor the feelings we shared. I knew from the depths of my soul that this was exactly what the Universe had planned, and I was all in.

For a time, I had felt that love was nothing more than a fairytale dream. I believed that anyone who said they were in love was crazy and kidding themself. Love was just a figment of their imagination. I was completely and wholeheartedly wrong in my thinking. I realized the true meaning of love; that two people can connect so deeply, surpassing the realms of logic, and create the reality that they desire. Love is more than just a word. It's more than just a simple emotion shared among lovers. It is our ultimate destiny to love another and experience true bliss in our lives.

That semester turned into two, and then into a year, and happily continues to this day. On our wedding night, I confidently told JB, "I will do everything in my power to have you fall in love with me every day." I had learned that *that* is what true love takes. It doesn't just happen. Each person in the relationship has to show up every day, first for themselves and then for their partner. I do my best to hold myself to this promise. If you do the same, you will find a love and devotion in your relationship that you didn't even know existed.

(JB) While in Barcelona, I celebrated my 47th birthday. I remember feeling the deepest love I had ever known; the love I felt for myself and the beautiful life I had created with my kids. I decided that if I was going to be alone for the rest of my life, I was okay with it. If what I had was all I was going to get, I was thankful. I felt a massive amount of love from my kids, my friends, and my family. I was living life on my terms and, for the first time, a true sense of contentment settled into my being. I was no longer searching for love and, when I stopped trying to find it, it ever so sweetly found me.

Standing at the airport waiting for Peter, Jorja, and Jackson to arrive, I shifted from one foot to the other not because I was nervous, but because I was excited. I told Peter he and his kids were a package deal and loving him meant loving them also. My heart had blossomed during my time with them, expanding past the limits of loving one person and growing into loving three. My deepest hurt had led me to find my greatest love; one I had always believed was possible but which had eluded me until I took the time to stop searching and start loving myself.

I realized that when we look outside ourselves for love, we don't see the greatest love there is: the one within ourselves. When we bask in that kind of love, we allow ourselves to love another more completely, succinctly, and profoundly. We see past the ideas and beliefs around love and we touch the very core of another's existence. We go beyond the thought of love and swim freely in the effortless bliss of one person's deep acceptance and affection for the other.

Finding love is yours to discover. You can travel the world or you can find it right at home. Regardless of where you go, deep, unabashed love begins in you and then radiates outward. Look within and you will find what you are looking for. Be willing to say yes when your head says no. Don't settle when you can have so much more. Take chances and trust that the Masters are always working diligently for you. Most of all, when you find the right and special person, promise to be Legendary in Love.

Epilogue

The next year, Peter and I took all the kids and traveled to Tallinn, Estonia to attend the same personal development event where we had met; this time happening in a new location. For 30 days, all six of us immersed ourselves in the top training on personal psychology, biohacking, self-development, and mindset. It was fantastic to see all the people we had met the year before in Barcelona and to witness their faces when they found out Peter and I had kindled a relationship together. Many knew we were roommates the year before, but not all knew Peter had packed up his life and moved to Canada where we were blissfully living as one blended family.

Those who knew us well were delighted we had fallen in love. Those who heard our story were inspired by the notion that one never knows when your perfect person is right around the coroner, and how powerful it can be to say *yes* to love. We became the beacon of hope for many, proving that you don't have to know *how,* you just have to believe it is *possible.*

In full fairytale fashion, Peter and I married each other that summer in Tallinn. He was dashing in his full wedding attire. I wore a sparkling pink dress fit for a princess with a blush-colored crown and delicate pink slipper-like shoes on my feet. It couldn't have been more romantic or perfect. In front of 800 people, the girls and I rode an open-horse carriage into the massive cobblestone square at the center of the city. Peter and I said our vows standing on the steps of a beautiful 800-year-old church where all our friends could witness us pledge our life-long commitment to one another.

Tears of joy flowed, cheers of celebration erupted, and when it was over, Peter and I descended into the crowd where our guests, all holding hands, surrounded us and formed one enormous group hug. Hundreds of people took part in that hug, squeezing the person next to them, coming closer to the center, moving inward so that every single one of them felt embraced and loved. It is hard to describe the elation I felt from marrying the man of my dreams with my magnificent children at my side while being hugged joyously by hundreds of people all at once. If I had to put it into words, I would say it was love in its truest, most divine form. It was the pinnacle of what love is; a treasured moment where everyone felt love, willingly gave love, and became Love.

That day was an Ignite Moment for many. Others saw the power of love being possible; Peter and I saw the power behind inspiring love in as many people as we possibly can. This book and the Ignite company was born from the embers of that day. Together we have made it our mission to Ignite others and impact humanity in dreams, possibilities, and love. We want every person on the planet to feel love on the deepest level and to know love as intimately as they can. We believe sharing stories about love will do exactly that. Love will heal the world. Through love, anything and everything is possible for every one of us!

Ignite Action Steps

Commit to putting in the work of relationship development. Having an exceptional relationship will not happen without work. Set an intention, then sign up for a personal-development conference, read a new book, listen to a podcast, and even seek out therapy. The bottom line: when you have things in your life that you want to get better at, know it will take work and time to get closer to your goals. It's not often that we think about relationships in this manner; doing so will help remove any barriers that will keep us from having the relationship we want and deserve.

Come back to what's best for your relationship. How you *should* be in a relationship is normally learned from the experiences of *other* people; i.e., parents, friends, even celebrities or just society itself. They aren't in your relationship; you are. Resist the trap of comparing what you have with what others have. Keep coming back to what serves you and your partner best.

Check-in on your relationship regularly. Set the intention to take your relationship to the next level and then continue to check in with it. Ask yourself if you are supporting your partner in the way they need. Set a reminder in your calendar to touch base and check that you are both on the same page. Making minor corrections now before they become full-blown issues will go a long way to ensuring your relationship is on track.

Giving your relationship your full attention is how love grows. You know what you need, so be sure to give the same attention and devotion to your partner. What you give, you get; so give full out.

Peter Giesin - United States of America
CTO and Co-Founder of Ignite
www.igniteyou.life

JB Owen – Canada
Speaker, Author, Publisher
www.jbthepossibilityqueen.com
www.igniteyou.life
www.lotusliners.com
 jbowen
 jbthepossibilityqueen

ALEX JARVIS

"The beauty of life is to love and be loved, so let love in."

My desire is to provide you insight into each different type of LOVE in Greek Mythology so you may begin or expand upon your journey to awakening to the LOVE in your own life.

LOVE IS LOVE IS LOVE

Love. Ahhhhh… they say it makes the world go 'round. But does it? Does it always make us feel all warm and fuzzy inside? Or does it sometimes cause us problems in our relationships? Well, the answer is both.

We have all had our share of relationship problems — especially romantic ones. And when people say to me, "Relationships are hard," I always reply, "No, not necessarily. They are not inherently hard. *It's the people who make them hard.*"

Humans are inherently self-oriented. We all want to 'win.' We want to get other people to understand what we want and give it to us. One key to healthy relationships is understanding everyone gives and receives love differently. We all have our own ways in which love resonates within us. We tend to give love to others in that same way, regardless of how the receiver of our love needs to receive it.

Though forms of love are driven by affection and attachment, each of them is distinct. In society today, we are awakening to defining different types of love. Our view has expanded. The ancient Greeks seemed to understand these concepts well — there are eight words in the Greek language that describe love in all its nuanced forms. With any luck, you'll be able to experience each form in your lifetime — if you haven't already.

The ancient Greeks studied everything from public speaking to the stars in the Universe, and they studied love extensively, classifying it into eight different types. Let's take a look at the different versions of love that so fascinated the Greek philosophers so you can better understand and be fascinated by your own relationships in turn.

Agape — Unconditional Love

"Agape doesn't love somebody because they're worthy. Agape makes them worthy by the strength and power of its love. Agape doesn't love somebody because they're beautiful. Agape loves in such a way that it makes them beautiful." — Rob Bell

First, we have Agape love (Ancient Greek ἀγάπη, *agapē*, pronounced *a-GOP-aye*). Agape is a Greco-Christian term referring to an altruistic, selfless, unconditional love. The Greeks thought it was quite radical, perhaps because so few people seem capable of feeling it long-term. Some people would describe agape as a type of spiritual love. For instance, Christians believe that Jesus exhibited this kind of love for all humans. He suffered for the happiness of others.

Agape is all-giving love, not only concerned with the self but with the partner or with people needing compassion. It is said to be relatively rare, 'the highest form of love, charity,' and 'the love of God for man and of man for God.' The concept of agape has been widely examined within its Christian context. Our world has many definitions of love, but we most commonly think about love in a romantic sense. What if love — true love — meant more than romance? What if there was a deeper, richer, more full expression of love that could only be found in God or the Universe? Agape love is love at the highest level. It's so much more than we could ever dream or imagine.

Eros — Romantic Love

"Eros will have naked bodies; Friendship naked personalities." — C.S. Lewis

Eros is the name of the god of love, the son of Aphrodite, and he represents romantic Love in Greek mythology (Ancient Greek: Ἔρως, "Desire"). Eros can be creative, a sexual yearning, love, or desire: "The new playful Eros means that impulses and modes from other spheres enter the relations between men and women." Eros is romantic and passionate. In this type of relationship, love is life's most important thing. It is usually associated with romantic, passionate, and physical love. It is an embodied expression of sexual wanting and desire. The Greeks were actually quite fearful of this love, strangely enough. They thought that because human beings have an instinctual impulse to procreate, this love was so powerful that it would result in a loss of control.

Although the Greeks regarded Eros as dangerous, it is still the kind of love that is associated with passion and sex. In modern days, some people believe that this kind of love burns hot and bright, but it burns out fast. At least in the earlier stages of courtship, when everything is crazy-hot and you can't get enough of each other. Eros can and does persist throughout the life cycle of a relationship if it is nurtured. Eros is passion, lust, pleasure. It's an appreciation for one's physical being or beauty and is driven by attraction and sexual longing. It describes desire and obsession and is most similar to what we think of as romantic, passionate love between life partners.

Philia —Affectionate Love

"Love is what you've been through with somebody." — James Thurber

The Greeks defined Philia (Greek /ˈfiliə/; Ancient Greek: φιλία) as 'affectionate love,' the love you feel for your friends, often referred to as 'platonic' love — love without sexual acts. Ironically, the ancient Greeks thought this kind of love was *better* than Eros (sexual love) because it represented love between people who considered themselves equals. While a lot of people associate the word 'love' with romance, Plato always argued that physical attraction wasn't necessary for love, that a great respect and admiration for the inner world of the person was, in fact, love unencumbered by Eros.

Philia is characterized by intimacy, knowing, and soul-to-soul bonds. It's encouraging, kind, and authentic — the stuff from which great friendship is made, whether it's platonic or romantic. This love is based in goodwill or wanting what's best for the other person. Philia is a connection akin to that of soul mates; one part destiny, another part choice.

Philautia — Self-love

"be easy. take your time. you are coming home to yourself." - Nayyirah Waheed

Philautia (Fila-ftia), the concept of self-love and loving oneself is hardly new; the ancient Greeks attributed a deeper meaning to the word. For them, it encompasses two concepts. The first is that healthy, care-based love grounded in compassion. This can look like small rewards or gifts, like buying yourself a new book as a gift for completing a big work project; or it can look like self-care, pleasurable indulgences to relax and take care of your body. The other concept of Philautia is one rooted in ego. It can be pleasure- and fame-seeking or highly concerned with status. It can even be the foundation of narcissism. Philautia is not negative or unhealthy in any way. In fact, it's necessary if we are to give and receive love from other people. We cannot give to others what we don't give to ourselves. Another way to look at self-love is by thinking about it as self-compassion. Just as you might show affection, love, and compassion to another person, you should also show it to yourself.

Storge — Familial Love

"Love is the chain whereby to bind a child to its parents." — Abraham Lincoln

Storge (/ˈstɔːrgi/, from the Ancient Greek word στοργή *storgē*) is the protective, kinship-based love you likely experience with family members. You might love your sister, even if you don't like her, for instance; and you might love your dad, despite the mistakes he made in raising you. Storge is driven by familiarity and need. It is sometimes thought of as a one-way love. For instance, consider a mother loving her baby before the baby is aware enough to love her back, or even before the baby is born. Storge can also describe a sense of patriotism toward a country or allegiance to the same team. Storge is a slow-developing, friendship-based love. People with this type of love like to participate in activities together.

Storge can be defined as 'familiar love.' Although that's a strange term, this type of love feels a lot like Philia — affectionate love felt between friends. However, this love is more like a parent-child love with a strong bond, kinship, and familiarity between people.

Pragma — Enduring Love

"Two souls but a single thought, two hearts that beats as one" — John Keats

Pragma (comes from the Greek term πρᾶγμα) is a pragmatic, practical, mutually beneficial relationship. It may be somewhat unromantic and is some-times described as 'shopping list love' because a partner is selected on the basis of a series of traits or requirements. The ancient Greeks define pragma as 'enduring love,' almost the opposite of Eros (sexual love), which tends to burn out quickly because of its passion and intensity. Pragma is a love that matures and develops over a long period of time.

The kind of old married couples who have been together since their teenage years and still hold hands... well, that's a great example of pragma. This kind of love is rare and precious. It is filled with a great amount of connectedness. This form of love appreciates the magnificence and beauty of the partner you are with and the ones involved work consistently at supporting and growing their love every single day. And after years of joyfulness, it is effortless with both people making allowances and each person putting a loving effort into embracing the other person's happiness.

Ludus — Playful Love

"Each of us is a lake of love, yet strangely enough, we are all thirsty." — Anon

Ludus is known as the 'playful love.' It describes the situation of having a crush and acting on it. It's rooted in having fun. Ludus is definitely the love you'd experience with a fling — casual, sexual, exciting, and with zero implications of obligation. The ancient Greek word 'Ερωτοτροπία' is a toying and flirtatious expression of love. It is full of games and teasing. It is flirty, playful, and can be uncommitted. A person who pursues Ludus love may have many conquests but remain unattached. Some may say that a better way to describe it is the feeling of infatuation in the early days of romance. If you've had a crush before, you know what I'm talking about. It's the butterflies in your stomach, the giddiness you feel when you see your love walk through the door, and the feeling of never wanting to be without them. Studies show that when people are experiencing this type of love, the brain is lit up and active just like someone who is literally high on a drug. Ludus makes you feel alive and excited about life.

Mania — Obsessive Love

"Present over perfect, quality over quantity, relationship over rushing, people over pressure, meaning over mania." — The Free Woman

Mania (Greek: μανία) is not necessarily a good type of love. It is obsessive or possessive love and can be extreme. It's the type of love that can lead some-one into madness, jealousy, or even anger. A person in love this way is likely to do something crazy or silly, such as stalking. This is because the balance between Eros (sexual) and Ludus (playful) is terribly off. Many people who experience this type of love suffer from low self-esteem. They fear losing the object of their love and it compels them to do things in order to keep them. If not kept under control, mania can be very destructive.

Love is love is love

Ask yourself how these loves appear and feel in your life. With that aware-ness, you can expand your life by noticing how these loves surround you. Play with them, immerse yourself in them, and share them to enrich your life and those around you. *Love is love is love… So love yourself first and then full out.*

IGNITE ACTION STEPS

The process of loving begins with knowing who you are. No matter what type of love relationship you are hoping to create, you must begin with the Self. Write your intentions for what you desire in all the relationships around you. It took many years for me to figure out how to create love and receive love. But not a day goes by that I am not grateful for the LOVE in my life — love of myself and honoring myself was my first step. It doesn't have to take you long at all; follow your desire to your dream love relationships. After you've clarified what you want, it's time to flow your energy toward that dream. That's why taking a look at your beliefs is so important. Have fun with this… think of many action steps to create love in all areas of your life.

Live life as if you are in LOVE — sing, smile, come from a space of LOVE — show up in the energetic space of LOVE.

Spread LOVE wherever you go — create a positive connection with as many people as possible. Offer to help someone in need. Use your voice, speak out, and have eye contact with your community to create a loving environment.

I love ME — Learn how to connect to yourself. Love yourself. Be compas-sionate toward yourself. Start looking for LOVE with real intention — getting a clear sense of what you would like to experience. Look inward and look at yourself in a new and deeper way.

Make a decision that you want to find LOVE with real intention — Be committed to the processing of releasing the old and making room for the new. Form a deeper, more profound, and more accepting connection with yourself. Be happy and confident, as you will attract love with people who are aligned with your vibrational state.

Ask yourself about your needs and desires in your quest to find romantic partnership:

- What 5-10 words would you use to describe what you really want in a partner?
- What personality traits attract love but also help to bring out the very best in you?
- How do you want to be treated by a partner? When looking for love, what are the behaviors that you will simply never tolerate?
- What are your deepest, most heartfelt passions in life?
- What do you consider to be your life's mission? What sort of partner can be a teammate on the road to achieving this goal?

Make time for self-care. Connect and tune into your own needs. When you make a habit of this, you're much more able to attract love with someone who will nurture you. One way to ensure you take better care of yourself while you're looking for love is to set time aside where you commit to doing things you love and enjoy!

Challenge your limiting beliefs. Look at the underlying assumptions that hold you back, limiting beliefs that might block you from finding love. Write them down. Identify where they come from. Most importantly, write down a contradictory belief that you can then turn into a daily affirmation. Embrace and trust that you have the answers within.

In Summary... Expect the unexpected. Embrace the uncertainty — that's the beauty of love. You might not find love quite where and when you expected it. Keep an open mind and be alert to signs around you. These might come in the form of coincidences, repeated imagery, or chance meetings. Trust your intuition. Be still, in the very moment.

Alex Jarvis – Australia
Interior Designer, Rose Alchemist, Speaker, Author, CEO
www.jarvisinteriors.com.au

KATARINA AMADORA

"How you show up on the dance floor is how you show up in life."

Love is a dance that carries you through life. Partners may change but if you find joy in the dance, you will never be alone. My intention is that you fall more and more deeply in love with yourself every day. I pray that you look in the mirror each day with love in your heart, seeing the soul-deep beauty of the person who looks back at you. May you carry this energy through your day, dancing through life and magnetically attracting all the Love that you deserve and more.

DANCING WITH LOVE

I remember the first day that I walked into Sweet's Ballroom in Oakland, California. It was a Sunday morning. I had heard about Ecstatic Dance from a friend in Portland years ago, but it was on the east side of the city and I lived across the river in Northwest Portland. Somehow I could never get myself out of the house that early on a Sunday morning to drive across the bridge and check it out. Now here I was, back from Shanghai and living in the San Francisco Bay area again after two of the most stressful years of my life, finally finding my way to Ecstatic Dance.

The one constant companion that carried me through the challenging years that I spent moving from place to place and country to country every couple of years had been dance. Every time I had been required to uproot myself and my family to follow my husband's career, my saving grace had been finding and connecting with a dance community. In each new location, from Singapore to the Bay Area, from Portland to Shanghai and back to the Bay, dance had been my refuge. It gave me a place to find community, to connect with sisters, and to have somewhere I felt at home. As long as I had a place to dance, I felt that I belonged. The community of women who danced resonated with me in a way that touched my soul. It gave me a way to find new friends each time my family moved because there was a universal call that brought us together.

I didn't consider myself to be a good dancer. I was not as nimble as I once had been. I had been dancing for over 20 years and in all those years, the dancer I was in my head rarely manifested herself in reality. Bad knees prevented me from doing many of the things the younger dancers could do, yet my love of dance kept me coming back for more. I kept trying. I welcomed opportunities to perform and sought out different teachers who could push me to the next level. On a few occasions, this led to having a breakdown on the dance floor, in tears at the back of the class, unable to go on. I cursed my body for what it could not do. In spite of this, I never gave up. I always came back the next week, the next day, determined to master the choreography and to gain the muscle memory that was required to be able to reach the next level in dance.

It was never my intention to be a 'professional' dancer. I danced because dance was *Life*. It was the canvas through which I expressed what was inside of me. The good, the bad, and the ugly. I tried performing, getting over the fear of being on stage, endeavoring to get the moves perfect in ensemble pieces despite towering above the other dancers. I found that this type of rote choreography did challenge me, yet it did not call to my soul. I loved solo dancing because I could improvise. I could allow the music to flow through me and inspire my movements without having to look like the younger, more agile dancers. I found dance as an expression of *My Soul*.

On that particular fall day, I had finally made my way to Ecstatic Dance, knowing that my soul craved the creative release that dance gave me. I came into Sweet's Ballroom, this beautiful, huge art deco ballroom that was one of the earliest homes of Ecstatic Dance in the United States. I remember tentatively looking around. How amazing that I could be so close to one of the oldest and largest Ecstatic Dance communities in America! Talking was actively discouraged on the dance floor and people would hush you if you tried to start a conversation. I hardly knew anyone. How could I even learn their names if we could not talk? My years of dancing helped me to overcome my shyness as I joined in the dance. I found release after months of trauma, having to hold space for a daughter who seemed hell-bent on hurting herself... cutting... suicide attempts, and a husband who valued his career over keeping our family together.

I remember noticing one particular guy that day who did not seem to fit in. He was not dancing; he was hanging around the edge of the room. I saw him looking at some bags and went over to check on mine. Everything was okay. There was my iPad mini and a dance belt as well as a few other items. I left my bag on the side of the room and went back to dance. It was liberating, transporting me for a few hours away from the stress of my daily life. At the end of the dance, I went back to gather my things. Something was wrong. My iPad was not in my bag. It was gone. I went to the organizer and another woman was already there reporting that her wallet had been stolen. After that beautiful day of dancing and reconnecting to the music, we spent the next hour in the Oakland Police Department reporting the theft.

Someone else might not have come back to Sweet's Ballroom. They may have stayed home, fearful of taking another chance. In spite of this negative experience, the next Sunday, there I was again — undeterred. I was careful not to bring anything valuable inside this time, but I knew my soul needed this. I needed to be here as much as a person in the desert needed water.

In those early days of dancing with this community, I still felt a bit like an outsider. I knew very few names yet I came to know their faces. I often found myself looking around, wanting to initiate a dance with someone yet not quite knowing how. Sometimes someone would approach me, which could be blissful, playful, or even sexy. Sometimes I was successful in initiating a dance with someone else, yet other times I would try to make a connection and the person would gesture 'Namaste' and back away, the universal sign that indicated that they were not open to dancing. Part of me would collapse, berating myself for doing it wrong, for not reading their cues right. I made it mean that there was something wrong with me that they were not open to partnering. It didn't stop me though; I kept coming back for more.

I have taken dance workshops from many teachers. In one class, I learned the non-verbal cues to look for to see if someone was open to dance. This workshop, led by a professional West Coast Swing dancer by the name of Shantala Davis, was a wonderful introduction to how to communicate on the dance floor. She led a beautiful, dynamic exploration which allowed me to play with varying levels of connection, from mirroring someone to exploring dancing in their negative space, and then from there how to initiate connection in a non-threatening way, and how to feel into the degree of connection that someone was open to.

In another workshop called *Dance is Life*, Gabriel Francisco taught me to play with energy in my dance, exploring all the types of movement we had access to from the playful to the sublime. His *Dance is Life* workshop opened new realms of playfulness in my dance and turned me on to how energy can be used in dance as you connect with another. It was wonderful and he remains one of my favorite teachers to this day.

Most importantly, I discovered Shamanic Fusion Dance™ with Anandha Ray. As I attended her very first Serpent Ceremony five years ago, I knew I had been called to this work. In that ceremony, I experienced Intuitive Technique for the first time; a moving exploration of the body through the six body systems... from the outermost fingers, toes, and top of head, in toward the center of the body, the Spine. My body resonated so much with this new way of moving, it felt like every muscle was lit from within with an inner fire. Our Waking Dreams Meditation that day seemed to be a message. My teacher, Sedona Soulfire from Portland, had led me there, and I saw her white wolf dog in my meditation, a symbol that told me that this was destined.

It was not an easy path. I did not have the flexibility that the younger dancers had and there were so many things I could not do. I had a particularly hard time with floor work because of my knees, and occasionally some of Anandha's feedback was difficult for my fragile ego to accept. I always knew that what she said was for my growth, yet sometimes it was hard to hear. I so desperately wanted her approval. I wanted to dance and perform with the younger dancers, yet the pain in my body stopped me.

I still remember the day that I had to make the difficult decision to let go of my dream of being part of the performance troupe. We were working on a piece that involved three dancers standing in a row as one, with the dancer in the second position serving as the arms for the first. Because of my height, I had to be in front, yet I could not contort my arms into the position that was required to make this work visually. I also had to bend my knees to bring myself closer to the height of the dancer behind me. This was painful. I finally had to tell Anandha that I just could not do it. Over the next several months, I watched the development of the dance which I was to have been part of. It was powerful. It was performed on stage at the last Tribal Fest and it was one of the most powerful pieces of the entire event.

In spite of having to drop my aspiration to be part of the performance troupe, I kept coming back. My tenacity kept Anandha investing her time in me. Even when sometimes my stubborn nature would lead to conflict, she came to respect me because I kept doing the work. Dancing with her in the Serpent Ceremony, I learned the fundamentals of Shamanic Fusion Dance™. Intuitive Technique unlocked my body in profound yet subtle ways, allowing me to move from a much more intuitive place, getting me out of my head and into my body. This gave me a flow that translated onto the dance floor at Ecstatic Dance and in any other place where I chose to dance. I learned to dive into that place of Silent Knowing where I became one with the music, not its slave, but rather using the structure of the music and its many layers as a playground that I could explore. My love of dance helped fill a void in me that I didn't even know I had. I had always looked for love and approval outside of myself, but it's like a person looking for their keys outside under the light when they've lost them in their dark house.

As my dancing evolved, I saw this translate onto the dance floor at Ecstatic Dance. I could feel the way my dancing began to blossom. I tried to get to Sweet's Ballroom as often as I could, to get my Sunday 'fix.' I loved starting my week with dance, as it always put me into the flow in such a wonderful way. Walking out of dance each Sunday, I would feel almost like I was floating on air. When I could do what I love, this would carry me through my week in such a wonderful way.

Month by month as we dove deeper, I came to know more and more about myself. Sometimes we would do Waking Dreams, which is a form of moving meditation that allows a person to discover things about themselves which lie deeply buried within the subconscious mind and thereby repattern them. Layer by layer, I healed old stories, old wounds, traumas that I had carried since childhood. Occasionally things came up in the tribe which were sometimes uncomfortable, but these too brought subconscious patterns to light so that I could look at them and heal them.

Transformation is like a spiral path. Relationships bring up your triggers so that you can see them and heal them. Whether it is in romantic partnership, in family relationships, or in my dance community, it is all the same. Every relationship is a mirror. It shows you what you need to heal. When you see something in another that bothers you, understand that in pointing your finger at another, there are always three fingers pointing back at you. Instead of looking outside of yourself and judging others for what they are or are not doing, look inside. What part of you is being triggered by what you see? Be grateful to this person for giving you the gift of this opportunity to heal. When you do this, you take back your power and have the opportunity to respond from a conscious understanding rather than reactive reflex. These were uncomfortable lessons that I learned about myself, understanding where I had given away my power by blaming others or by playing the victim. Ceremony by ceremony, I shed these layers, coming to understand myself more deeply and accessing where in my body this trauma had been stored.

In every moment, we each have the opportunity to choose Love, to embody Love, and to take full responsibility for how we show up. There is power in this. As you fully own your reactions and responses, you take back your power. You become unflappable, or as a favorite mentor of mine says 'unfuckwithable.' Through my years of training with Anandha, I have continued on my spiral path. Time after time I will find my way back to the same trigger, each time wondering, "Haven't I healed this yet?" This is the nature of all transformation. It is like an onion. Each layer that you peel away brings you closer to your true self. Like an onion, each layer is usually cleaner than the last, yet sometimes it takes a while before you get to the core of the problem or the belief. Eventually the goal is to come into closer alignment with the person who you were meant to be.

As I have danced through these years with so many amazing dancers and mentors influencing me, I have come to see the dance floor as a microcosm of all life and all relationships. How you are on the dance floor is how you show up in life. Do you dance to the beat of a different drummer? Are you attuned to others around you? Are you oblivious, bumping into others like a bull in a china shop? Are you timid and meek? Are you respectful of others? Do you dare to take up space? Can you be unapologetically you while still honoring and respecting the space of others around you?

To me, the dance floor is like swimming through eddies of energy, playing in the current, relating with others and then letting go. All the work I have done on and off the dance floor has helped me to recognize how I was always looking for approval outside of myself. It has helped me to see that sometimes in reaching for connection, you push it away. Whether on the dance floor or in a relationship, when you grasp at what you want, it eludes you. People can feel that grasping energy even if you are not aware of what you are doing. It comes from a space of lack, and when people feel this Push-Pull energy, they pull away. Whether you are on the dance floor or dancing through life, the skill of non-attachment will serve you well.

When you finally feel comfortable dancing and being in your own skin, it becomes contagious. You may not be for everyone, but those who see your Light, who behold the unbridled Joy in your Dance, will gravitate to you. You will not need to chase what you desire as it will come to you. This may take patience, but when you can be in your Yum... when you can finally fully let go with Joy and dance with all the love in your heart... the right type of people will be drawn to your Light. Never dim your radiance for anyone. Radiate your love and light so brilliantly that you become a supernova. Take Joy from the pure pleasure of being in *your* body on *this* planet at *this* time. Shine your radiance so bright that others can sunbathe in it. When you can do this, you can live ecstatically in Love and Joy. You can let go of grasping for what you want because you will attract those who are aligned with your vibration.

I know that sometimes waiting for the right person to find you can be frustrating. We are social creatures. We are healthier and happier when in community and in relationship with each other. Just remember that your most important relationship is with the person in the mirror. Love him or her. Accept him or her. Praise him or her. When you Love yourself unapologetically, you teach others how it should be done. You become 'unfuckwithable.' When you can do that, you can create any life you wish.

IGNITE ACTION STEPS

- Get out and move your body! Whether you dance, do yoga, or other forms of exercise does not matter. Moving your body helps you to come into your body more fully. When you are fully embodied, you can be more present and more able to handle whatever comes at you. Being embodied also makes you more attractive to others.
- Seek out opportunities to dance, particularly in drug- and alcohol-free environments such as Ecstatic Dance or 5Rhythms. Use these dance floors as a laboratory to explore how you relate to others. Notice your responses when someone initiates contact with you or when you initiate contact with others. What comes up for you? You can learn much about yourself in this moving laboratory.
- Sign up for contact improv classes. Get outside your comfort zone. Learn from different teachers. Learn to love your body and be grateful for how it carries you through life. Nourish it well and take care of yourself. Meditate, do mirror work, start a gratitude practice, create a vision for what you want in partnership, and don't settle for anything less than what you really want.

Katarina Amadora – United States of America
MD, Certified RTT Hypnotist, Certified WildFit Coach, Rev. Priestess
Tantra Facilitator at Temple Amadora
www.AmadoraTransformations.com

TARA LEHMAN

"Unapologetically asking for what you want never goes out of style."

Do you believe that a REAL experience is within your reach? That's my acronym for *R*ocking, *E*xplosive, and *A*mazing *L*ove life, and my story is the intimate journey of what it took for me to claim it. My wish is to reassure you that you can as well. It's a tale of both drama and love that left me no choice but to shine a light on the hidden (and not so hidden) corners of my life which, unexpectedly, brought my love life full circle. My goal is to share how powerful investing in ourselves can be, to ask for help when you need it, and proof that once you get out of your own way, the love you thought impossible becomes possible.

SHIMMY & SHAKE & SHOES

Opening my hall closet, I saw what, to date, is one of the best tales in my dating history. One shoe out of every pair I owned was gone. I assumed that my shoes, from the glorious sparkly high heels to the $5 flip flops, were shoved into a stinky garbage bin, scooped up by the man I hadn't forgiven for breaking into my bank account. I could envision his rage, vindictively stealing my shoes before he flew out of town, drunk as usual, never to be seen again.

Feeling more inconvenienced than angry, I considered the fact it was December and updated my Facebook status to, *"All I want for Christmas is size ten shoes."*

My real love life began in a coffee shop in Newfoundland a couple of years earlier. It was a glorious sunny afternoon on the east coast of Canada and my mom had been helping me shop for a new belly dancing coin belt. We found the perfect color to add to my collection. It was bright orange with countless silver coins ready to jingle on the dance floor and I envisioned it pairing perfectly with my favorite purple dance top. With my purchase complete and my regular coffee shop only one block away, we decided to stop in. Immediately I saw a dance instructor friend sitting at one of the tables. Knowing he'd love my new purchase, I whipped the orange beauty out of its bag, tied it on, and stepped up to his table. I started shimmying my shoulders and shaking my hips. He burst out laughing and I could see the thought pass through his mind: "Yup, there's the Tara I know!"

It was then I noticed he was not alone at the table. And there I was, shaking and shimmying in my orange and silver glory, all before he could even introduce me to the person he was enjoying tea with. Had I noticed the extra person at the table, I wonder if I would have given that silly dance show? Probably not.

Let's refer to him here on out as 'my guy' because, as I learned years later, he had fallen in love with me two weeks prior to my impromptu dance show. How was this possible if I'd never met him? It turns out that two weeks earlier, he had definitely noticed me when I stopped for a coffee. He wanted to get to know me more. He made more frequent stops at the shop, hoping to meet me. My mini dance was the beginning of me bumping into him at the coffee shop all the time. We began sitting together, me sipping on strong coffee, him on Earl Grey. It seemed he spent even more time there than I did, (which was a lot) yet I'd never noticed. We knew a lot of the same people and our conversation was always interesting, easy, and witty.

Within less than a month, he began helping me with simple errands, offering to fix my computer and even helping me move which was thoughtful for someone who didn't know me well. But keep in mind that I was still on the slow side, unaware he was attracted to me. Then, a shift happened. I noticed a chemistry was evolving that I couldn't explain. It was warm, curious, strong, and exciting.

Years later, I still have a vivid memory of getting ready to see him one beautiful summer evening about a month after we had met. It was the first time I was doing so with butterflies in my stomach. In an attempt to look sexy in an unobvious way, I had chosen a beige button-up, knee-length skirt, bright white t-shirt, and sandals with a bit of bling. Walking casually down the sidewalk, I remember feeling as though I couldn't get there soon enough. It surprised me that I felt that way. We were meeting up at his place of work — he was the sound guy at my favorite bar (again, making it hard to believe we hadn't met before my shimmy and shake performance) — and I felt nervous walking through the doors. Now I was the one falling in love and each weekend, without fail, resulted in me dressing up to the nines so I could dance all night with friends, knowing he was watching nearby. I'd start getting ready at 10:00 PM and close the bar at 4:00 AM making it easy for him to drive me home. And so our friendship glided into something more, which was filled with both beautiful and regretful moments. I was devastated to learn he was already in a long-term relationship. It was a situation that hurt him as much as it hurt me.

We hadn't said the words 'I love you' to one another, but it was obvious all the same.

Humans aren't built to walk away from what they want. We were drawn together like the strongest of magnets in a way that was almost scary. He was who I wanted to spend my days with. The entire situation was heartbreaking. Scientists are right. Our brains register the emotional pain of heartbreak the same way as physical pain. I lacked my usual energy, would cry on a whim, and felt like I could see an actual crack in my chest. Who we desire is driven by powerful forces we can't control, and as such, we weren't perfect at following the socially expected boundaries. It was impossible to imagine him not being in my life, but we did finally reach the point where we were able to completely avoid one another with the exception of occasionally working together, as we were in the same industry.

We had gifted one another with the experience of true connection and there was no going back. And that meant any other man I invited into my life didn't stand a chance.

That's why the shoe story happened. That's why I thought moving away from the east coast, all the way across the country to be near my brother would make things easier. It's why, after binge-drinking shoe-guy, I attracted yet another unstable alcoholic into my life. Then, for a grand finale, just two months after meeting online, I moved in with a man and his two kids to start both a relationship and a company together. Things were going so well that I thought he was the one I'd marry... until I woke up to an email one day while he was out of town on business that unveiled the disturbing truth of who he really was. There wasn't an ounce of validity to who he claimed to be and, to give you a snapshot of how shocked I was, hiring a private investigator was up for serious consideration. That would have been an expensive, pointless exercise though because even the most amateur sleuth could see he was a thief, a fraud, and so conniving. By the time he flew home, my bags were packed with my parents' couch calling my name. We'd had countless screaming matches over the phone that were my introduction to the sneaky, emotional abuse of gaslighting my insecurities and the interesting experience of watching a narcissist desperately trying to cover his tracks.

Consequently, he destroyed our brilliant business, left our dedicated staff unemployed, investors drained, lawyers well paid, and his children confused. Not to mention what my family endured physically and mentally. As for me, I started working with a relationship coach who little by little was piecing me back together.

Yet still, despite me walking away from the company and enlisting the help of a coach, I let him remain in my life. He pushed so many buttons I didn't know I had that I turned into a person I didn't like. He succeeded in making me wonder if I should have believed in him more. He made me feel guilty that his children were left without *my* parents, whom they had come to love. My health rapidly declined and my common sense was evaporating to the point that one friend threatened to kidnap me until she talked sense into me, and another wondered if my ex was drugging me. It took five months to escape his web. Looking back, it resembles a darn good Oscar-winning performance that left him with the short end of the stick and me ready to play BIG.

Now, back to that relationship coach I mentioned.

I had no hesitation in committing to several sessions with the coach, once a week in her home office, sitting in a comfy chair and sipping tea as we talked. Our sessions always ended with us gently clasping hands while repeating phrases she felt my heart needed to hear. Statements such as "I have the right to unapologetically ask for what I want" and "I have permission to forgive myself" and "His behavior is not my fault," I needed to hear those *a lot*. I was allowing this man to make me second guess every good decision I made. My coach and I would reflect on my emotional heritage and how to work it in my favor so I could rid myself of self-doubt and ready myself for a healthy relationship.

I always went to my sessions alone; however, one day, my ex banged his way into her office so quickly and without warning that I doubt anyone could have stopped him. He was aware that I was enjoying my sessions with her and he knew that meant he was losing his grip on me. That afternoon, instead of spending the day trying to hold the company together, he drove clear across the city to display behavior that resembled a 40-year-old grown man stomping his feet like a child because he couldn't get his way and didn't understand why. Knowing she was successfully lifting me up when all he wanted to do was push me down triggered so much anger in him that he paced, vibrated, and yelled about how I had no right to make him look like the bad guy. It felt as though even my coach had never witnessed such a performance. I'll never forget her calling out to her husband, a coach himself, that he needed to cancel her next appointment because she was afraid to leave us alone together.

Meanwhile, the main investor in our company, being kept awake at night by the epic business disaster that was unfolding at the same time, offered to fly me anywhere I wanted for a well-deserved break as the relationship ended. I could take his travel points and disappear. When my ex got wind of our meeting about it, he executed yet another fantastical banging into a room performance, yelling at both me and the investor about how unfair it was. However, since I understood the wreck of my love life and our business wasn't my fault, I was able to dismiss and even laugh at his attempt to shake me. Two days later, without realizing how much those flight points would change my life, I flew to my happy place: St. John's, Newfoundland, Canada.

My best girlfriends met me at the airport with great fanfare, flashy pom-poms and all, and I was whisked around to a few pubs where old friends awaited me. We crashed a birthday party at one and found a good friend bartending at another. And then I unexpectedly spied my guy's car. I knew what pub he would be in and I froze, not sure if I should text him and say I was nearby. My girlfriend, knowing how I felt about him, pulled over to the side of the road while I debated what to do. So, I texted him. He said to come to join him and a rush of excitement flooded over me. My friend and I walked down the very familiar stairs to the pub and, upon opening the door, saw him right away. I immediately felt as though I had come home.

I hadn't intended to find him. In fact, I didn't expect to see him at all, as we had given up on the idea of being together years ago; like star-crossed lovers. But when I opened the pub door, we were magnets once again. He pulled me into his arms, both of us grateful to feel one another. My recent ended-relationship drama was non-existent at that moment and our conversation quickly led to the fact we were both single. He'd finally left the woman he had been with. I didn't fully comprehend what that could mean for us until the next day. I was sitting on my friend's couch doing work online and it just hit me like the most obvious thing. I could work from anywhere, so why couldn't I move back here, back to this town, to give this long lost relationship a real chance?

The next evening, my guy and I had a long-overdue date at our favorite pizza joint. We caught up over the good, the bad, and the ugly we had each experienced since last seeing one another and, ironically, my ex called me in the middle of dinner. He couldn't handle knowing I was having fun without him but I simply ignored him. He wasn't going to be granted the power to ruin the high I was experiencing with my guy. We fell right back into the past as if nothing had changed between us except the fact that we were both free to finally explore our full emotions. All that wasn't working before was percolating into perfection and we spent the night together. Curled up in bed, just before falling asleep, he laid his head on my chest and gently asked what kind of relationship I wanted. His question, so carefully and delicately posed, was unexpected. He's not one to express his emotions as easily as I do. A woman thing I guess. His question reverberated through me. I immediately recognized that how this conversation went could determine whether or not I would be moving back to give our relationship a proper chance. I asked him why he wanted to know and he replied without looking at me, "Because I love you and know we should be together." And those words were my Ignite moment. They were what I always wanted to hear, and combined with the time I'd taken to better myself, made the stars and the moon align. Finally, I found my R.E.A.L life: *my rocking, explosive, and amazing love life* And it was only just beginning.

We spent the next three weeks of my vacation together and that time with my guy was *glorious*. I was in constant awe, and still am, that my love life had come full circle within hours of stepping off the plane. It made the nonsense in my previous relationships seem trivial. When my vacation came to a close, I flew back across the country, made my last appointment with my relationship coach, and now it was me bursting through her door! But it was with complete joy versus the tears she'd grown used to. With her gentle prodding, I reported that I was proof that the moment we get out of our own way, everything can really fall into place. Joyfully, I packed everything up and said goodbye to my west coast family and friends. They were baffled by my abrupt departure in the name of love. After all, they hadn't heard of my guy before then. It would have been rather pointless for them to hear of and meet the love of my life since he wasn't available, right? And yet, here I was, coming back from a vacation and telling them that I was moving back to Newfoundland.

That flight back to Newfoundland three weeks earlier changed my life. Once I returned, my guy and I had no idea where we'd live together, so we moved into the Delta Hotel for nearly a month. The idea of living separately, like most couples do prior to moving in together, wasn't an option — it was all or nothing. We had no idea if one of us had idiosyncrasies such as hogging the covers, leaving socks on the floor, or never replacing the toilet paper roll… and it didn't matter. Past relationships had taught us each what DID matter, and that didn't include making each other feel wrong and suppressed. Most people don't believe this, but not once have we raised our voices to one another. We bring our issues up when they happen and, because of that, typically there isn't a problem that can't be discussed and understood within moments. It means we can spend our days, which had already been cut short until now, enjoying one another versus wasting our energy on pushing our feelings down. Even strangers have pointed out how happy we look and our single friends often comment on how much they love our love story. As silly as this may sound, it feels like a fairytale come true.

I am living a rocking, explosive, and amazing love life with my guy and now that I have it, I can't imagine why I would accept anything less! Like Cinderella, I have gone from losing my shoes to finding my prince. I've made my own transformation from looking for love to feeling love deep within. The actual outcome of what it takes to find our dream relationship is never 100 percent of what we envision; however, there is a simplicity to living your best love life once you are with the right person. We each can make peace with our past, respect the power of timing, and act as if we are already living the best love life possible. Fairytale relationships do exist beyond Disney movies! After all, I'm living proof that fairy tales do come true.

IGNITE ACTION STEPS

*"When you love a person, all fear disappears and
when you are afraid, all love disappears."*
~ Osho

- Decide what a rocking, explosive, and amazing love life looks like for you.
- NEVER stop unapologetically asking for what you want.
- Act as if you are already living your best love life.
- Understand and believe in the power of timing.
- Invest in yourself whether it be through coaching, reading self-help books, etc...
- If you feel trapped in an unhealthy relationship, know that you aren't alone and there's no shame in asking for help.
- If you suspect a friend or family member needs help with their unhealthy relationship, check in on them, even if it feels awkward. They may feel too ashamed to ask for help or not even realize they need it.

Tara Lehman – Canada
Event Coordinator
www.geteventive.com

Natalie Syrmopoulos

"True love is to love unconditionally — beginning with self."

My wish is to help you see for yourself what took me so long to realize: unconditional love brings peace and freedom. This journey has but one condition: it *must* begin with self. Accepting all that you are while evolving to all that you can be — this is the key to true love.

The Conditions of Unconditional Love

As I sat on the uncomfortable green armchair across from the family therapist, I was distracted. She attempted to speak words of kindness and compassion, but I had a lot on my mind and my impatience grew. I was tired of the same bullshit, trying to understand how to break free from the dysfunctional cycle I was in. My morning with my daughters had been rough, my husband and I were bickering at each other, and my health hit a new level of detriment. Just hours before, it had finally been confirmed: I had thyroid cancer — it hit me like a ton of bricks. I was still processing my new reality. All I could think was, "I can't keep living like this."

For a year, I had been seeing a family therapist while completing a course that focused on parent-child security and connection. Prior to that, I had read several books, done research, and counseled with the pediatrician. Although many of those helped, the relationship with my children was not improving enough. During this life-changing session, my therapist asked me a question that caught my attention and shook me to my core. It was pivotal and sent chills down my body.

Two years before, I was playing outside with my children on a warm autumn day. I was tired but making an effort, wanting to take advantage of the weather as winter would soon approach. We were out in our front yard by the large maple tree, where swings hung on the sturdy, thick branches. I was steadily pushing my girls while keeping an eye on the time. The cool breeze rustled the leaves, which were changing from rich green to beautiful red, orange, and shimmering yellow. The fallen leaves crunched under my feet. We were having fun, smiling, and laughing! I looked at my watch and saw it was getting late. And a familiar feeling began to flare up in the pit of my stomach.

"Okay girls," I had announced hesitantly but with hope, "it's time to go in!"

"NO! I don't want to!" yelled my eldest. My stomach started to twist in knots; my jaw began to tighten. Everything with her was a struggle... a negotiation. She was the most persistent, tenacious, and difficult four-year-old I knew.

I slung my one-year-old over my shoulder and tried to reason with her sister. "I know, but we've been playing a long time and I need to go in and start dinner." She didn't like that. That's not what *she* wanted to do.

She twisted her mouth into an angry frown and glued her bottom more firmly into the swing. "You're a stupid Mommy!"

The knots tightened and my face scowled. Keeping in mind that my neighbors might hear me, through clenched teeth, I told her to get inside. She didn't move. In the pit of my stomach, a fireball of anger started to form. I began growling the classic parental countdown. She wasn't budging; my hands began to sweat and my heart raced. Using every ounce of restraint I had, I yelled, "You better follow us inside, otherwise you'll be outside by yourself!" Finally, after what seemed like forever, she dragged her feet to the front door. Embarrassed, I slammed the door and locked it behind us. I couldn't push the flaming volcano of anger down any longer. It trickled up my throat and I screeched, "Why are you so rude? How dare you call me names? I don't say them to you! You're so disrespectful! Why can't you just do what you're asked?"

"I'll rip your head off!" she snapped back with a seething look.

My heart wrenched in pain from the stab of her words. How could I love someone who speaks to me like that? Is this what loving your child should feel like?

I was so fueled with anger and yet so deflated by exhaustion. This dysfunctional dance had been going on for a couple of years now: she does something she's not supposed to do, we get angry, everything escalates. I worried about various scenarios. My biggest concern was what would the dynamic look like when she was a teen? Or an adult? It was overwhelming to think about.

For months our relationship continued to falter and she continued to act out. There were dark, trying moments when I would question if I had the capacity to love her — and that weighed heavily on me. I didn't know what to do — I was at a total loss. Feeling run down and desperate, I sought out a family therapist.

While sitting in her green armchair, lost in frustration and worry, she repeated the question she'd asked me and it took a moment to register: "What makes you the 'right' mom for your kids?"

And it hit me, like a big slap across my face. What am I doing? My breath was shallow. I sat sunken in my seat, shoulders curled forward, looking down at the worn-out gray carpet. I felt small. I frantically thought about what it was going to take for things to really shift. My mind was going a million miles a minute, fearful of what would happen if I didn't get my shit together. I can't keep going at this rate. Clearly, from my newly confirmed diagnosis, my body was fed up. And so was I. The hard reality was, the cards have been dealt: I was the mother of two feisty, strong-willed girls, and clearly, I wasn't playing my hand very well. Things don't just happen by chance; nothing is coincidence. There is a reason I am a parent of these two incredible girls.

Slowly, I looked up, shifting in the green chair. I straightened my back, lifted my chest, and took a deep breath. I paused and pondered, "As life goes on and my daughters get older, would they be inspired *by me* or *in spite of me*?" Authentic inspiration comes from a place of love. I knew that — but I wasn't living it.

At that moment, I knew I needed to make a difference in my life. I no longer wanted to be surviving and fighting but thriving and evolving. I wanted to morph, emerge into something I hadn't experienced before. I needed to explore a path I had never walked. That pivotal moment was when my Ignite journey began. I felt like I had been given permission to get back in the driver seat and head toward uncharted territory. I felt a mix of excitement, fear, and possibility! As I left that session, I began to formulate a plan that would alter the course of our lives.

Throughout my life, I was often coined as a machine: hard working, head-strong, full of passion and drive. When I set my mind to something, I made it happen. In fact, that was my motto: "Make things happen." I was the driver in my life, doing what I wanted, trailblazing with impatience and callous with people in my way. I had an urgency to accomplish whatever I could with any available minute. I was in a race against time and hated anything that wasted it, including myself. When I didn't deliver, I didn't give myself much grace. Those were the conditions I set for myself. When unmet, a barrage of berating comments would enter my mind: Can't I do better? Why didn't I make a better choice? Why am I such an idiot? After would come a flood of unhappiness, sadness, and disappointment. I felt incomplete and empty. Restless, I would find opportunities to do better.

I was continually reaching for the next destination, rarely enjoying the journey, always impatient. Upon reaching my goals, I would feel temporarily satisfied and then empty and hollow. Once again, an uneasiness would engulf my stomach. I hated something about this cycle; I just didn't know what it was. What was wrong with me? After building a career, owning my own place, having great friends, and living a good life, I was still left with a sense of unhappiness. I needed to fix this. I didn't like this about me. In fact, I hated it.

So I did something about it and learned how to be better. And things were progressing! I fell in love, got married, and then... shit got real in a profound way: I became a stay-at-home mom who gave up her career. My life turned upside down, and the gut-wrenching cycle of uneasiness started again. I realized there was a pattern. A recurring theme: this notion that things weren't going as they should, my expectations weren't being met, and I was disappointed with my life, again. I was tormented with the familiarity of this insane sequence.

Right from the get-go, I struggled as a mom. Increasingly, I became frustrated and exhausted, often angry and screaming at my kids. I felt like I wasn't heard and I had little control. I grew resentful; I didn't love being a parent. But wasn't I supposed to? And, if I didn't, clearly I was doing something wrong! Maybe I wasn't meant to be a parent! Why couldn't I just be grateful? Why am I such an asshole? Once again, the berating commentary flooded me, overtaking my mind.

This time, the magnitude of my pattern was unbearable, largely based on what I *thought* was the reason: my kids!! Especially my eldest — who was a complete reflection of me in many ways. It seemed to me that I wasn't the problem — it was THEM — they were the issue! I began reading all the parenting books and going to counseling. Something needs to be fixed with them! Or so I thought.

I'd often hear life coaches advise, "If there is a toxic person in your life, don't let them be in your life!" But what if that toxic person was your kid? Or your spouse? That advice didn't seem right. This way of thinking made me the victim of my life; I understood that and knew it couldn't be the answer.

Theoretically, I was *supposed to be* responsible for all that was in my life. But why would I have manifested such stressful and disconnected relationships with my loved ones? Why would anyone want a life like this? Something else was going on, a common denominator in this recurring pattern I had yet to fully acknowledge.

You see, children are our biggest mirrors. Whatever it is we don't want to face will stay staring at us until we are ready and willing. That pivotal Ignite moment signaled to me that I needed to make a profound and sustainable change. I had to break free from the pattern I created. I realized that this evolutionary journey had to begin with the willingness to look at the one thing I had most control over: ME. I had to own and accept responsibility for the recurring and unsettling thoughts I had: something is wrong — there is something I don't like about my life. I finally acknowledged *I* was the common denominator.

In the past, when I didn't like something about myself, I would fix it. All the while, making these improvements, the underlying current was: I didn't accept myself. In fact, I disliked so many things about me. I hated how angry I could get. I hated when I didn't meet my own expectations. I hated those expectations. Why did I have so many conditions on myself? Why couldn't I love myself unconditionally?

Somehow the child in me never learned to completely love herself. My parents loved me immensely, but times were tough and they worked hard to make ends meet. We didn't have the luxury of spare time. There were too many things to do around the house and farm! The expectation was we needed to behave. If that expectation wasn't met, my father made it clear: there was no time for that bullshit. He was stressed and understandably so, working two jobs, tending the farm and trying to build his business all while supporting his family. It was a lot. And I didn't always follow the rules. Being strong willed, I veered off course often, which was routinely met with impatience and anger. Here originated my pattern, which strengthened throughout my life. In some ways it served me; but in many ways it didn't. And now, as a mom, the latter became clear.

Kids are that mirror that you can't run from. Anytime my daughter wasn't behaving nicely or respectfully, I would be disappointed. My disapproving look and tone shouted dismay and disgust at her, even without me saying so. When I was really frustrated and impatient, my automatic reactions echoed that of my father's from when I was a child. I wanted to evolve and break my generational cycle. Determined to give my girls peace and freedom, I needed to love and accept them for who they are and *all* that they are — unconditionally.

That precise moment, sitting in the green chair of my therapist's office, set me on a new trajectory. As I began my Ignite journey, I viewed her question with a different lens: Who do I need to become so that my daughters could look at me and see that unconditional love is possible for them?

How could I do this when I've never experienced it? After all, I had been living my life in a particular way for many decades. So I thought, if I wanted a profound change and to cut the cord of my continual pattern, I had to do something uncharacterlike. Instead of resorting to my usual: fixing myself, I began to do the opposite. I began to *accept*. I began to *love*. I began to accept and love *me* — unconditionally. Then the real work started to unveil; I had to practice it.

Today when I think about the therapist's question, I know that I can confidently answer her: I AM the right mom for my children… simply because I *choose* to be. I decided from that moment to lead a life where my children will be *inspired* by me. To be the person that will love them — unconditionally — no matter what.

As I embark on my uncharted path, my awareness grows, and this journey becomes more comfortable and comforting. I practice letting go of my expectations and trading them in for appreciation. I also do my best to treat myself with compassion and forgiveness. And I use that same perspective when interacting with my children. When my daughter screams in protest or when she yells in defiance, I practice embodying *unconditional* love. I pause. I practice patience and do my best to stay calm. I take a deep breath to center myself, recognize the pattern I *could* fall back into, and make a conscious choice to thoughtfully respond. I tell her that I love her, I'm here for her, and I offer a hug. If things have escalated, I communicate, "I'm starting to get angry and I need a moment." Sometimes, to maintain the space, I softly repeat my mantra: "*love unconditionally.*" Then, when we're both ready, we'll have a conversation, discuss what we can do better next time, and acknowledge that we're learning together. I'll wrap her in my arms, embracing love and gratitude, feeling warmth and hope.

Since my Ignite moment, I continually practice walking this journey, imperfect as it may be. Through this process my children will know what true love feels like and the peaceful freedom it brings. They will know that *all* of them are loved: all their behaviors, all their emotions. Side by side, we embark on this journey to *become* the humans we were meant to be. My Ignite moment shines a shimmering light on how I will continue to parent. With crystal clear vision, I know, it all begins with self and *unconditional* love.

In this journey the biggest fulfillment you will experience is the loving relationship you create with yourself. When you let go of unreasonable expectations, you can start to love *unconditionally* — and that is powerful. Beginning with self is the sustainable pathway to true — *unconditional love* — giving you the freedom to just be. There is peace of mind knowing you are whole and complete. And as you continue to evolve into all that you can be, you will feel your whole world magically shift. And — I can say with confidence — it feels damn good.

IGNITE ACTION STEPS

Awareness: Start with pausing. Practice mindfulness by being aware of your thoughts and your body's reactions.

Acceptance: Of who you are — fully and completely — fragmented but whole.

Compassion: Toward yourself — you've been operating a particular way for many years, unlearning to relearn takes time.

Practice: Consistency is key in evolving. You don't need to be perfect, you just need to *believe* in your higher self and do it anyway!

Forgiveness: Forgive yourself often.

Community: Surround yourself with supportive people who love you.

Breathe: Take a breath. And do whatever it takes to shift your energy forward.

My Mantra: Accepting all that you are while Evolving to all that you can be is the key to living a full, loving life.

Give this gift to yourself – you have that power!.

Natalie Syrmopoulos – Canada
Curator, Educator, Coach
www.evolvingwithnatalie.com

Tracy Finkel

"Our main purpose on the planet is to be Love, and to be loved."

My wish and desire for you is that my wee tale gives you hope, reminds you of possibility, and helps you recognize your worthiness while instilling the knowing that you're deserving of being loved and loved well. I hope you find your unique style of playfulness, live in a deep sense of gratitude, and experience a soulful, loving connection between *you* and *your* person.

Love, Loss, and Life Interrupted

My heart-stopping, life-changing Ignite moment occurred fairly early in this story. Not to say that there haven't been many since, but that one unexpected moment when I knew in an instant my life would be changed forever? That's what this is about.

I was in my early 30s, living in St. Louis, Missouri, United States, the 'Gateway to the West.' It is the city where I was born but had never really felt at home. After years of hoping, wishing, and desiring to meet my dream man, I had become disillusioned. Sitting across the table from yet another bad date, I was so bored within the first minute that I wanted to poke my eyes out. I decided to take a break. I was no longer going to spend one second more looking for my 'person.' I put all thoughts of meeting a man out of my head and redirected my energy into me.

I guess that now is a good time to mention that about a year prior to this decision I met a new friend at a Sondra Ray relationship workshop. We instantly felt like kindred spirits. She had this hoarse, gruff voice and was dressed funky, not conservatively, and I loved her instantly. We both lived way out in the suburbs at the time and started hanging out together. We'd sit around drinking wine and smoking cigarettes… pot might have been involved too… quelle surprise!

We would sit outside and discuss life and of course men. She was married with kids and I was casually seeing a rather young, rather dumb guy who was good in bed and was really into me. One day early in our friendship, she said she had a guy for me. He worked with her husband in the live music business. Ok, that sounded like potential. But then she mentioned that his wife had recently left him and taken their daughter with her. My heart sunk; I knew even if I liked him, he wasn't close to being ready to meet me… or anyone, for that matter. He hadn't had time to mourn his daughter being taken away to another state or the end of his relationship.

My friend and I continued to hang out together and every once in a while she would give me an update about 'the guy.' I knew if we were meant to meet, we would, so I didn't pay much attention, although there was one time she told me that he wasn't ready for me… yet… because he was dating a six-foot tall, redheaded cocktail waitress from a local casino. I replied, "That's called a hooker."

Time went on. About a year in, I had moved to midtown to be closer to the action, less suburban, so of course the opportunity to finally meet 'him' came up. My girlfriend was having an open house as her sister was coming to visit from Minnesota. He was invited. This coincided with my decision a week prior to take a break from meeting men and I already had plans for that night. I was having dinner with my good friend, who was also my neighbor, and her parents who were visiting from New Jersey. I literally would have a half-hour window to be at the open house. I'd committed to myself that I would no longer wait, change plans, or drop anything to accommodate meeting a potential guy. I had a full life, I was fabulous, and I wasn't putting anything on hold, on the off chance that I might meet someone.

That night, even though I had no reason to, I started feeling a little nervous. I'm actually very shy and facing the idea of finally meeting this guy, my nerves were getting the better of me. I walked into the party, stepping into a room full of people holding drinks, laughing, talking, eating, and I saw him through the sliding glass door off the kitchen. I knew it was him. He was sitting alone on the deck at a picnic-style table. My friend's husband, who I had also never met until that moment, came over to greet me and to my surprise, grabbed me by the arm and almost dragged me out to meet his friend. He introduced me to him and the hair on the back of my neck stood up. I could tell that there was a buzz among our friends about my meeting this guy and I knew they were all waiting to see what would happen. After the introductions were made, we were left alone.

We were both wearing all black and had inches of silver bracelets going up our arms. He had a ponytail, I had a shaggy haircut, and over the next 17 years when we would tell the story of our meeting, he would say that my haircut was so shaggy on that first meeting that he couldn't see my face and had no idea what I really looked like. It took a few dates before he really had a clue of what was under all that hair. He was darling and funny like that. At the time, we were actually both rather shy… I know nobody believes that, but it was true. That first meeting, we barely talked.

If you're lucky you may know the feeling of 'being home' with someone… of having a soft place to land. That was how I felt… I don't know how to describe it other than that. At our first meeting, I spent exactly 30 minutes with him. He walked me out and stopped at his car trunk to hand me some concert swag. It was a very cool-looking Depeche Mode t-shirt. The only thing I knew about Depeche Mode was that it was a band. We were a match made in heaven in that opposites attract. Actually, we weren't opposites, we were almost exactly alike… except for the fact that he was in the music business, a huge music lover, and music wasn't my currency. But that only made it better.

It was also the weekend before Memorial Day weekend 1994. It was a very busy time for him because the concert season was getting underway. There was no doubt I was attracted to this cool sexy guy in the live music business. As we said our goodbyes, I said we'd have to do it again soon. I told him to let our mutual friend know when and I would provide the food.

I left then, heading off to enjoy my planned evening with my friends, my head still spinning from everything that had just happened. When I got to their apartment that evening for dinner, I walked in, looked at my neighbor and her mother and said, "I just met the man I'm going to marry." And I meant it.

Something about being with him, as little as we actually talked, made me feel like I could exhale. I was giddy with delight, light and buoyant, bouncy and exuding joy all over the place. And I was going to marry him. I couldn't have been more serious; I felt it in my soul. It was all the more surprising because I never imagined that I would get married, and I certainly didn't think I'd meet someone in St. Louis.

The next time we were together was about a week later back at the friend's house. This time I brought the food… including edible flowers for the salad.

At the time I didn't realize it, but the flowers were just fodder for more of his stories in the coming years. In telling the story of how we met, which he was inclined to do, he would say that he knew he really liked me when he ate flowers the second time we met. He'd go on to say he thought I was trying to poison him… and spin it into a much greater story than it really was. But he was darling when he told it, and funny, and it would crack me up!

I left that evening knowing we would be together. I trusted that it felt right and was right. He called me the next night and we made brunch plans. That first time alone together just confirmed the feeling deep in my soul. One of my favorite quotes is "Your heart and my heart are very, very old friends." (Hafiz) and it actually describes perfectly how it felt being with him.

We were together almost every night from that night on and for the next 17 years until he died in my arms — but that's a story for another time. This story is about big love and as I go deeper, it's also about unconditional love, about hope, about possibility… and most importantly, about how when something is right, it feels like ease.

Not long after those first few dates, he wanted me to come out to his amphitheater for a concert so he could show me where he worked. I was excited. And I was nervous about passing the test of meeting the many, many people who worked with him making the concerts happen. He sent a limo for me. That in itself made me feel special but all the more fun because right before I was in it, Jerry Seinfield had been in it. I know this because he left a bag of books on the seat and of course I had to ask whose they were. Once I got there, like gnomes coming out of the woodwork, his employees and friends kept popping up to get a look at me, wanting to see who it was that was making their boss act differently. Act happier than normal. Apparently I passed.

After that, on most show nights I would go out and see him, even if just for a few minutes, so we could spend some time together. He was this cute, young, sexy, single guy in the music business… trust me, he was in demand. His picture was in the official concert program the year we met and every patron got a copy. Random women were constantly sending him notes and other trinkets, trying to get his attention, to get him to find them so they could meet. But I knew he was already mine.

I had not one second of concern that he was or could be interested in anyone but me. Once I really got that, it was another subtle Ignite moment. For the next 17 years, I felt honored and adored, but most importantly I didn't have to spend one second questioning his commitment to me or our relationship.

When we first got together, everything I was feeling was so intense that I told him that I couldn't imagine having sex any time soon. To clarify, I was no saint and had had more, many more, than my share of one night stands. So I wasn't uptight or prim and proper. I was often left breathless by how good it was when we were together, already close to feeling overwhelmed, and I needed a little time to get used to that before we added another element. When I told him that, he said that he'd wait as long as it took. This was 1994, well before #metoo, but to him, there was no urgency. It doesn't mean there wasn't intimacy… we fooled around plenty, always filled with laughter and fun. The slow unfolding actually led to an intimate playfulness that we might have missed had we jumped right into the main event. He had actually started sleeping over every night within about two weeks of our first date, but it was about six weeks before we had 'sex'. I know, crazy right??

It's said that we marry one of our parents; or, our spouse is here to teach us lessons, to be our mirror to reflect back to us and hold space when we aren't able to. They are all true. He was a combination of my mother and both grandparents, and he loved me like they did. He loved me as much as a person can love someone and that's how I felt about him. And the best part was… I knew that… I really felt that always, even when we wanted to kill each other. (Yes, we were human, that still happened.) Looking back, I see that our biggest fights almost always occurred on the afternoon of an event of mine he didn't want to attend. Here's a tip… pay attention and notice if there is a certain pattern for when the shit hits the fan in your life. It took me years to notice that pattern.

We showed our love in a thousand little ways. He would always take my hand when we were walking and I would feel him squeeze three times for 'I love you'; I'd respond by squeezing back twice... 'me too'. We were once watching an episode of Anthony Bourdain's *No Reservations*. He was in Vietnam with his handlers when they headed up into the mountains to a remote village. The proprietress had made her specialties for his visit and when he asked what he was going to eat, she said 'Squeezle.' No one knew what Squeezle translated into until Anthony pulled a porcupine quill out of his mouth. From that moment on my pet name became Squeezle. I knew that it was the sweetest term of endearment, and the bonus was every time he said it, we cracked up. Those were just a few of the darling ways he showed up and made me feel special and loved.

He loved me any size, preferred me without makeup, loved that I loved hardware, tools, and big box stores… He loved to shop, I loved that. I liked a loaded SUV and an old pick up truck, and he loved that about me too. He loved to collect things. He loved to go to flea markets and auctions, and I loved that about him, loved doing that with him. He really was the yang to my yin.

People that met us would say they never saw two people that more belonged together. They were right. The only problem was that it wasn't long enough. But still, 'grateful' doesn't begin to express how lucky I am that I experienced that at all… it just was that we expected to have more time.

He saw me through some of the lowest lows in my life… when I say I don't know what I would have done without him, it's not just an expression. His calm, his ever-present self got me through the 18-month period when my dog, my mother, both grandparents (who helped raise me), my paternal grandmother, and my oldest childhood friend all died. He was the epitome of grace under pressure. More than once I called him from the hospital, hysterical, thinking my mother was about to die, and both times he flew out of meetings to come and be with me, even though it was a false alarm. He came when I needed him, no matter what was going on.

He was amazing in so many ways and taught me so much. But knowing I could feel safe to be my truest self, who I really am...demons and all...was an amazing feeling. There is another quote I love "We are all searching for someone whose demons play well with ours." Everything of ours played really well together. It was an indescribable feeling knowing someone had my back without reservation. It allowed me to feel like I was breathing… really breathing… for the first time. It was such a gift with a big bow on top.

My divine love left me too soon. It was cancer. We kept him alive and thriving for almost three years after a stage IV diagnosis, with, as crazy as it sounds, lots of fun and adventure along the way. But actually it was the treatment that killed him as is so often the case. And that's another story for a different book.

Our magical relationship really taught me about how worthy I am of being loved and adored, how there is always hope, how your person is out there somewhere… if you want one. But probably most importantly, when it's right, it feels like ease. Your relationship flows and unfolds in the most beautiful way, it feels fluid. You know that there are no games, no posturing, no trying to figure it out because it just is. I truly believe that our main purpose on the planet is to be Love and be loved. I've had it, I miss it, and I want it again. Only this time I know it will be even better……….

Ignite Action Steps

Here are a few suggestions if you, too, want to have a magical relationship. First, know that you are worthy of the mad, passionate, toe-curling kind of love with your best friend… it's worth waiting for.

Expose your belly… a little homage to my dachshund (he loved dogs too), but it's really about being all in, being willing to expose your most sensitive parts… the right person will only love you more for it and you may just get a belly rub… ok massage, out of it.

Be and stay playful… Have your own secrets, together…or rituals, or traditions… something fun, playful. We would be in a grocery store and I would walk down to the other end of the aisle looking for something; the next thing I'd hear was, "Head's up!!" and a four-pack of toilet paper would be flying toward me. I would laugh so hard I almost wet my pants… Things like this were a common occurrence.

Be your truest self… it's too exhausting remembering where your 'dark secrets' are hidden. If you can't be your true, honest self with someone, maybe you need to work on that before you find your person.

Have a lot of shit in common. It's easier if your core beliefs are in sync. I love a spirited discussion, but at the end of the day, I want to spend my time with someone whose worldviews I respect and for the most part agree with. I've found that if we start in alignment, it makes for a greater feeling of ease and flow.

Tracy Finkel – United States of America
Complicated Human
Tracyfinkel@gmail.com

CAPT. DIONYSIOS DRAKOGIANNOPOULOS

"Find the strength to compete with the sun."

I want to inspire you to gain your courage, to stand up, to claim again and again your dreams until you make them happen. Be strong, don't make excuses. Discover yourself and the fears you have inside. We sometimes make our decisions based on fear, and I want to encourage you to make your decisions based on Love. Remember the feelings you had when you first fell in love and act from those.

CHASING THE SUN BETWEEN THE SEA AND SKY

My story starts one relaxing June afternoon four years ago. I was working at my office in Athens when I received a phone call, a call that a port captain never wants to receive. It was from the captain on one of my surveillance vessels. He briefed me that he had had a severe accident in the Suez Canal, one of the heaviest traffic places on the planet. His vessel, one of the biggest in the world, had run aground. I was stunned. It is the worst-case scenario for a vessel, and it could shut down the entire Suez Canal for days until we could get the vessel clear. I immediately gathered my things, left the office, and flew to the Suez Canal to lead the refloat operation and undertake the repairs in the nearest repair yard.

A few days later, after my team and I managed to re-float the vessel, we sailed her to Dubai for the repairs. There, the weather conditions were deplorable. We had to work in cramped, enclosed spaces inside the vessel's wounded hull where the temperature would get to the unbearable heat of 69°C or 156°F.

We had to suffer under those conditions from 6 AM to 7 PM every day, scribbling notes on paper as we tried to figure out how to solve the complex technical problems onboard, as our electronic devices failed due to the heat. New challenges popped-up every day, increasing the pressure we were under. We had to make the vessel ready to sail by a tight deadline; otherwise, we would lose a half billion dollar deal. The tension was super high and I barely slept. For the first time in my career, I felt that I had reached my stress limits. It felt like a war-zone; it was the definition of hell.

In the second week of the project, we finally had a small window of relief. We succeeded in finding a way to make the redelivery deadline. My colleague and I decided to celebrate with a drink at a local bar. I invited a friend from home in Greece, who was working as a pilot in a local airline, to join us later along with his colleague.

Sitting at the bar with my friends from work, I luxuriated in the icy freshness of a mojito when all of a sudden I spotted a breathtaking woman coming our way. She was one of my pilot friend's associates. She stopped right where we were sitting and said, "You must be Denny!" My heart was racing, my mouth was dry, I felt myself sweating, and my breath became short.

I thought to myself, "God must be playing tricks on me! This is not possible!" Facing me was one of the most beautiful and elegant women I have ever laid eyes on, with a smile like those we see in advertisements: curly dark long hair, big beautiful cat's eyes showing a passionate fire and at the same time a calm sea. Using all my energy, I replied bursting with confidence, "Even if I weren't — I would say yes, Denny here!" She rewarded me with her captivating smile. I can still recall that moment. She was wearing a sleek black dress and black Louboutin heels, pearl earrings, and a necklace with a single white pearl. We talked all night long, paying practically no attention to what our friends and colleagues were saying nor to whatever else was happening around us. I had an intense desire to get to know her as much as I could. I absorbed every single word she said, and I loved the way she talked and moved her beautiful lips. Her eyes locked on mine, very bright and full of longing. I could not take my eyes off her. It wasn't only her eyes or her breathtaking beauty that pulled me in; it was also her elegance, the tone of her voice, the way she moved her hands… everything about her.

From that point, my Dubai days transformed from hell to heaven. Somehow, the weather seemed a little cooler, the wind a little tamer, and the project not so difficult. That was it, my life's point Zero.

Throughout the three incredible years that followed, I discovered more of her virtues every day. She was an equitable, very organized, practical person. She was faithful, emotionally stable, self-conscious, intelligent, and trustworthy. She was a fantastic cook with a great sense of humor. She was never late, she never criticized other people, and she was kind and humble. She loved brunches in the Hamptons when the weather was pleasant and the balcony was open. She loved pearls and Hermes accessories. She liked to feel free with the wind in her hair. She was a Persian leopard who could not easily be tamed, but when under pressure, ran away. She moved so fast that no one could reach her and she did not turn back. Life without caring about anything was her ultimate goal, although she wouldn't admit it then and still does not today. She became my angel, the brightest star in my sky, the center of my universe, my everything.

Except we both had a second center to our personal universes: work. Due to our crazy demanding professions, we both had to travel around the world on a weekly basis. Sometimes we were in the same city and so busy we could not see each other. Other times we met for a few hours during an airport layover. We tried to find a way to spend more time together but it was never enough. "How can I quench this thirst of love?" I thought. We were spending our work leave to see each other. After several weeks apart, we would stay awake for nights when we met, trying to win the battle over time for one more hour, or even for just a few minutes more.

We were both well used to flying and to the goodbyes that come with it, logging hundreds of flights each year, but our hardest moments were at the airport departure halls. I found myself standing at the airport and my heart would literally feel pain, yet we tried to show each other that we were strong enough to control our emotions. When we would finally lose sight of each other's figure, only then would our tears roll. Our souls were singing and we were languishing like a blooming flower that was left without water, exposed in the sun. It's not easy to leave someone so important behind, but you must find the strength to do so until the next time. Usually, before boarding our return flight, we would start counting the weeks and days until we could meet again.

In those years, my life was excellent and everything was amazing. We were dreaming about and planning our future, and we couldn't wait to live what life had prepared for us. Then one night, a few days before our summer vacation, we were talking on the phone about our future and I said something which I later realized was very insensitive. It was our first conflict and it destroyed *everything.* Two days later, just before I boarded the plane to meet her and start our holidays, my phone dinged with an incoming email. I looked down and saw it was from her. I opened it quickly, wondering what she had sent, and after reading the first few words, I felt my heart stop. Her email explained why she could not join me for our holidays. Reading further, she wrote that our paths were to split. She thanked me for every beautiful moment we lived and asked me not to contact her ever again. Her words froze me to the ground.

I cannot clearly remember how I found the courage to board the plane that day. My hand kept drifting to my pocket where a small box holding an engagement ring lay heavily inside. On our holiday together, I was planning to ask her to make me the happiest man on this planet by marrying me. I had arranged everything, the best hotel, our flights, everything, but all of that made no sense anymore.

I was so in love at that time. I couldn't eat. I couldn't sleep. I couldn't work. I was losing my mind. For most of the next 28 days, I was thinking based on my fears. I was trying to understand how I got to that place and thought I could find the answers by drinking until mid-morning every single day. At the bottom of each drink, her figure was there. The lyrics of all the songs suddenly became meaningful and I was reeling. I was discovering what rock bottom means. I wrote to her, called her, texted her... all without success. She had blocked me even from the postman.

A few weeks later, I managed to open a small crack in a communication channel when I sent my best friend in Dubai to 'accidentally' meet her, but the damage was already done. Our relationship couldn't be repaired.

After my vacation period ended, I returned to Shanghai, China, where I was stationed at that time. I was trying to find peace with my new reality without alcohol, without friends to pamper me, and without other distractions. On one of my sleepless nights, tossing and turning in bed, I felt the need to run until all of the angry voices in my head subsided. It was three o'clock in the morning, there were no cars, there were no people. For an hour, the voices got louder and louder. My emotions moved from hurt to angry, from disappointment to frustration, from sad to mad. I was going to lose control, so I kept running. Two hours later, my legs gave up. My heart was beating at its maximum and the oxygen that I was breathing was not enough to cover the demand. Unable to run one more kilometer, I gave up; I was so broken.

Exhausted, I lay there on the Pudong riverside and watched the sunrise through the trees. That was the first time after four weeks that I felt a warm touch. As I lay there watching the sun for about twenty minutes, I realized for the first time that I had to find peace with myself, to evolve, and become a person that I would love to be. This was my Ignite moment. I had to be consistent, focus on the goals that I would target, and battle the fear that controls my decisions from time to time.

That morning, I made a bet with the sun:

Every sunrise for the next five months will find me running. I will write a book about our relationship so as not to forget a single beautiful moment that we lived together, I will start learning piano, I will join the next Ironman race in Greece, I will change my job, and I will learn to embrace my emotions.

When I told my best friends my goals, they thought that I had lost my mind. My dear friend Petros, who was living in China as well, told me, "Are you crazy, mate? Chasing the sun in China? WHAT ARE YOU THINKING!!! Here it dawns at 4:30. Why sunrise? Please consider sunsets instead." My brother briefed me that it is hard, if not impossible, to train for such a demanding race as the Ironman in such a short period, that people train for *years,* and that I should consider a marathon first and maybe an Ironman race for next year.

The more they tried to convince me, the more stubborn I was. I was not afraid of storms; this is how I learned to sail ships. It is predetermined when the sun will rise, and it can not do anything about it, but I can. Not giving up was a way to prove how much I wanted something, how committed I was to it, and I wanted to become a better person for me, for her, and for our future family.

The early morning run became my drive. It energized me. Most of the time, I was waking up before the 4:20 AM alarm, determined and excited. Despite the initial concerns of my friends, I felt lucky to have them and my brother supporting me on my journey. They were calling me every day to follow up on my schedule, observing my training program and progress. Over the next eight months, we connected more than we ever had before through this unique adventure.

During that period, I worked hard every day to be a better person. Sometimes I fell short, but I didn't give up. I spent 294 hours training. I swam 50 kilometers, cycled 4,949 kilometers, and ran 825 kilometers. I was confident, determined, and happy with myself.

One by one, I fought all my fears with the support of a fantastic friend and therapist, Renia. She helped me reconcile with myself. I discovered that within us, we all have a weak child who has fears and desires. I understood from this journey that fear is an emotion, a fundamental and straightforward emotion, and like all simple things in life, it's very complicated.

After three months apart, we started talking again. I was flying from Shanghai to Dubai, and since we were going to be in the same city, she agreed to meet me again. The moment she walked into our favorite restaurant, I knew in the core of my being that she was my other half. Everything I had done up until then made sense. She was the cause and the force behind everything for me. Afterward, when I dropped her at her apartment around 4:30 in the morning, with my whole body vibrating from the energy of our encounter, I went for a run. I ran the best 10 kilometers I had ever run. Had you seen me, you would have thought I was crazy. I talked to the sun in my excitement. It was everything. I had won back the love of my Persian leopard.

I was reminded of Odysseus, the legendary Greek king of Ithaca and hero of Homer's poem *The Odyssey*. He was driven off course by storms, he got captured by the Cyclops Polyphemus, he crossed the ocean, and reached the end of the world, passing the six-headed monster Scylla and Charybdis. He lost all his crew and it took him ten years to finally be reunited with his faithful wife Penelope after the Trojan war, and Ithaca became a land of peace and order again.

Like Odysseus, my life was amazing again. I had everything that I could dream of, and my life looked more beautiful and meaningful every day. I understand how Odysseus felt, after 20 long years wandering, being challenged, and then finally returning home. His drive during this astonishing adventure was his love of his wife, Penelope. He managed to make it home because he kept fighting for his dreams, and maybe because he was a bit lucky. As was I.

After a year and a half of being together again, everything was going as I had dreamed. Our relationship was wonderful, I had a new position as manager back in Greece, I ran an Ironman, a marathon, and we were planning to get married within the next two months. Everything was on track until the conditions of our relationship became more complicated and she started losing ground to her fears, doubting our relationship and, again like a Persian leopard, running away, but this time I was better prepared to handle the situation, my fears, and any feelings I had.

Through my self development journey, I have found how beautiful a daily routine can become when you love. I learned that it is essential in life to deal with fears and act out of Love. I have become a better version of myself through this experience. I have found peace in myself and the person I am today. Whether or not she is with me tomorrow, I know I will be alright just as Odysseus was; piece by piece, stone by stone, I will build my own Ithaca again filled with peace and love.

Elytis, Nobelist in Literature 1979, major exponent of romantic modernism, writes: "Only he who fights the darkness within will the day after tomorrow have his own share in the sun." Life is a beautiful voyage with heavy and calm seas, as well as sunbathed sunrises and beautiful sunsets. How you will sail it will depend on the route you choose. Get out of your comfort zone. Decide based on Love, not fear. The moment you dare, you evolve.

IGNITE ACTION STEPS

- **Just live situations.** Do not plan them. The unknown scares us because we are afraid of how much more beautiful the 'tomorrow' can be. Things will never go as you have planned. Feel, explore, experiment, fail, cry, laugh, learn from your mistakes, and try again.

- **Be stronger than excuses.** It is impossible to live without failure unless you live so cautiously you might as well have not lived at all (in which case you fail by default). Better an 'oops' than 'what if' later. 'Don't give up' is something you develop; we are not born with it. It is not easy. It needs discipline and self-knowledge, but you've got this. Be real, not perfect.

- **Be proud of your journey**, of your failures, and your achievements. Discover your passion. The passion is contagious, so manifest it, do not restrain yourself!

- **Be kind to others and to yourself, always**, no matter what. Be loyal to the romantic emotions that get you into it in the first place, love yourself, love others... Love with all your glory!

- **Find your own sun and challenge it!**

Good luck with your love adventures.

Capt. Dionysis Drakogiannnopoulos – Greece
Master Mariner, AFNI
⊙ captaindennydiary

CASSANDRA FOX-PERCIVAL

"Take the mask off and be the real you."

I want to teach you the beauty, joy, and bliss of finding someone who wants to know the *real you*. If you really want to find *love*, you have to see what that person loves in you, and then love that more in yourself.

JOURNEY OF LOVE

"God has given you one face, and you make yourself another."
~ William Shakespeare

All of my life, I never opened my heart up to love. I was always afraid of showing my real self and not being lovable. In my mind, it was safer if I never showed my true face to lovers. I was always happy-go-lucky and fun but never the real me. Relationships were light and easy, but they never quite connected on a deeper level.

I've had only one long relationship in my life and it was with a beautiful Italian man. He was handsome, intellectual, a baroque musician, and a food and wine connoisseur. We lived in Thailand and had a great time playing music, traveling the world, drinking fine wine, eating amazing food, and talking about the meaning of life. Unfortunately, at the time, I hadn't truly discovered what love was and therefore part of our relationship lacked true passion. It was a beautiful friendship for seven years, which helped me grow immensely, and I will be forever grateful for the time we had together. Eventually, we split and, although it was my choice, I still felt broken and confused about what love really was.

Four years ago, I decided to go on a journey and write a book about love. My home base was Thailand, but with six months holidays a year, the research for my book mostly took place in India, Greece, Spain, Portugal, and Cuba.

I began in India and purged my very tarnished soul on Indian hilltops for a few months. It was there I learned to love meditation and dance. Then, I passed through the small island of Santorini, Greece, for a small promiscuous midlife crisis, where thankfully all the men look like Greek statues. There, I learned to love my body and study the art of being desired. A year later, I went to Spain where my heart finally got its first taste of grown-up love. Physically and emotionally, it was intoxicating; but the intoxication was not sustainable because of his mental illness. I went on to experience love again, but it was always missing something. It took me many attempts at love to piece it together; but finally, I realized what I was missing from my relationships — that I so desperately needed — was support, trust, equality, and partnership.

Over these last few years, although I did find love in many places, it was always in short stints, a few days, one night, or a couple of weeks. At the time, I thought it was just circumstances that made everything so abruptly short term. However, in hindsight, I realize I was unconsciously keeping men around who for the most part didn't have the ability *or* desire to know the *real* me. There are a myriad of reasons to follow, many were consumed with their own lives or were workaholics. A few were mentally ill. Some were seeing multiple people and didn't have time for frivolities. Others had language barriers that really couldn't allow them to have deep conversations about feelings and life. In truth, I was the one choosing these people because I was afraid of love and commitment. My long-term relationship had ended and in an overcorrect I ran in the complete opposite direction. I had found my freedom and was enjoying life and my new sexual adventures to the fullest. I had a deep desire for simplicity and anything that was complicated was free to go. I was at a stage in my life where I just wanted to laugh, dance, and be joyous.

If I did choose men for longer than a couple of days, which was rare, they were people who just fit into my life without me having to change anything. Kind of like a Ken doll. I could travel, do, and see everything I wanted and they came along for the ride. It was a way for me to keep my freedom and have companionship at the same time. The problem was the people who had this kind of freedom to fit into my life were not exactly the right kind of people for 'partnership.' They were, in essence, just people who had a lot of free time on their hands. We had great fun, it was easy going, but we never connected on a deeper level.

A few months ago, after another broken heart because someone didn't have time to fit me in their busy schedule, I had written in my journal that I was ready for a *change* and wanted someone to make 'long-er' term magic with. I had written: *I want another amazing human being who is leading their own interesting life, stands on their own two feet, and wants to come together with me and make magic. Send me someone who enriches my every day for the better, and has the time and desire for me to be in their life. A person who is as excited to see me as I am them.* In my mind, I couldn't really decide what long-er meant, but I thought a few months would be nice. It was almost as if I had put all the good karma I had been collecting into one lottery ticket purchased from the Universe. *Dear Universe, give me the best you've got.* It sent me Apollo.

We met at a club one night when I sat down to have a cigarette next to him. "Hey do you have a light?" He gallantly pulled out a lighter from his pocket and lit my cigarette. "Thanks." I said "You live here?" "Yep," he replied. "You?" "Yep," I was pretty surprised because most people I meet in Bangkok don't actually live there. "Where are you from?" I said. "Guess?" he smiled. He talked funny so I knew he had to be Australian or from the UK. I said, "UK?" He laughed, "No Australia." He said, "We are going dancing; you want to come?" I was alone and the place was tiny so I said, "Sure." The two of us were fast friends, hanging out, laughing, dancing, and being silly. We were attached at the hip in no time. He was with some friends, but he made sure the whole night I was never far from him. It was nice to have a friend.

I have partied for the last couple of years around the world in beautiful places like Ibiza, Barcelona, and Mallorca but I have always partied alone. I never found the patience to hang out with other people, let alone a group. I have a system that I have perfected over the years that so far has worked pretty well. I go into a club, walk straight in front of the DJ, dance until the end, and then am the last person to leave the dance floor. Rinse and repeat. I've been to over 300 raves and every rave I started, I have finished. If there were raving Olympics I would definitely be a gold medalist.

It was about 15 minutes before our club was closing; Apollo walked up and said, "Hey, we're going for an after party; come if you want." And he walked out the door of the tiny club. I stood there staring at the empty space where he had just been standing. I knew because it was late, that the door was already locked so he couldn't come back in, and if I went out neither could I. I thought to myself, "No, I'm not going to break that record after all this time." My inner child piped up, "Yes, but we were having so much fun with him." The music was so good that I didn't want to leave. I knew if I didn't move soon he would be gone and I would never see him again.

I have had many signs from the Universe in my life, and I knew this was one of them. I saw the temptation hanging in the dimly lit doorway. I knew that if I walked out that door, my life would be changed somehow, my record would be gone and my habit would be broken, but I didn't know what else. I knew I wanted a change because I had asked for it already. In that moment I had a choice; I could either keep going as I had been for the last few years, instinctively keeping my mask on, everyone pushed away at a safe distance and living in my world of one. Or I could jump in, eyes closed, and go for the mysterious unknown Universe option. In a huff I walked out that door. I found him sitting on a bench outside waiting for a taxi. "Hey, Cassandra's here, we can go."

From that moment on, he was my person. We were inseparable; whatever he did I did. Slowly but surely he earned my trust and we began to build a friendship. For one month, I was raw, all natural, sweatpants, no makeup, and the real me. He was kind, supportive, loving, funny, and inclusive of me in his life. I wasn't used to this kind of friendship where I was accepted all the time, could do no wrong, and was never judged. It was a space where I was always free to be me, and no mask was needed. Our priority was having fun, and wow, did we ever have fun!

He became this wonderful partner in my life and the world became our playground. We made banana pancakes for breakfast while Jack Johnson played on the radio. We made dinner while wearing animal pajamas. We had endless dance parties in silly costumes with disco lights. We drank wine and had deep conversations about life. We stayed up to watch the sunrise and took morning walks exploring the city. We had candle light dinners of sushi and swam in the sea under the moonlight. Apollo had appeared in my life and filled this puzzle piece of support I didn't even know I was looking for, wanted, or needed. I trusted him and he opened me up to so many beautiful things in this world I never even knew existed.

The first thing he taught me was friendship. Through his trust he was able to open a space where I felt comfortable enough to have friends and be my authentic self. I was an only child and growing up, my mother was always my best friend. Since then I had spent my entire life by myself or with a lover, because it was all I knew. No one had ever painted a different picture for me until the day Apollo came along with his boatload of friends. Truthfully, I probably would have run away if he hadn't been there by my side.

He held my hand, as I tip-toed uneasily into the world of friends. At first, I watched from a distance unsure of the situation. But little by little these beautiful people impressed me with their love and acceptance. My previous misconceptions about groups, friends, and young people slowly began to disappear. Our collection of eclectic friends was away from their loved ones, so we created our own family. We did so many fun things, like having home-cooked dinners at each other's houses and baking cakes at all hours of the night. We had impromptu dress-up parties. Our friend had a box of silly costumes, with giant sombreros, silly hats, and colorful wigs that we needed very little excuse to get out and use any day of the week. We would come together and dance all night with great joy. I had not found these friends by myself but I did ask the Universe to please surround me with good people who keep my vibration high.

I realized there's so much more love to give in this world when you open yourself to platonic love in addition to physical love. I had never in my mind distinguished these two things before. I learned from these great masters of what can happen when I'm in a trusting and caring environment. I felt myself expand and become a more kind and loving human being. If I ever became afraid or worried I wasn't able to receive this love, those feelings would always pass. And with time and practice I realized I wasn't those fears anymore.

Next, he taught me Love. Eventually our friendship turned into romance. It was a bridge I didn't want to cross because I was so happy with my new friends. I didn't want to jeopardize these new beautiful people in my world if something went wrong. Also part of me felt trapped, because he already knew the real me; I couldn't reverse time and go back. It was uncharted territory to go into being lovers without my mask on. But I trusted him, and where he went, I went. So I followed, while he led the way and it was truly breathtaking. From the first night we were together as lovers I knew this partnership of support was the same for love. The way he held me and cared for me. The way we made love and it wasn't in a hurry. Everything was about learning, enjoying, pleasuring, and of course Euphoria. He called it a treasure hunt and my body was a wonderland. I was his goddess Cassandra. At the beginning, he had said, "This love is not good enough for you because it's not long term. I am not free at the moment." And I knew he was right but I didn't want to miss a second with this magical human. So we agreed to live every moment as if it were our last.

What I had feared most, being in love without my mask on, ended up being one of the most liberating experiences of my life. I was so deeply connected with this human who was not only accepting of me, but loved every part of me, and daily wanted to know more. This connection was only able to happen because I was being my true self.

He taught me how 'to live in the moment,' and be liberated. It was here I learned to let go and be me. Anything with this human was an adventure because we believed in each other. He loved everything about me and always thought my crazy ideas were awesome. Should we whirl in circles until we fall down? "Sure!" he would say. Should we pretend it is Christmas and decorate the house plants with Christmas ornaments in the summer? "Ok!" Should we walk around the city and pick different directions on the street corner to see where we end up? "Yes!" We egged on each other's inner child to be free. I felt like I could do no wrong. He was my biggest fan and truly believed his life was better because I was in it, and I felt the same way. I was building a stronger confidence in myself with him by my side. For every fear I had, he held my hand and guided me through it. For every dream I had, he held me up while I reached for the stars. I felt like we were magical beings playing on borrowed time.

Lastly, he taught me the art of how to 'love without attachment.' All of this love we had shared was coming to an end and we had to return to our normal lives. It was so hard to say goodbye to this beautiful human being that I spent all this time with, gave all this wonderful love to, and made so many memories with. But, I knew I wouldn't have traded a second of it for the world. Not everyone is meant to be in your life forever — no matter how painful that may feel at the time. Some beautiful souls drift into your life only for a moment, just long enough to pick you up, show you the way, and then move on. To know that you will love with all your heart and, when the time comes, you let go with grace, because ultimately everything needs to breathe and change.

I have learned from those beautiful few months that if you really want to discover what love is, you have to find someone who wants to know the real you. A person who will always see the good in you no matter what. A friend who raises you up and keeps you safe. A partner who believes in you, your goodness, your heart, your soul, and your love. A playmate who pushes just enough to make you think you can fly. A teammate who chases your happiness with you. A guide who sees your brilliance, your good deeds, and your soul shining like a star. Someone who looks through your chaos and sees beauty. When you are truly loved by someone like this, you become *love*.

I am happy for the time we spent together because my perception of love changed for the better. My expectations on love multiplied. My ideas on relationships morphed from taking what I could get, to knowing what I deserved.

And through the beauty I saw in his eyes, I raised the price tag on myself and began to know my worth was much higher than I had previously valued. It was like I had gone through life with blinders on and once I saw love with his devotion, those blinders will never go back on again. He showed me that I deserve the same love that I give... and that is priceless.

Although I could not keep this love forever, I was happy to have a wrinkle in time with him. I learned that there is no longer a need for the mask I hid behind for so many years. In essence, this love I had been internally yearning for did not happen because I wasn't being my *true* self. What I did learn is, love is always there if you just look for it. When that person looks beyond this blonde hair, crazy dancing, meditation loving, and traveling queen, this is where you will find the real me. And... I love her.

Lead your life for yourself, your pleasure, and your bliss. Forgive yourself for the past and give yourself permission to be happy.

Thank you for believing in me and reminding me I am enough. Thank you for showing me the gift of friends. I shower you with gratitude until the end of time. Thank you for this eternal love we shared in this wrinkle in time. Although the moment has come to say goodbye, maybe for a while or forever, I know our hearts will meet again. Life is too short to carry sadness. Remember the good, and always carry a piece of me with you.

IGNITE ACTION STEPS

- Find your people, find your vibe. Find those people who raise you up, support you, and keep your vibration high.
- Every morning ask the Universe to give you the people you are supposed to meet and the experiences you are supposed to have — the things that will best serve you on your journey.
- Look around and find beauty somewhere in your surroundings. Could be a person, nature, clothes, or even food. Be creative, just find as many beautiful aspects as you can. Radiate love.

GRATITUDE, FORGIVENESS, HAPPINESS, LOVE

Cassandra Fox-Percival – Thailand
Classical Musician, Joy Giver, Happiness Researcher
cassieaf@gmail.com

Toma Vichanov Molerov

"It's our decisions, not our circumstances, that govern our love lives."

My intention is that you go deeper into understanding which decisions have led you to where you are right now and see which ones will lead you to where you want to go. When you take a closer look, you'll see that you've chosen it all — every single step of the way. I wonder what decision you'll make by the end of this story...

Experience Love Wherever You Go

It was the year 2017. It was hot outside, very humid and yet romantic when the sun would set behind the horizon of Kuala Lumpur, the busy, metropolitan, yet dusty capital of Malaysia. I had lived in the country for four months already and had recently been hired in one of the largest — and in my opinion coolest — companies I could ever work for. As a customer support representative, I would answer emails, often highly complicated ones, 40-60 of them a day. However, my heart was still in the cool air and homey European environment of universities and cafés around each corner that I was used to in Vienna, Austria. I had come to Asia as a student, feeling stuck and desiring to learn a lot faster and a lot more than I thought I could anywhere else. That decision had a price. I left behind friends who I really enjoyed spending time with, an apartment with five other people, whom I had grown close to, and the first woman who had accepted me and whom I loved for a full three and a half years. But the student life ends at some point. And with that ending, one has to begin to make decisions for the future.

There I was, sitting at my desk in the company I always wanted to work for, and I had tears in my eyes. I was surrounded by inspiring people from all over the world. Answering one email after another but thinking about the end of my first relationship with the woman I loved. I needed to make sure that nobody saw my tears. I never was a fan of crying in public and this time I didn't want it to be me who was known for it. I finished the last email, packed my bag, and went back to my condominium apartment.

It had taken me three years to fall in love and make it work. Before my first love, I had zero relationship experience. I was 23 years old and living in Vienna, the most *liveable* city in the world and, honestly, I was pretty sure something was wrong with me until I met her.

In my teenage years, just as much as in my early 20s, I kept a highly optimistic attitude. I would flirt. I would date. I would have a lot of fun and always believed that at some point it would just work out — that I didn't need to do anything about my relationships. I was convinced that it would magically unfold without me needing to read up on it. And yet, when I started to really like somebody, I would get nervous, start behaving like I was an alien, and turn into a highly insecure boy who just wanted to be accepted. To my surprise, the girls I met didn't want to date a boy, they wanted to date a man. On top of that, I defined myself as somebody who is very picky. I didn't want to date *girls*, I wanted to date women. And not just any woman — I wouldn't simply start a relationship unless I was really attracted or in love with that person.

But that year, I had just started my final year of my University Bachelor's degree. I was standing in the Metro, banging my head against the door, asking the Universe why finding love seemed to be so hard for me. My last date had just ghosted me and I was, frankly, done with it. I didn't want to wait any longer. In my mind, at that very moment, I decided: falling in love and making it work was non-negotiable. I was going to conquer my insecurity and find love, a beautiful relationship — and everything else — no matter what it took. That simple change in perspective allowed me to stand my ground for what I wanted — romantic love.

And it worked. One week later, I fell in love! The woman I grew to adore felt the same and we spent three wonderful years together exploring the world, ourselves, and each other. It was beautiful.

With my recent move to Kuala Lumpur, I had not only left Europe but had also broken up with my first loving relationship. At the time it was hard for me to understand why. It was my first real connection and now it was over. When I understood it was ending, it was as if a big amount of love that I had contained and channeled for one person expanded and got unleashed! I remember walking through my office on the verge of crying and, at the same time, overwhelmed by the amount of love that was pouring out of me. For three months, I would indulge in my emotions, look through pictures of the past, and play songs that reminded me of my old home and my old life. I was wallowing and I knew it, but it felt like the right thing to do.

Then in December something changed. I was at home in the beautiful but crammed condominium apartment I shared with two flatmates. It was a Friday night. I had just received a message from my friends to go out and have a drink. As I was sitting on my bed working through a few files on my laptop, I caught a glimpse of an old photo of me and my ex-girlfriend. Seeing that one picture brought everything back. Most of all, it triggered a decision that until then I had taken subconsciously: Would I go out and enjoy the evening or would I look through all my photos from the past, feel nostalgic, sad, cry a little, and eventually watch a movie and fall asleep? I realized how tempting it was to choose sadness. And this time I knew that it *was* a choice. A choice I could make. And... how I needed to fight to go out and enjoy myself.

That night, I chose to stay inside and indulge in my sadness. Feel sorry for myself. Appreciate the past and go to bed.

The only difference that time was my understanding that I had chosen it. I could have distracted myself, gotten out of bed in a moment and forgotten all about it. But no, I chose to be sad! And I really liked it. *Interesting*, I thought. When I gave myself that space, I understood many more things about myself and my relationship.

I became aware that it ended because I moved away. I had chosen this path to Asia — unconsciously it seemed. But somehow I knew it was right. I always knew that it was the right step to take but I was resisting it and denying it, and right then and there I was ready to make peace with it.

A few months later, on New Year's Day, I sat refreshed and reflecting — I always do that on New Year's Day — in a very comfortable café in Kuala Lumpur. My life had changed dramatically in the past year and this was the moment where I could slow down and appreciate everything that was. It had been about four months since my break-up and I felt grateful for everything that happened.

But what now?

I had met people who experienced similar heartbreak and theirs lasted for over a year. One friend of mine had gone through a particularly rough break-up when the person she had loved moved away. As she followed him to get closure, it only ended in a fight and in more hurt. She was telling me that story as if it were yesterday, but more than a year had passed. I was frozen and shocked. One... entire... year?!

I had only been single for four months. One year was such a long time. I didn't want to feel sad for the next eight months. I didn't want to even wait one month. Being in love was amazing. Why would I wait? As that thought occurred to me, a new energy streamed through my body. My soul was taking control, lifting me up and all of a sudden, I was ready.

I remembered how it had taken me three years to fall in love the first time and actually create a relationship around that feeling. But before I could start a new relationship, there were a few more things I needed to overcome. I was still very sexually insecure. As a man, you regularly feel that pressure to excel in the bedroom. And if you don't deliver — chances are your partner may not stick around for long. I wondered: Would I have to wait another three years for my next experience? Would I have to wait until my confidence was higher? I was ready now!

The café was very comfortable. Palm trees were set up around me, blocking the sound of the cars. A fresh smell of cake and coffee filled the area. I was sitting there by myself, looking at the greens, the sky, and the wind. Then, a rare moment: I felt a new fresh breeze coming through. In the tropics, this rarely happened and, if it would, the fresh breeze would make you sweat. But not this one. It was as if it spoke to me, telling me that a new year was about to begin. That a new me was about to emerge. I looked at everything that I was grateful for. It gave me appreciation. And it allowed me closure from the past. It made me realize I had been subconsciously waiting for permission to begin living my life full out. I looked down at what I had written in my journal. And that's when I made a few bold decisions. Here's what I remember writing:

Decision 1: I would travel Southeast Asia. I was already living here. Everyone was exploring the world. Why would I need to stay at home in Malaysia? That moment, I booked three flights to the places I always wanted to visit.

Decision 2: I would fall in love again. I would feel love regularly. I didn't care what was normal or what I experienced before. This was my way to say 'screw you world, I do what I want.'

Decision 3: I would overcome sexual insecurity by having a lot of mutually agreed, respectful, and loving sex that would leave me and the person I slept with deeply connected.

I looked at my decisions and was pretty satisfied. Rarely had I declared my decisions on a piece of paper and been so convinced that this is what I wanted. Those words on that paper were burned into my very being. You'd expect I would have carried them around wherever I went, but, honestly, I never looked at this paper again. Because I knew it would be okay.

Here's what my three decisions led me to:

I traveled to nine countries and experienced flow like never before. Traveling isn't so hard, I noticed. All you need to do is book a flight. Everything else will then fall into place. I ended up going to Thailand, Laos, and Japan — places I had wanted to visit all my life. I traveled to Estonia, to Los Angeles, made a stopover in Austria to see my old friends. I impulsively went to Egypt — a fun roller-coaster ride that was completely unexpected — before I finally returned back to Malaysia. There wouldn't be one single month where I wasn't going to do something that would excite me. And somehow, in every single place I'd visit, I would meet somebody, someone I would fall for. I noticed that it's actually quite easy to fall in love.

When you fall in love with your own life, you'll start loving all the people that are part of it.

My career made a U-turn, as well. I'm still in awe of how traveling and saying, "Yes" to myself first allowed me to thrive more than ever before. Each trip was followed by an exponential learning and performance curve that to this day is, to me, somewhat unbelievable. I worked less and doubled the revenue I was making in my new marketing role. My sexual insecurity had disappeared, washed away after I realized how compatibility plays a role in our relationships and how practice and radiating love makes you truly master anything.

Insecurities don't just disappear like that. We're usually self-conscious about something that we're not very good at. It would be something we would like to be better at but haven't really mastered yet. Sex is a specifically tricky subject, because it has so much dogma and anxiety attached to it. I always felt like I needed to perform in bed. This year, I realized that sex wasn't about that at all. It was just like life, every minute is precious. It was about the journey, much less about the end result. I also realized that some people really like the same things in sex, while others don't as much. And to my surprise, I found that to be okay. Sex was an insecurity for me because I didn't know much about it. Marketing was an insecurity for me too. That year I had decided to look them both in the eye and say, " I'll get better at this." You know what — I will be *amazing* at this. And slowly, step by step, the insecurity started to disappear.

It seemed like every single place I went that year, I fell in love, experienced something magical with that very person, moved on with gratitude, and looked ahead to the next adventure. The women I met were way out of my league. Strong, smart, beautiful, and downright mesmerising — but with respect, a smile, and a clear understanding of what I wanted, they seemed to magnetically engage with me.

I'm in a new relationship now. Loving, playful. It feels like I'm experiencing my first love all over again — but different. Did you believe that was possible? I didn't back then either. But I do now.

I learned that year that love is like a boomerang; when you send it out, it comes back to you, guaranteed. I realized my decisions are way more powerful than I thought. And that my life has been going 'according to plan.' Everything was my decision, whether it was staying comfortable or taking the risk. I learned that working less and tracking your time will drastically increase your output and recognition. Most importantly I learned that you can fall in love with anyone at any time and that it could literally happen tomorrow.

Don't fear it will be over, because if it has to, then it will.

Don't fear that you won't find anyone, because if you really want to, you will.

Instead, ask for what you want, so you get it.

Trust the path you're on because the clarity will carry you.

Become aware of the decisions you've taken, and I hope that you — just like I — will experience love wherever you go.

IGNITE ACTION STEPS

Up until my Ignite moment, I had been waiting for permission to fall in love again. From whom, I do not know, but I was. I hope you see that breaking free of that idea is important for you, for your journey. That by doing this it will lead you to make some big decisions and live full of wonder.

Begin by understanding what you really want. Create a non-bullshit one-page letter to yourself where you state what you truly want *right now*. What is it that you desire to experience if *everything* was possible? And I mean EVERYTHING.

Raise your vibration. Create a list of what you're grateful for in your life, be it your friends, experiences, ex-partners, etc. Then create a list of why your ex isn't the right person for you now. Take your non-bullshit letter and take *one step* that makes one item on that list inevitable.

Decide what will happen for you this year. Make it non-negotiable. This is happening one way or the other. Make your three decisions for the year. Do not think about who you need to ask for permission or whether it will be possible. Decide that it will happen and ask for forgiveness later. Act before you doubt yourself. Ask for what you want. And if you feel stuck, send me an email :)

Toma Molerov – Germany
Relationship Coach, Science-Fiction Author
www.tomamolerov.com

Danya Katrina Yusep

"A mysterious courage awakens when you arrive on the step of forgiveness."

I have come to believe God brings us angels along the way. An invitation to remind us of who we are and where we are going. It's when we are brave enough to step back into our power and connect to the people and places where we felt most free we rise to something more.

Rooting for Her Rise

Her pain is big, visible, and revealing. She is trying to hide this from the people she loves, but it's really hard because the battle is real and it's very dark. She doesn't know how to get off the merry go round; it's moving too fast and now she is moving too slow. Her body aches. She is tired of feeling shameful and fearful in this place.

She no longer recognizes the woman she has become. She is laying in a fetal position on the couch in her photography studio praying to God. "Please send me women who can lift me up. I need help; I can't do this alone anymore." She realizes she is in a very toxic cycle, at first in danger, but now dangerous to herself, to the people around her, and it will not have a good ending. She needs to get off this ride. Mathew 7.7 is the verse that keeps going through her head. *Keep on asking, and you will receive what you ask for. Keep on seeking, and you will find. Keep on knocking, and the door will be opened to you.* At that moment, in her safe space surrounded by her armor, her cameras, lights, and props — the things she has tried to hide her pain behind — a vivid vision comes to her mind's eye. She sees herself carrying a light onto a stage. The seats at her feet are filled with women, daughters, mothers, and grandmothers...

In her vision, the light in her hands is full of hope. She had isolated herself from her friends and her own passions slowly over the years. She had lost herself in trying to please him, to be someone who she thought he wanted her to be. She works hard to un-see the danger before her because it will ruin everything she has wanted all her life. She is trapped by so many things. She needs to get out; it is inevitable that he will strike again, it's only a matter of time. The thunder of his anger is deeply rooted, a beast he can't control, a fragile young boy inside who must have been broken along the way. Staying keeps her light on dim, soaked in pain. A crowded place filled with sadness and isolation. This was not her. She was not this. She was so strong, so full of life, of energy... a visionary. A bright example for others and her daughters. How did she get here?

A week after that fateful angelic prayer, she would come home to a beautifully wrapped box on her front porch. It was a snowy January day and she had just spent the afternoon with her mother watching the movie *Wild*. She was deeply moved by the story about a recently divorced woman named Cheryl who decides to start a new life by hiking along the 1,100-mile long Pacific Crest Trail. She feels connected to the mountains, to the imagery, to the solitude and the adventure. To Cheryl's journey and her brave spirit. Little did she know at that time that her own story was about to parallel with *Wild* in the most profound, painful, and beautiful way.

It had been Mom's idea to go to the movies. Her mother was forever putting books in front of her or inviting her to shows, mothering her in little ways no matter how grown up she was, showing her new vistas, new avenues for exploration, and sharing her strength. Her mother had raised her sister and her on her own. In the 70s, divorce was still somewhat of a taboo, but her mother's strength and determination had carried all three of them through. There was, of course, a strain at times, as there always is between strong-minded women from different generations. Distance through the years, she admired and loved her mother deeply, knowing her as a woman of independence and grit. But, also knowing her as private and not very sensitive; a challenge for her who needed a mother to soothe her through the fall of her own marriage and her own demons.

She, who wanted to shelter her *own* children, to shower them with as much love as possible, connect and communicate with them even when the story was hard. She needed that woman who provided the pinnacle moments in her life, the mother who was always pulling her back to who she was.

The timing for the movie invitation from her mother and the box left on the porch would be a day that would shift everything for her. Inside the pretty box was a note: "Where have you gone, my friend? I miss you dearly, we have so many more memories to make. I love you." The box was filled with a stack of old handwritten letters from her beloved childhood best friend along with an embroidered handkerchief.

The words had been passed back and forth between young girls growing up. Memories of Vancouver Island, of them in high school and university. Funny, heartfelt exchanges shared from the ages of 15 to 23. The two girls were glued together in those magical years, living out a bond so strong it held them locked together like a daisy chain in their souls. They were soul sisters. As she cried through the words wrapped in the box, she knew it was time to let go of the wrong dream and grab hold of herself again. It was the start of a chain of events. It would be the beginning of many angels coming into her life just at the right time.

The box is a beautiful lifeline — a rescue ring made of love thrown across miles to find her sinking heart and pull it to the surface. She reaches out to her friend and tells her how beautiful the gift is. How she is a guardian angel and the gesture has come at a desperate time. Her friend, her soul sister, tells her to not lock up the words any longer in a box; that there are plenty more memories to make.

She decides to be brave like Cheryl in the movie. To team up with her soul sister to climb a mountain called Knox for 30 days straight. They would laugh as they hiked and talk about the book they were both reading by Brene Brown, *Rising Strong*. They fell effortlessly right back into that place where they left off, as soul sisters do. She feels good in this place, it's easy and lighthearted, she can be herself with her friend. She is back with her people. Her friend tells her she is still industrious, brazen, bold, beautiful, magnetic, and bursting with love to give.

She is doing hard things, *good* things... and her prayers are being answered. The hike up the mountain is not easy. Every step of the climb opens her up and makes her feel awake again. She blooms more each day as she walks, day after day, petals opening to absorb the radiance of the sun and the earth on her feet. Hard grueling work, but nothing comes free, she reminds herself as she completes every single one of the 30 days.

She has just done this giant thing, this momentous chain of step after step after step, with only a scant few left now until completion. She feels she is walking back to the daughter her mother raised her to be; she thinks of Cheryl again. And on that last day, in those last remaining steps, something shattered. Literally. Her phone, secure in her hand, falls from safety and hits the ground under her feet, splintering into a thousand pieces. And in that shattering, something *Ignites* in her. She knows it is time.

Craving more adventure after her completion of the hike, the girls ride on their momentum and decide to leave for a conference in Los Angeles to walk on fire with Tony Robbins. After chanting, "Yes, Yes, Yes!" at 2 AM in the morning on the first day of the event, she knows it's finally possible to break free. To break free from her past wounds, to break free from her limitations. From her guilt. From him.

This break won't be clean. He likes to battle; it's his specialty and he is ruthless. This will be a massive endeavor more complicated and enormous than she thought.There are dark rabbit holes, old patterns, temptations for comfort, and road blocks everywhere. It's when her fear pulls her back another angel appears. A spiritual mentor has a vision that she is a black bird drenched in black tar, but it's ok because the bird is starting to shake her wings free. This gives her more affirmation that she is being guided by something higher than herself. She needs to stay the course and stay fearless.

She sets out on another 30-day goal to walk the loop in a beautiful park called Springfield. She needs to focus again and follow a routine for inspiration. As she walks, she collects magical pieces of nature from the path and forest. She is excited to photograph them in unique ways and eventually makes a collage with all her treasures. As she moves in the beauty that surrounds her, she listens to the wind. She listens to the trees and the sounds of birds and squirrels. She is becoming more like her old self, healing her spirit through exercise, creativity, and a constant connection with God. This path becomes her sanctuary as it provides her with a chance to be creative and connect with the people she loves the most. A chance to dream again, to study, to have meaningful connections and conversations when friends join her.

On her walk one day, she sees a young woman in her twenties with a blonde ponytail and a white tank top running. When she passes her on the stairs, she is captivated by her beauty and strength. The forest feels enchanted, magical, this particular day empty of others except for her and the woman. She wonders if this person is real or is a ghost from the past. After a second passing from the woman, she felt shivers and goosebumps come over her entire body.

Walking on, this encounter with the woman is reminding her of memories where she felt happy and connected to herself and her purpose. It was in the mountains where she felt like a bird, soaring on her snowboard beneath her strong legs as she carved her edge deep into the powder snow. She feels this power and connection also on her mountain bike. Steep grinding climbs up picturesque mountain peaks with exhilarating winding descents through lush forests. She smiles as she remembers the years in the wilderness planting trees all over western Canada, alone on the cut block, one by one as the seedlings go in, just her, her spade and her bag of trees. She felt most at home in her body in those days, one with the earth and Mother Nature.

With the pony-tailed woman lingering in her memory, she continues on her loop, the bright memories fading and the dark ones creeping back in. She walks on and another memory comes: she is on the side of the road, apples heavy in the branches, grapes in the vineyards ripe for harvesting; she is screaming, asking herself why she stayed for so long. It's the same road where her mother was in labor with her. The same road her father is buried. There she stood years ago, her eight-year-old self and her mother and sister, the tiny child she was, standing beside her father's grave. She hears her mom's voice, "Don't let them see you cry, girls. We need to show them we are strong." Her mother's voice rings in her ears, "Pay attention to the signs; they are all around you."

The last dark memory comes with so much pain. She sees herself beside her mother at the hospice where the fountain outside is crying its tears. Her mother is dying. But she can't be dying, she is finally through that awful divorce and her Peachland angel told her she saw her dancing, wearing yellow, and healing this year. It's supposed to be time for her to reconnect with her mother, make more memories, travel, and laugh together. Her word for the year is 'Shine.' How can she shine and dance without her Mom.

She can hear her mother's words, that beautifully loved body beginning to get cold, turn purple, and shut down slowly in the hospice bed. "Danya, you have so much potential, so much light. Don't waste your gifts. Look for the love and joy." She makes a promise to after that, just as Cheryl did, to not dismantle the good parts of herself any longer through this new loss. A heartbreaking scar so different than any other she would experience. She never loved her mother more than the moment she was gone.

She had a dream the night before her mother died that she pushed her hospice bed into a pristine lake, toward the Starlight Inn. The Inn was the place where her mother and father first met. As her mother dove off of the bed into the water, she transformed into a beautiful mermaid. There was an explosion of all the colors of the rainbow mixed with sparking light beaming on her as she swam away. She was no longer sick; she was free, free as she had always been her entire life, a true untamed magical spirit.

When the woman with the ponytail passes her a third time she knows she needs to to stop her. She tells her that she had a vision about standing on a stage holding a light. She explains she has inspired her on this path because of her strength when she runs. She also shares the memories she has had about the dark and the light. She tells the woman she now knows that without the dark there can be no light; they can't exist without each other. She realizes in that moment that she wants to document her story through a film, a story about how God brings us angels along the way, an invitation to remind us of who we are and where we are going. The young woman shares some of her similar struggles and dreams. Both are inspired by the stories that are shared.

As the two souls part on the trail, she can see the sun setting up ahead, streaking the sky with its warm tones of gold and orange. Her arms begin to rise, stretching high to the clouds. She pictures her inner child in a field with long brown hair, green eyes, singing in a white cotton dress to the words from *Rise Up,* by Andra Day.

And move mountains
We gonna walk it out
I'll rise up like the day
I'll rise unafraid and I'll do it a thousand times again

It's starting to get dark in the forest as she approaches the stairs that lead her home. As she comes to the final two steps she stops to reflect. She calls the second last step before the path the step of *Forgiveness*. It is forgiveness for her mother, for him, and for herself. This step frees her from the illusion of time and moves her onto the last step she calls *Purpose*. She knows what her calling is: living in love, staying true to that mountain bird. It's now up to her to take action and use her light to guide others.

She envisions hundreds of women living in love, angels, lining the path, holding lanterns of hope harboring the way. The light is always there; we just need to look up ahead one step in front of the other, seeking what is true in our spirits. She, who she is now, vulnerable and revealing, is twice as beautiful. She is You.

Ignite Action Steps

I believe something beautiful and magical happens when you commit to something for 30 days. Try it, and I promise you there will be clues and signs along the way.

Hike for 30 days. Walk for 30 days. Meditate for 30 days. Eat clean for 30 days. Journal for 30 days. What you do doesn't matter. Just do anything for 30 days.

Look for the third way. My mother coined this term in our little family and now I teach this to my daughters. "There is always a third way." If something is challenging you, think about a third way to work it through. Not their way, not your way, but a third way.

Soaking. Find a quiet space, lie down, and soak in music for 20 minutes. I usually tune into Bethel music for this or faith-based music, but use whatever music resonates with you. It's my go-to for clarity and connection with my *Self* and Holy Spirit.

Danya Katrina Yusep – Canada
Photographer, Film Maker
www.loveyoudanyaxo@gmail

FREDERIC LAFLEUR-PARFAITE

"Raise your standards and the Universe will meet you there."

If you take anything from my story, know that we are all learning. There isn't a set recipe for ensuring love. Good relationships don't happen overnight. They take commitment, compromise, forgiveness, and most of all, effort. There is not a single one of us who has it completely figured out, but I am confident that by learning from each other, becoming vulnerable, believing you are worthy of love, and more importantly, choosing to love fearlessly, we can get closer to the relationship we desire.

CRASH AND BURN

I fell for her potential, bound by her charms, and I woke up in a sea of red flags where smoke and mirrors were my reality. I had been blindsided. My world had collapsed. I felt alone and ruined. My eyes got blurred. My heart stopped. How could I have been so clueless?

My story started in the summer of 2018. Happily single, I had just arrived in the beautiful Istanbul airport, coming from Romania, and in front of me was a discouraging sight: the longest immigration line I had ever encountered in my life. It did not help that I was sleepy and friends were waiting for me on the other side of town with an expectation of dinner. I tried to race ahead to get in line, zipping in front of the grandpa in front of me, only to find myself coming to a halt as the immigration line was not moving. I had no choice but to be patient. I was dazed and tired, and the only thing I wanted to do was to end this dreadful line and shut my eyes in an Uber. The more I went through the serpent line, the more uncomfortable I felt. I was being stared at by the three party guys adjacent to me, the intensity of their looks making me feel naked and violated. After the line snaked around for the third time, I realized they were not looking at me but the woman right in front of me.

I sighed with relief and burst into laughter at how silly the situation was. Then I became even more disgusted by their chauvinism and made the worst joke I could think of to the lady in front of me. That joke will haunt me forever, "How does it feel to be a piece of meat?" I asked her. She laughed and to my surprise turned around to reveal the most gorgeous green eyes I had ever seen. There was something so pure and genuine that emanated from her. I was smitten instantly.

I was compelled to introduce myself. Her name was Zaya and she was traveling from Eastern Europe. I noticed her cute charm bracelet and trying to start a conversation said, "My niece has a similar bracelet." It worked! We continued talking about our summer adventures as the line fell away from my awareness. I'm sure the three party guys were probably kicking themselves, wishing they were in my place. She went through immigration and waited for me to have my passport checked. We exchanged Instagrams and, with a rush of adrenaline, I took her hand and told her that we were going for our first date. She smiled, her excitement was evident. She had a layover for a few hours and we had no cellphone reception so ditching my friend Jack for dinner was a no brainer. Plus, I was blinded by her beauty but confident that Jack, a foodie who had undoubtedly planned a fabulous meal for us, would understand.

She joked about going to McDonald's. We settled for ice cream at the airport café. The sweet cold treat was delicious and I impulsively asked the server to take a photo of the two of us. Sitting there at one of the plain little round tables, we chatted for hours. We filled every minute engrossed in one another until she had to depart to her next destination. She shared details of her summer adventures and in turn was fascinated by the car racing I had been doing. I was happy to talk about my passion for it. At one point, she used her phone to check out my Instagram and to my dismay, I realized that she was seeing a stream of endless photos of me with a hundred different very fast cars and various gorgeous women. Her eyebrows lifted at the sight and her demeanor changed in an instant. I was quick to explain that I was on an adventure to fulfill a bucket list dream and that the person I was portraying on Instagram was not necessarily who I was. At her boarding gate, I got her WhatsApp number and I watched her until she was out of sight. A strong connection had been formed, and I knew right there that my world would never be the same.

The next day, as I was thrilled by the chemistry between us, I convinced a few artist friends to sing her a song as we cruised on the Bosphorus lake in Istanbul. I immediately sent her the video and waited excitedly for her reaction. Thereafter we talked every day. Even though it was one day further from the last time I saw her, it was one day closer to the next time I would. My friend Jack thought I was nuts as we did not even live on the same continent. I was falling hard for her as we used all the social media channels possible to stay in touch.

To me, love means knowing that no matter what, you have someone to count on. I have always been the man who loved love and could devour a marathon of romantic movies. I enjoy officiating my friends' weddings and spending time with my female friends to select the best decor for their "I do's." I had grown up to become completely in touch with my feminine side having been raised by strong, independent women. And having grown up in seven different countries across five continents, I always had a love of nurturing a very international life and cross-cultural relationships.

I wanted to be face-to-face with Zaya again. Therefore, I made it a priority to meet up and invited her to Paris for the most romantic 10-day trip ever in the following month. I told her, "Just show up with your luggage, I will take care of everything." At the same time, I also booked a trip to Miami for months later, knowing that it would be a great surprise for her birthday. That's the planner in me. What could go wrong!? It was either going to be a great love story or a good lesson to learn! Plus, it felt right.

To my sorrow, her family did not share my feelings of a grand gesture of romance at first. They thought she would fall victim to human trafficking in France. "What random guy flies you to Paris after meeting you once in an airport?" they had asked her. It sounded like a remake of my favorite movie, *Taken*. To remedy this, I shared our complete itinerary with her family and it allowed everyone to feel at ease. The day our trip began, I was bouncing on my toes with excitement. I ran all around Paris, going from shop to shop due to a national holiday, looking for a florist who was open so I could welcome her at the airport with flowers. I even made up a sign. I was thrilled that we could pick up where our first date had left off in Istanbul. Together, we sought out a cute Parisian park that sunny afternoon. We celebrated with ice cream and a passionate first kiss. She could have been a bad kisser but she wasn't. It was electrifying! The moniker between us #peace, love and ice cream was coined.

We painted Paris with our passions. Our time together was exciting like an episode reminiscent of *The Bachelor*. I did not hold any stops and the hopeless romantic in me finally had someone to spoil. I was elated. I hired a photographer to take epic shots of us near Paris monuments to cement what could only be described as magical. The days were amazing, the nights even better as we discovered not just Paris but each other.

Our courtship continued around the world. I invited her everywhere I was traveling for work. Despite my executive duties, we found time to paint up the town. She was finishing her Master's degree and able to travel at a moment's notice and join me, so we joyfully collected surreal experiences together in as many cities as possible. I loved doing new things and so did she.

As a child, I rarely saw my parents exchange gifts and always feel the sadness my mother felt when another birthday slipped by, uneventful. It was even worse for me being a Christmas baby. I didn't want my partner to feel that way, so buying gifts for my girlfriend was important to me and my way of showing love.

After five months together, I wanted our eternal bliss to continue. We both agreed that long distance relationships can only work if there is a deadline. Hence, we put a date on living in the same city. Plus, I had mastered enough Russian to convince her parents to let her finish her studies wherever my career opportunities would take me. We settled for living in the United States and went to Miami to finally celebrate her birthday — the trip I had meticulously planned months ago. It was an exhilarating three weeks of pure fun: skydiving, plane rides, horseback riding, and boat trips… before flying north and making a home together in Washington, DC.

Only a few days after moving into our new home, I had to travel again on a week-long trip. Before leaving her, I made sure that her every need was met and that she knew how much I cared for her. And she was angry with me. It made no sense! During this separation, we had our first argument stemming from the fact that I had traveled by myself and not taken her with me. We spent a lot of time talking and trying to resolve this unexpected bump.

I came back from my trip and found her a dream job in the city, and coached her how to get it. This gave her more money than she had ever made before, a working permit to start in her career, and the opportunity to stay in the United States while she finished her university thesis remotely. I had delivered what I thought to be the impossible in record time. I would have done everything for our relationship and to take care of her. I wanted that true-partnership, do-anything-for-the-other-person type of love with a best friend that I could build an empire beside.

In our third month living together, a different side of her started to emerge. Her sweet innocence had slowly disappeared and morphed into a manipulative person who was being unveiled right before my eyes. We often argued about her reluctance to use contraceptives. I wanted to collect experiences together around the world, not raise a family right away. Then it was about money. She sat on the couch and I paced the room in front as we discussed our spending. We traveled every month and, although she had been working, I was financing everything from our lifestyle to her trips to the hairdresser. I asked her to start contributing just a little and, to my shock, she refused, stating whatever she was making was for her 'own entertainment.' I was flabbergasted. I had become her wallet. This was far from my vision of a partner who could dance by my side through thick and thin. She could not hide her real nature anymore.

How did I end up with someone so selfish?

Our relationship wasn't equal or mutually healthy. Zaya would play to my desire to rescue her and bring me all her challenges to solve. She would only focus on the support she wanted. It never felt like enough. I had fallen under her charm and failed to recognize that I was with a taker. I am a giver not because I have much, but because I know exactly how it feels to have nothing. Generosity was my way of life. But you can't love someone into loving you. This was the moment when I realized our values differed. My flawed definition of a relationship was staying committed and putting the other person first no matter what she did or didn't do to me.

Like the calm before the storm, it did not take long before cracks emerged. She had put a shock into my system. We separated over a weekend but I could not help but be sucked back in with the promise for change and a flimsy future. I wanted to believe that our story was meant to survive the rumbles.

My friend Jack was getting married in Italy in May of the same year, and I thought it was the perfect opportunity to rekindle our romance in Florence. There was no shortage of amorous things to do there. From watching the golden sunsets on the Arno river and strolling in the Bardini gardens, to stealing a kiss in hidden squares. It could not have been a better destination.

At a garden party just before Jack's wedding, I listened to my friend of fifteen years talk about his fiancée. He described a connection that was deep and strong, shining with admiration and respect for the woman who would be his wife. And it was then I realized that I could not envision Zaya that way. I could not see her as my wife. I realized instead that something was amiss. This was a profound moment for me. We had drifted apart to live in the shadow of happiness where petty arguments kept pointing out her immaturity and our 17-year age gap.

This is when I started to pay close attention to my own growth and review our relationship vision. I could not count on her when I asked for help. Her incessant lies were amounting and pushing us further apart. I hung on for as long as possible until it was more hurtful to stay. I had become miserable. I was now living with a stranger in my home. I could not trust her. I felt used. One year after it began, our story ended.

After the bitter scent of our farewell, I fought hard to shake that feeling of darkness, that song of death, my bruised ego. Counting my blessings, I leaped to the rapture of living and the infinite possibility it held. I had to remind myself that I had fully opened my heart and peeled away my shell of vulnerability. I had given my all. This alone allowed me to avoid the burden of regrets.

What seemed like a failure to identify 'the one' was actually a lesson in patience.

The first step was to let go of my faulty definition of love. My life didn't need to be worthy of Hollywood Blockbuster narratives. There was no point in rushing it because it's not about an end goal. In rushing into a relationship with Zaya, I didn't leave enough time for her to reveal to me who she was beyond our infatuation stage. We had talked about everything and I believed I knew her intimately, but in fact, she had only been telling me what she thought I wanted to hear. I had fallen for her potential. But the problem with potential is that it's based on who we think this person could be, not who they really are. We had incompatible beliefs and couldn't agree on fundamental values. I had forgotten that love, like friendship, is a feeling that expresses itself in action. What we really feel is reflected in what we do. Love is an ongoing decision to act in a loving way.

In the weeks that followed, I felt impassioned to transform my heartbreak into something positive. I sought knowledge and wisdom to bring light to my shortcomings. To help in my quest, I interviewed hundreds of married couples to gain an understanding of how they view relationships and how they solve issues as a pair. I did this in the hopes that it would help me become the perfect partner for my future soulmate. Yet, it was much more insightful. I came to terms with the possibility that finding true love may be worth the risk of not finding it.

After seeing trends and patterns, I created tools to share my learnings with others around the world. My quest to understand Love became bigger than me, positively impacting several relationships among those I interviewed. I transformed my findings into AmourKit.com, a free app to improve relation-ships. A way for people to become their own Relationship Guru. It was my hope that people would find that information as useful as the couples I interviewed gratefully did.

Love is about discovering when what you want is never important. But what the other person needs and wants is always paramount. If, like me, you have started a quest to find someone who can complement your life, consider that your search for love only ends when you truly understand that there isn't a set recipe for ensuring it. It is in the living when we keep learning, believing we are worthy of love; and more importantly, *choosing to love fearlessly* so we can get closer to the relationship we seek.

L'amour n'est jamais perdu.

IGNITE ACTION STEPS

- Fall in love with yourself first.
- Live in the now by being committed to inner peace, gratitude, and expansion.
- Be clear about your core values to avoid settling for less.
- Create a relationship vision and use it as your guide.
- Question assumptions. Recognize red flags and ask questions if you are unsure.
- Don't take things personally. Shift your focus by seeing the positive intentions in the other person, and when that fails, give yourself empathy and talk about it.
- Use the free tools in AmourKit.com to cultivate compassion and deeper communication in your relationship.

In the end, we only regret the chances we didn't take. So, take them all, and bring your best life into being with your intentions.

Frederic Lafleur-Parfaite – France
Chief Love Officer
www.Amourkit.com

Cherrie MacLeod

"Let your belief be bigger than your fears and you will Ignite the desires of your heart."

Sometimes the journey to love demands you be willing to army crawl through the trenches in order to reveal the silver lining of blessings. My intention is for you to break free from the constraints of what the world tells you love should look like, to believe you are worthy of that earth-shattering love your soul desires, and to courageously go after what you yearn for deep within your heart.

From Ashes to Grace

One gloomy mid-November afternoon, I was aimlessly wandering the streets of Toronto, Canada. The wind was blowing the leaves off the trees and the crisp winter air sent chills down my spine. I shoved my hands deeper in my pockets, searching for warmth. The city was bustling all around me, but all I could hear was my own footsteps echoing loudly on the pavement. I wasn't sure where I was looking to go or what I wanted to do; I just knew I needed to escape.

I felt empty. At the same time, incredibly heavy. So many thoughts were whirling through my head, crowding my mind and weighing me down. That feeling I had was not something I had experienced before; yet it was eerily and uncomfortably familiar. Deep within my subconscious, my intuition was sounding an alarm bell; but too afraid to deal with it, I blocked it out. IGNORE. DISMISS. DELETE.

It turns out this cold winter afternoon would be one of the most pivotal moments of my life. For the first time *EVER* I would choose to make a decision to do something solely for *me*. Something that put my needs, my wants, my hopes and dreams… first. It was a decision that ultimately would turn my world inside out and upside down. It would bring me to the lowest of lows, crumbling me to my knees, and shattering my heart into sharp, jagged fragments, like pieces of broken stained-glass window scattered across the floor. Yet this was the catalyst that would catapult me to discovering the truths I only wished someone had shared with me long ago.

As my footsteps carried me along, my mind kept wandering back to my idea of relationships. When I was little, I was mesmerized by the Disney princesses. Cinderella. Sleeping Beauty. Little Mermaid. Rapunzel. Beauty and the Beast. In my naive mind I thought our life goal was to find '*the one*,' fall madly in love, and live happily ever after. All my life, I have been fascinated with the idea of love.

I began studying the love around me and felt incredibly deceived. The relationships I witnessed in my world always ended in heartache, anger, and resentment — nothing at all like Cinderella's courtship with her Prince Charming.

I remember every month I would anxiously await the latest issue of my *Cosmopolitan* magazine subscription, the cover plastered with dreamy headlines like "How to Get a Man and Make Him Fall Head Over Heels in Love With You." From those articles, I believed I had learned the missing ingredients that would help me avoid the marital woes I saw all around me and escape the fate of having broken relationships. A hopeless romantic, I also binge-watched shows like *The Bachelor* and *The Bachelorette*, daydreaming about the passion, intimacy, and romance in my fantasy love life.

Inspired by all of these shows and magazines, and with the life-long study I had done on relationships, I set out on a quest in search of love. It didn't take long for me to fall for a charismatic bad boy named Trevor. The relationship with him was easy. He was forever taking me on fancy dinner dates, surprise outings, and giving me lavish gifts. It was fun and carefree. Within the first couple weeks of dating, we became inseparable.

Eager to start my grown-up life and begin following my passions, I was applying to schools across Canada. When I got the acceptance letter from a school in Toronto, I jumped at the chance even though it meant moving from one end of the country to the other. And in the two weeks after getting my acceptance letter, while preparing for my move, I found myself living my own real-life episode of *The Bachelorette*. After a lovely dinner out at a fancy restaurant, Trevor took me for a stroll along the sea wall and pulled a ring from his pocket. It was his grandmother's engagement ring. He told me he had arranged to get a transfer with his job just so he could be there to take care of me. Was this my fairy tale love story coming to life? I wondered.

Deep down I just wanted to be married, to buy the house, to have the babies, to get the fancy car, to have all the things. This is what I thought love was supposed to look like. I felt left out when I realized many of my friends were checking these things off their 'to do' lists and I was determined not to be the last one walking down the aisle.

We settled into our apartment in Toronto. It was tiny but cozy. We established a routine. Things were good until one night, I woke up at 4 AM to find myself alone in our bedroom. Trevor was nowhere to be found. Intuition told me to look outside and I saw him sitting on the sidewalk talking to someone on the phone. Talking to a buddy was what he told me at the time, but he really wasn't. I later discovered he had been having an affair for the past year and a half with a woman who would end up becoming his wife, taking the role that was supposed to be mine.

The pain, the hurt, and the betrayal was so unbearable that I indulged in whatever I could to numb the heartache and escape reality. Intoxicated was where I ended up most nights of the week, and I distracted myself with rebound relationships in an attempt to revive my self-worth. My original quest for deep connection and intimacy was now a jumble of emptiness, abandonment, and worthlessness mixed with lust and other stimulants just so the adrenaline could keep me functioning. I felt used and alone, and I struggled to comprehend how the man I was going to marry — who supposedly cared for me so deeply — would end up breaking my heart so badly.

I quickly spiraled into depression. Slowly, after a year of grief and pain and with an immense amount of effort, I pulled myself out of the deep melancholy. My closest friends reminded me that I was worthy of being with someone who respected me and that any man who truly loved me would not hurt me the way Trevor did.

I timidly resumed my quest to find love. However, now in my late 20s, where was a single lady supposed to meet a quality guy? Like many others, I hopped online and swiped my way through dating apps like *Bumble*, *Christian Mingle*, and *Plenty of Fish*. I was kind of skeptical at first because the guys I connected with were either incredibly socially awkward or would flood my inbox with unexpected dick pics after the first hello. I really didn't think I would find anyone worthy of having a serious relationship with since 99.9 percent of them only wanted to get laid. And then I simultaneously swiped right with a guy named Josh.

Our interaction started with a 'normal' conversation and our first date was about 12 hours long. He was chivalrous and kind, and the relationship looked promising; however my heart was still unsure. After all, it had just been mended back together and my gut screamed, "Navigate with caution!" I became ultra-observant of Josh's character. For the first time, I realized I needed to ask the hard questions. What was he *really* like with his family? What reputation did he have with his friends? Was he someone who kept his word with the little things? Were we both looking for the same thing in a relationship? And… what was his relationship like with his ex-girlfriends? This last question was probably a bit taboo, but I *needed* to know. I figured if he had nothing to hide, he wouldn't have any problem sharing his past. After all, being in a relationship requires honesty and vulnerability.

Our relationship continued to progress as Josh proved his trustworthiness. We got along well, and I didn't sense any red flags as I evaluated him. Life was just ordinary as we went through the motions, running the rat race every day. We had been together for three years and had briefly talked about marriage. Since neither of us were getting any younger, I felt it was the next logical step. Little did I know he had been secretly conversing with my parents in Vancouver, asking for my dad's blessings. Josh's proposal caught me off guard, but with the looming pressure I felt to 'keep up' with all of my friends, the word "Yes" spilled out of my mouth.

We had a cozy and intimate engagement party with just our closest friends and life continued on as usual, until that windy mid-November afternoon where I was aimlessly wandering the streets of Toronto. My mother had called a week before to tell me my aunt, battling stage IV leukemia, had almost died. Mom suggested it would be good if I came home to Vancouver for a few months to spend some quality family time together.

A huge part of me wanted to be there for my family, especially for Dad, who's mental health challenges were being intensely triggered by my aunt's illness. I had almost lost Dad once before to depression and I couldn't bear the thought of reliving that again. But deep down I was scared that if I went home to my family for an extended period, it would rock the boat with Josh and potentially jeopardize our engagement.

I found my way to a church, empty and peaceful, and sat down on one of the pews. It was calm. It felt warm and comforting. I felt that sense of peace that

I wasn't able to find anywhere else. I still didn't know what to do, but I felt a sense of relief. Leaving the church later that night, I still had no answers, but I felt for the first time that there was hope. I went back again the next day, and then the next, and somewhere in the midst of all the stillness and calm, I found myself. For the very first time, I listened to my gut on what I *truly* wanted to do. Despite my fears of the aftermath, I made the decision to go home. I *knew* that it was what I needed to do.

Josh was surprisingly very understanding, reassuring me that I had his support every step of the way, even though I wasn't able to fully articulate the jumble of emotions I felt inside. I left for Vancouver a week later, intending to stay for six months. After a month had passed, while in Vancouver with my family, I received an unexpected text message from Josh. It read, "We need to talk." followed by a long message that ended with the words, "It's over." My hands shook and I could hardly read the words on my phone. It had happened *again*. I was devastated. Suddenly that eerily uncomfortable feeling that had engulfed me as I walked the streets of Toronto made sense. Intuitively I already knew this was destined to happen.

Too ashamed to face the world, I slept my days away, becoming a prisoner in my childhood bedroom at my parent's house. The only time I ventured out from under my covers was to go to the bathroom or when my parents would force a few bites of food in my mouth. All that kept running through my mind were things like: Was I really so unlovable? Was I such a terrible person that I didn't deserve to be happy? What had I done to deserve having my heart stomped into pieces after I vulnerably gifted it to not one, but two men I loved? Something must be super wrong with me to be engaged twice yet never make it to the altar. I was certain I was destined to be alone. If I had fears about being abandoned before, now I had *proof* that people always leave.

What I didn't realize was that every relationship I had emotionally invested in up to that point in my life was essentially the same relationship with a different face. I was so desperately searching for someone to love me that I morphed myself into being whoever the other person wanted me to be. I did all the things I thought would make my partner happy, yet there was never any open communication or dialog about what was working and what wasn't in our relationship. I certainly did not dare to voice the things I wanted or needed for fear that if they didn't like what they heard, they would leave me. The reality was, they left me anyway.

My epiphany came when I realized that instead of jumping from one person to the next, searching for that intimate love that my heart yearned for, what I actually needed was to focus on falling madly in love with ME. No one would ever be able to love me if I didn't know how to love myself. Heck, I didn't even know who I was or what I wanted.

I vaguely remember teachings from church about being 'complete in God,' and so I delved into my Catholic roots for answers. When I felt the most hopeless and helpless, when fears paralyzed me, I learned to turn to prayer for guidance. In prayer, I found answers to my worries coupled with resounding peace. In this peace, for the first time in my life, I believed that I was worthy of a deep loving relationship, and that I didn't need to settle for whoever was conveniently around just to avoid being by myself.

Freeing myself from this fear of being alone brought so much clarity on what I truly wanted in my dream spouse: what traits and characteristics am I attracted to in a man, what my non-negotiables are in a life partner. Rather than get caught up in the honeymoon phase where hormones, attraction, and lust ran through our bodies, I started asking questions: How do I want to feel when I'm around him? What types of things would we be doing together? How would we be bringing out the best in each other? This became the checklist I used when I met potential partners so I could discern whether they were the one my heart truly wanted. I also realized that when I gave my body away in search for love, what resulted was always clouded judgment and a false sense of intimacy where we ended up in the relationship for all the wrong reasons.

Despite the pain of the breakups, what tore my heart to pieces was the exact thing I needed to grow. The earth-shattering love that our heart yearns for is possible if we dare to dream. That perfect-for-you spouse is out there if we quiet ourselves enough to let our intuition guide us and not rush to make decisions from a space of fear or lack.

The saying that 'things happen when you least expect it' is something I've always believed. After learning these hard truths about love and relationships and shifting the focus to working on myself, I unexpectedly met the man of my dreams while I was away on a retreat in California all alone. Like the fairy tales, this man was my Prince Charming but not for all the Disney princess reasons. No, he didn't sweep me off my feet on our first date. No, he didn't pick me up in helicopters to go on romantic reality TV-style getaways. No, our courtship was not all rainbows and unicorns.

In reality, the dating phase of the relationship with my now husband was full of peaks and valleys, ones we had to learn to weather together. It was actually during those challenging times when we were army crawling through the trenches together that our relationship grew even stronger. While I was previously afraid to speak my truth for fear of abandonment, this time there was nothing we couldn't talk about. Clearly and openly communicating whatever was on our minds, working through challenges as a team, and selflessly loving each other when we weren't our best selves was the foundation that led us to a lifelong commitment to one another.

Even though the world may tell you love should be a certain way, YOU are the author of your unique love story. Believe that you are worthy of that earth-shattering love your soul desires, and don't settle for anything less when fear creeps up. Have courage to follow your heart, and be patient as you listen to your intuition guiding you to what it is you need and want. One of our greatest gifts as human beings is learning how to love and how to be loved. Pour your love into you and, when you are ready, the most amazing relationship will present itself. From there, go write the next chapter of your happily ever after exactly as your heart yearns for.

IGNITE ACTION STEPS

- The journey to love begins with you. Write out a list of positive affirmations beginning with **"I AM"** to affirm your worth. Make a decision on how you choose to show up every day.
- Go on **dates with yourself** and enjoy the feeling of being alone. What activities do you really enjoy doing by yourself? What can you do to pour love on you?
- Make a **checklist** of all the qualities you desire in a partner. Be as specific and descriptive as you can. What are your non-negotiables?
- Have you been hurt in previous relationships? In a **journal**, free write whatever comes to you relating to that relationship. Are there any silver linings?
- Write a **letter to your future self** in 10 years describing what your perfect love life looks like. This will help you get clear on what you want and create the space for those desires to come to life. Write as if you are living it NOW.

Cherrie MacLeod – Canada
Founder of Parenting Littles; Life, Marriage and Family Mentor
www.parentinglittles.com

ANNABELLA
AL-NAFUSI

"Magic is when we care to speak each other's love language and deliver a message for the heart."

I would like for you to have the most amazing love life. I want to share with you how important it is to be aware of your own needs for reassurance that you are truly loved. You can ask for it consciously from others. I encourage you to be curious about the nine Lost Love Messages that can bring you a feeling of being deeply loved. Love can become a game, when the goal is to make everyone a winner.

FINDING THE LOST LOVE MESSAGES WITHIN

I was in the middle of attending an amazing speaking academy in Oslo, Norway. I had stepped away for a few moments to make a phone call home to Denmark. During that week-long training I wanted to share my message about the importance of the *Lost Love Messages* — those same lost love messages which probably saved my marriage. I wanted to be on the biggest stages I could find because I wanted to save many other marriages all around the world. Yet surprising to me, I found out my own marriage was lost.

It felt like everything stiffened in that instant, like an invisible shell tightening in on me. It made a painful crack and revealed a deep felt truth. A truth that seems to have been there before I even realized it. On the phone, despite my husband's happy voice in my ear, I knew right then that I needed to get a divorce. I knew it on a deep level, one connected to a peaceful place within me, even though my bodily reactions were not at all peaceful.

And there I was at this conference, realizing that my marriage wasn't saved — it was doomed! There was no solution. On our 20th wedding anniversary, two months later, we made it known to all our family and friends by posting a selfie on Facebook.

"Frank and I have our 20 year wedding day today! August 2 has always been a day of joy. However, we have decided not to take another 20 years, and this day has now become our official divorce day. We support each other and can happily appreciate the many good years we have had together. We are aiming for a strong friendship to be our future. Thank you to all of you who have helped us share our good times. ❤ *"*

We then went out to share a delicious lunch together and celebrate the beginning of our new relationship. We transformed our marriage into a loving and supportive friendship through the tears of letting go of what was.

Precisely a year before the divorce, I decided to love my husband unconditionally. I knew that he noticed the change in me because a few months later he told me that I'd become "very loving lately." The result of my unconditional love was that I'd stopped mothering him and started respecting his choices. He had been sick with heart and lung disease and he could get sick again. He hadn't changed his ways to live a healthier life, but I decided that he knew of the dangers and he was old enough to make his own decisions. It was not up to me to decide for him any more. And it never really was. Loving him unconditionally meant that I would have to let him die if that's what he wanted. I had told him, the doctor had told him, and his body certainly had told him. As he always said, "You can't make a man do, what a man won't do."

It felt good to finally let go of worrying so much about his life and again see him as the gorgeous man he was, rather than seeing him as a man who depended on me saving him! It's a miracle how we come to re-appreciate the people closest to us.

With unconditional love, he was my man again and we found a refreshing happiness for a while. Through our last year of marriage, there was much loving, but at the same time it became more obvious that we had grown apart and stopped being interested in each other's lives. We had given each other freedom and had embraced our separate ways. And we didn't try to solve it anymore. Instead we stopped acknowledging our feelings of separateness, until we had an unavoidable realization that we had reached what had to be either the end or a new beginning. We decided that we had done well until then and that we would divorce in our own way — as lovingly as we had been together.

Not that our marriage was an easy road…. The truth is, we were living with addiction for years.

We met when we were studying to become teachers and lived in the same student housing. I fell for him after months of friendship and smoking joints together. Our way of flirting was a bit odd but very romantic to us; we would find new ways of scaring and surprising each other every day. I loved to feel outsmarted and entertained by him.

When I said my "Yes" in the church, he turned to me and whispered, "Got Ya!" I had gotten myself a loving, fun, caring, intelligent, interesting man who adored me. I had also married into addiction.

We eventually found a way to fit into the norm of having family, jobs, and a home. But we still smoked joints during the weekends and the holidays were a nightmare — my saddest times because they disappeared into haze and nothingness. I didn't reach out for help. I was ashamed because I found it unbearable to feel the weight of failing to live up to my own standards. For years I felt alone with that pain. I would take the dog for long walks and secretly kneel to the Universe and cry in my helplessness.

Mostly though, we were having fun together. The jokes that brought us together came from an ability to look at the bright side and make life worth living. We had a habit of cheering each other up and made an effort to see a smile on each other's faces.

For those first 10 years of marriage, I thought that I was the only one silently suffering. He mostly seemed happy and content, while I was often struggling with doubts whether I should stay or go.

I know that our loving marriage was inspirational to some people, and our journey toward this required lessons in conditional love first.

We experimented with the pleasures of marriage. We converged and departed — only to converge again! We found mutual interests. We challenged each other to understand new things. We forgave each other's limited views and perceptions. We had kids and shared our joy with them.

He was more easily satisfied than I was and didn't feel the need to change things that were working fine. But to me, it was never enough, because I had profound fears of being stuck in a polite and sad marriage. Not that I enjoyed being dissatisfied, but more because I loved to improve, to create something even better. That was my joy!

Until one magical Sunday morning, I had no idea that my husband was doubting my love for him. Had you asked me if he felt my love, I would have sworn that he did! Because I did. And because I made an effort to make him feel loved all the time... so I thought.

That Sunday morning I walked into the sunlight-covered kitchen. He was dressed in white and was haloed by the sun shining from behind him. I kissed him and we hugged. I turned to cut the bread. Nothing out of the ordinary. And then he said, "Can I ask you something? Why have you never told me that you need me?" I shook my head several times, as if to connect all the brain signals to make sense of his puzzling question. "What? Of course I have... We have been married for 10 years and I love you!" But he persisted, "No, you have never told me that you need me." I turned toward the bread, the knife gripped tight in my fist, and tried to say the words... then whisper them to myself, "I need you." But I couldn't even do that!

To my big surprise I couldn't tell my husband that I needed him... and I had no idea why.

I thought that I was able to do anything, and still I couldn't give him that? I decided to avoid the topic in my usual cheerful way and gain some time, "Oh honey, don't worry about me. I don't need anybody..." But this time, he didn't let me go that easily. "I know sweetie, you are cool. But can't you just tell me that you need me?"

And that's when I knew I needed help. I asked for a moment, and I hurried to the living room and fetched my book *The Wisdom of the Enneagram*. I instinctively looked upwards and pleaded for guidance. "Please show me what I need to know," I whispered. I then opened a random page that showed me that my Enneagram type has objections against being addicted to anyone and anything. I felt strongly that this was an important moment. And it was clear to me that the restriction was in *me*. I had a hard time being in need of him, because I had a fear of leaning against someone who would be able to leave me — to become sick or even die.

This explained my own restrictions, but I knew that if I was to give my husband what he was longing to hear, and to change my ways on a deeper level,

I would need more motivation. I looked upwards and asked again, "Why is it that he needs to feel needed?" My experience with other people needing me were not pleasant ones... they were about people who craved me, kept me in a tight grip and gave me a heavy feeling. I had no idea why anyone would wish for that! With that in mind, I opened the book, and what I needed to know was right there in front of me! It said that his Enneagram type has a deep wish to be included and to know that he matters to the tribe. It also said that he has always longed to hear this message but may never have felt that he heard it his whole life. And it said that, when these messages are given, it feels so overwhelming, that we might even reject it or protect ourselves against receiving it. We humans are living paradoxes.

I was now ready to give it a go. After all, the *Wisdom of the Enneagram* had been my bible for years. I decided to trust the truth in what I was shown and try it out. Then I thought, "Well, how is his need translated into my Enneagram type?" I looked at my type, and it said that I was longing for someone to say that I was being taken care of. I couldn't believe it. I have never needed anyone, so what was this all about? I didn't need anyone to take care of me!? I decided, that — holy moly — I had found the one mistake in the *Wisdom of the Enneagram*! There it was! And for sure, if it wasn't a mistake, then I would definitely discover something new about myself!

I went back to the kitchen where my husband waited patiently. I told him that I'd try to tell him that I need him, and I asked if he would try and tell me that he would take care of me. Even now, remembering how he sat there in the kitchen, patiently looking at me with warmth in his eyes, my heart is pounding. His face took on a loving glow and I'll never forget the way his voice filled up the whole room, slow and thick and rich, as he said from his heart, "Of course I'll take care of you. I love taking care of you. There's nothing I love more than taking care of you."

Those words were magical. I let them own into my system and penetrate all my cells. The feeling was so amazing that I forgot to breathe. My heart was pounding like mad and my legs disappeared under me. I grabbed the kitchen table before falling to the floor. It felt like a total body orgasm. I had never experienced anything like it, and when I came back to my usual self, I looked at him in awe and sighed, "What was that!? If this is what it means to you, I will definitely have to learn to tell you that 'I need you'!"

We practiced giving these messages to each other. He was really good at it. Whenever I would ask him to do this or that, he would bring me the coffee saying, "Here you are Love, I'm taking care of you." Or "Let me take care of you." And each time he said that, I noticed how my demanding approach softened and I felt that he was giving me more than coffee. The coffee wasn't the important thing; in fact, I felt that I could get my own coffee! It was the love message that came with the coffee that mattered. Whenever he told me that he would take care of me, I was the happiest wife.

I was a little slower at giving the message to him. For a long time, I could say, "Thanks for the coffee – that was just what I needed." But gradually through the years, with lots of support from him, I became better at letting myself need him.

Our relationship gained a deep softness. We were playing with it, longingly wishing to hear it, and constantly tapping into present moments, where it would be the honest thing to say. I am convinced that it prolonged our marriage by another 10 even happier years. After recognizing the magic of these simple love sentences, I thought of my children. I wanted them to grow up hearing those messages. So I waited for authentic moments to share love messages with our children as well. The responses I got from my two boys receiving the Lost Love Message were so heartfelt that I melted.

For a year I thought that this was just something that we had found that worked for us. But then I realized that maybe I wasn't the only woman who had a sentence that worked magic for her. And maybe I wasn't the only woman who would have a slightly bitchy and indirect way of asking for it. And I probably wasn't the only woman who could learn to love better. So, I decided to share it with friends, and the feedback I got was amazingly powerful. One woman told me that these simple words represent the reason why she got a divorce from a man she loves and still lives with as friends after four years. Another told me that these words could describe what a man gave her while she was with him for 10 months, even though she didn't really like him!

I call these the *Lost Love Messages*. It is as if these sentences can penetrate the walls around the heart and we feel deeply loved and appreciated. These are what the heart calls for and soothes the soul. If you say one of these to your spouse or children, you will witness the real person you love.

- Type One: You are good.
- Type Two: You are wanted.
- Type Three: You are loved for yourself.
- Type Four: You are seen for who you are.
- Type Five: Your needs are not a problem.
- Type Six: You are safe.
- Type Seven: You will be taken care of.

- Type Eight: You will not be betrayed.
- Type Nine: Your presence matters.

These small words have a massive impact. Try it yourself. Let your heart open up to hear the messages. Ask to hear them from your spouse, from yourself, and from the Universe. Ask someone to tell you the words, yet that it be done in honesty. Speak the messages your partner needs to hear also, trusting that the more authentic the moment, the more powerful the message will resonate in their heart. Give the messages to yourself. And meditate on receiving them from the love of the Universe.

I have learned that love speaks in many languages: friendship, buddies, co-workers, parenting, siblings, and lovers. Each one of those connections can blossom by using the Lost Love Messages. When you use them, the other person will never, ever forget how you made them feel. Try them all out and see which one resonates. Say them with honesty and authenticity.

IGNITE ACTION STEPS

1. See love

Complaints become openings for love, for it is when we don't feel loved that we ask for it the most.

2. Let go

When we let go of things having to go our way, we can perceive what the Universe has invested in us. What we perceive with an open heart is always better than what we thought we wanted.

3. Let love

Be true to what comes from your heart. If you can sense a contraction in your heart and body, honor that feeling. Always be true to whatever sensations you feel. Let your attention flow to others. Make an effort and give it all you've got!

Annabella Al-Nafusi – Denmark
www.Nafusi.dk

Natalia Słoma

*"Within our reach is a world of divine connection
greater than anything we've ever known."*

This story is my personal invitation to the incredible world of tantric connection and conscious intimacy. I encourage you to be open, to surrender to a deeper, more fulfilling bond with yourself and your partner. I would love for you to use the practical tools within my story to take your love life to the next level... and beyond. I invite you to experience the vast expansiveness of an intimate connection and create heaven on earth experiences in your everyday life.

Heaven on Earth in Your Bedroom

"This is going to be the most sensual exercise of our entire Tantra retreat," our trainer said, his dark eyes sparkling as he smiled mysteriously. I looked around the circle at my fellow participants and my entire body shivered. I wasn't sure if I should be scared or excited. It was already the seventh day of our love-journey on the magical Thai island of Koh Phangan. I had arrived on my own, ready to dive deep into the art of tantric connection. So far the experience had been both ecstatic and liberating. But it was also deeply challenging. The first few days were about healing past traumas, accepting ourselves, and filling our hearts with self-love. My boundaries were pushed to the limits and I had to confront all my fears around relationships. I knew I was onto something big though. Something that might change my life forever. Now we were about to explore the art of touch and sacred sensuality. I couldn't wait!

Our trainer told us to pair up with a person of the opposite sex on our right. I turned to my right and drank in the sight of a charming blonde-haired man. He smiled at me flirtatiously, a dimple playing on his cheek. All the ladies — aka 'Goddesses' — were asked to then blindfold our 'Gods.' We were about to play a game to awaken all five senses, and I felt the arousal start to inch its way up my spine at the thought. Ok, now I was officially excited!

First, we focused on the sense of smell. I started to tease my partner delicately with scented tissues. I danced them over his face, allowing the relaxing scent of lavender and the stimulating smell of peppermint to activate his energy. His body began reacting, trembling gently. The scent appeared to spread throughout his entire being with each inhale and exhale.

Next, we were given chocolate and were told to feed our partner erotically. I let him enjoy the sweet aroma of it first. I slowly waved the chocolate in front of his nose, letting the air currents bring the rich and velvety flavor to his body. Then I delicately started caressing his lips with the sacred ambrosia. From his lips I slid the chocolate inside his mouth, massaging his tongue. That pleasant arousal rose from within my pelvis, strengthened and continued its journey to my core. As if on command, his teeth sank into the chocolate. The tension rose.

Our next exercise was to breathe sensually into our partner's ears or give them compliments. I took a deep breath in. As I exhaled, I knelt down and began gently breathing in his ear. Over and over, I breathed in and then exhaled into him. With each breath, I relaxed into it more, sinking deeper into my knees and into the experience. As if beyond my control, longing moans began to escape my body. I felt safe — safe enough to express my desire from the depth of my being. I felt as if the room was ours, we were alone, lost in our own pleasure and ecstasy. I could feel the strong, powerful energy in my partner's loins growing. A deep fluttering moved through my own body in response.

We were then guided to use feather-like touch to keep the fire burning. I let my fingertips drift over him, starting with his arms and shoulders. I could feel all the little dips and curves outlining his strength. His ribcage rose and fell under my palms as his breath deepened. With firm strokes, I caressed his abdomen and the tops of his thighs. His mouth fell open as his breathing expanded. It was as if I was resurrecting a king-of-kings from a deep sleep. It was now time to awaken his sight.

I removed his blindfold. His eyes were bright and wild with excitement. His body looked like it was ready to explode. We were instructed to dance for our partner in our own version of a 'mating' dance. As I gyrated and let my body flow around him, he watched with animalistic desire. He appeared ready to hunt me. To take me to the depths of my being and ravish me, allowing me to expand into the sweet nectar of love. Both of our bodies were vibrating. The excitement was intense. All the sensual movement, the sounds, the tastes, and the smells had switched our senses on. At that moment, I felt we were unlocking our unlimited potential… we had unleashed something sacred and powerful within these love rituals and I knew that my love life would never be the same…

I first turned to Tantra in my early 20s as I wanted to heal my sexual blocks and overcome my insecurities. I was desperate to try anything that could make me feel more open and more confident. From my early childhood I felt a huge sense of body-shame. Even as a two- to three-year-old infant, I wouldn't allow my parents to let me run around naked. It was unbearable. I would often burst into tears and wouldn't stop until my parents comforted me. I never discovered what made me feel this way. All I knew was that for my entire adolescence I was carrying this huge body-shaming-baggage combined with the inability to express my needs, my desires, and most importantly, my boundaries. This created intense anxiety and awful panic attacks. As if that wasn't enough, I didn't feel like I deserved to be loved, let alone have a fulfilled sex life... or to even have a sex life at all.

Hence, I was desperate — REALLY desperate — to find a remedy and feel better about who I was. I wanted to prove my worth. So I started with what seemed like a solution: I started using sex as a tool to boost my self-esteem. This only worked for so long. I wasn't aware of it at that time, but sex without deep connection was leaving me with a terrifying feeling of emptiness that I was surpressing. It took me a few years to realize that I was actually hurting myself rather than helping myself. Allowing these compulsive behaviors was suppressing my true needs and deepening a wound that I was carrying from relationship to relationship. That was when I decided I was ready… ready to start my healing process by whatever means necessary.

My journey to healing was an adventure of a whole new kind. On top of various forms of therapy, meditation, energy healing, and shamanic sessions… I discovered Tantra. Tantric tools and teachings turned out to be beautiful guides to connect with myself and my body. They helped me start treating my body with love and respect, and worshiping it as my sacred temple… Little by little, I was learning to raise the bar for how I wanted to be treated by my partners. All of these tools opened me up to a new level of connection and helped me re-define love. Finally I understood what it was like to truly love myself.

The deeper I dove in this mysterious world of Tantra, the more I learned about the ultimate power of genuine loving connection with both myself and others. I was fascinated by how intimate sexual experience can go beyond just the physical realm and become an emotional experience. How sex can be way more than what we see in movies (including the ones for adults). How it can be a union of two bodies, two souls, two energies.

I was in my mid 20s when I decided to start attending tantric retreats and exploring all these theories and practices — an exploration I would continue for the next decade. That memorable tantric retreat in Thailand was where the magic truly happened for me. I remember laying on the grass after one of the sacred love rituals, crying the happy tears of deep forgiveness and liberation, and feeling my heart full with love. Love for myself, love for my body, and love for all the people in my life who made me who I am. I remember looking at the night sky, covered with stars and promising myself that I would not only continue this journey of self-love, this journey of treating myself and my body with the love and respect that I deserve, but that I would spread it further.

Before that retreat I had no idea that I could feel so ecstatic, so radiant, and so blissful. I had no idea that there were tools that can take your love life to such a whole new level. That was the moment that led me to starting a movement called *Zentra*, spreading the message of deep connection and conscious sexuality. A message of love and self-love. A movement that is taking thousands of people on a journey of relaxation and bliss while empowering them to reach greater self-acceptance and self-awareness.

In that moment when I was bathing in starlight on the grass, I also promised myself that I would not settle until I attracted the partner with whom I experience the deepest loving connection and the most mind-blowing intimate life. I felt I was finally ready for the love that I deserve. The love *we all* deserve. I got up from the grass and walked into a new world of complete and divine conscious intimacy — with a heart full of trust and self-love.

Three years after that remarkable tantra event, I was sitting in front of the most amazing man. A man whom I promised myself to manifest and with whom I literally 'knew it from the start.' A man who I experience stories with that proves romantic movies can indeed happen in real life. He is someone who treats me like a queen, reflecting the self-love that I was lacking for such a long time. Somebody with whom making love is a heaven-on-earth experience, a divine connection not only on the physical, but also emotional, energetic, and God-knows-which other level… It is a far-beyond-words experience.

The levels of connection I now share with my partner are those I've studied for years in various tantric sources. I had always wanted to explore them so badly, and now I have discovered that anyone can have them at their fingertips every day. Oh yes, they are real and so worth being learned and experienced! These levels show us a new realm of intimacy and connection... a new dimension of a love life that we all deserve and we all are capable of experiencing.

It took me many years to let go of the baggage of my past. To develop the feeling of loving myself and knowing that I deserve a true, deep love, and to attract a partner who embodies it all. Our relationships act like a mirror, reflecting back to us opportunities to grow. And yes, this might sometimes be uncomfortable as well as frustrating but that's a part of the process. Knowing this, we can choose to Ignite our love life by bringing our senses inward first. Self-love is the place we all must go when searching for love. Without love for ourselves, it becomes very difficult to find healthy, deep, loving relationships that feel fulfilling.

When we truly love and accept ourselves, we don't settle for anything less, in our life and in our partners. The same goes for sex. I spent a lot of life shaming myself for something I knew nothing of. Not respecting my true needs and using it as a tool to feel better about myself. But once I went inward and unleashed my true power within, I began to discover the divine nature of union and the orgasmic fullness of a partner that penetrates beyond the physical surface. The beauty of this tantric practice is that the power of sacred sexuality can be explored with yourself and with a partner.

Within your reach there's a whole new realm of divine intimacy. You *can* have a deep ecstatic connection that will allow you and your partner to melt into oneness; a connection that feels like you are making love to the Universe. Let this be the beginning of a sensual journey of discovering you: finding love and self-love. Let it be the spark that Ignites the flame in you, the flame that continues to burn brightly and guides you toward deeper, more loving connections and powerful intimate experiences.

Ignite Action Steps

At *Zentra* workshops and in the Zentra mobile app I guide our beloved students through a set of empowering and heart-opening meditations for both solo practice and for couples. I would love to guide you through one of the most beautiful connection exercises. This simple yet powerful tool will help you truly open up your heart, become more vulnerable, and connect with your partner on a deeper level.

Find a peaceful quiet place and sit comfortably opposite your partner. Allow your body to feel relaxed and at ease. Close your eyes for a moment and take a few deep calming breaths. Try to let go of any expectations, just open up to the experience with curiosity and accept what comes.

Slowly open your eyes and look deeply into your partner's eyes. Give each other a tender gaze and a warm loving smile. Offer your partner your full attention as if they are the only person in the world.

Notice the mysterious depth of your partner's eyes. The colors, the sparkle. Our eyes are the gateway to our souls. They allow us to enter into divine connection together. To melt into oneness… Look into your partner's eyes as if they were revealing all their unspoken secrets, uncovering the softness and vulnerability, beautifully balanced with their strength and charm. See your partner's true self. Whisper gently, "I see you, the real you." Take a deep breath to become even more present with each other. And let yourself be seen. Give yourself a loving permission to be fully visible in this moment. To be vulnerable. To unveil. You are in a safe space.

Allow your partner to really see you. With all your perfect imperfections. If the tears appear, that's completely normal. Feel how with each and every breath you're opening your hearts more and more.

Notice how beautiful this person is. How adorable. You're looking at a piece of art, at pure perfection. You are perfect exactly the way you are. With your smiling loving gaze let this person know they are beautiful. Let them feel your full acceptance for exactly who they are and how they look. Send this acceptance and pure unconditional love through your gentle gaze. And as a receiver — take in the love. Let your heart melt. You deserve it. We all deserve to be loved and accepted. To be cared about and appreciated for exactly the way we are.

You can put your right hand on your partner's heart and take your left hand and cover theirs. Surrender into the warmth of your touch, the delicate sensation of your heartbeats and the loving energy flowing between your hearts. Take a few deep soothing breaths with a loud sensual tension-releasing exhale. Look at each other in the most tender and trusting way. Breathe deeply. Feel the connection.

Smile at each other and express gratitude for your partner's presence, acceptance, trust, and love. Be grateful and proud of yourself for opening your heart and being truly vulnerable. Give each other a big warm loving hug or, while still keeping the eye contact, move to a long sensual kiss...

I highly encourage you to keep practicing this exercise with your partner especially in an intimate setting. Try kissing, love-making, and experiencing pleasure while looking tenderly into each other's eyes. Breathe deeply. Be mindful of each and every touch, breath, and sound. Also, try out the five-senses exercise and enjoy the magic happening.

Be present. Be open. Be curious. And keep Igniting your love life every single day.

Natalia Słoma – Poland
Founder of Zentra, Meditation & Tantra Instructor
Head of Mindvalley Certified Trainers
www.myzentra.com
f *myzentra*
○ *myzentra*

ANA CUKROV

"Love limitlessly. That's the only way to live."

I want to remind you that love is all there is. It has no end, no boundaries. You can access it anytime, no matter how deep you fall or how empty you feel. There is no limit on the currency of love. You can't spend it, so use it freely, abundantly; there's always more where it comes from. You *are* loved limitlessly and you *can* love limitlessly.

LIMITLESS LOVE

Once upon a time there was a sweet young maiden. She was cared for, held tenderly, and loved gently as a baby. She was played with and raised with love. She was admired and respected and she knew how important and special she was. Her path was set for love, abundance, and happiness...

Every story has its beginning. Mine began as a fairytale, with moments that touch threads of many known tales, as most of our stories do. Human lives are all similar when it comes to basics. We are all heros and heroines of our lives. We live, we love, we suffer, we grow. And what better way to embody all that than a story? My story is about a pursuit for romantic love, a journey full of challenges, dynamic plots, and interesting characters. A tale that hasn't been completed yet, but has introduced me to *Love* itself and made me fall in love with it.

It was supposed to be like this: they meet, two fabulous people, whole and interesting, defined and attractive... their eyes lock, time stops, everything else is a blur... they know that the moment is precious, unique, one that will determine the course of their lives... they decide, independently, to go for it... tingles and everything... they click... a deep connection is there ...they feel safe and accepted for who they are when together... he tells her how precious she is to him, that there is no other...she inspires him, assures him, makes him feel whole...they grow with one another...you know the rest. Happily ever after.

That was the picture I had built in my mind, the dominant idea of a love story. I always wanted to understand love and nothing gave me a better answer than Disney movies. I stuck to that fantasy because I liked it more than any other and because it resonated with something written deeply in the core of my being. We all carry a glimpse of happily ever after. In my early childhood I received some answers about love, but many questions remained unanswered. Mostly, how can two people in love fight so much? Will they remember that they love each other? I must have known instinctively, despite all my questions, that limitless love is possible.

My parents met quite young, married quickly and secretly, and soon my twin sister and I were born. I guess love was unclear to them as well. They needed to learn how to approach love, how to negotiate, how to forgive, and how to heal. They didn't get along and this was painful to me as a child. I was never told why and how they came together, nor why they separated. Sure, I knew the divorce circumstances, her leaving with another man, feeling unsatisfied, unfulfilled, him mourning over that fact and trying to cope. But the true dynamics of the relationship? I didn't have a clue. I didn't get to see them together, because my sister and I grew up with my grandparents for the first few years of our lives. Nor did I understand the way it works between men and women, how it looks when the days are filled with mutual respect, passion, work and fun, food and sleep, partnership and parenting included. It took awhile for me to uncover the mystery.

What I did know was limitless love. I knew it well because I lived it, I felt it. I knew love well because of how it makes my heart beat, how it makes my eyes sparkle, how it gives me shivers when I look at my loved ones. I remember from the earliest age how it felt to want all the best for those around me. I know so well that blissful uplift of energy just by watching someone I cared about do or say something that made them happy, fulfilled, or proud. I came to the world equipped with this tool, this organ for love. It is my ingrained feature and I know it. It came handy later and God knows I needed it.

I felt loved since my young days. My first impressions are so loving: my mother holding me tenderly, nursing me. My father, carrying me gently, lifting me up, providing the feeling of security, and encouraging my curiosity. My twin sister, looking at me openly and sincerely, with full trust, holding hands with me, being present with me all the time, and I mean all the time. My grandparents were so calm, focused, gentle, peaceful, and trustworthy. A family friend, a retired professor, reciting poems as I sat on his lap. My babysitters and teachers, so careful, encouraging, dynamic, and trusting.

But when it comes to men, I have to be honest and have to admit I don't know what a love life means. Sure, I have had love stories, I have met love. Some of my love experiences were beyond imaginable. Some were wild, the others kind, some were short, the others very long, some passionate, the others affectionate. But to truly know love is to live a lifetime with a person. One whole man, one whole woman. Growing together, even while one or both of you isn't willing to grow. Both working together through the hardships and peaceful times. Until the two of them can understand what was going on, can forgive one another, even laugh about the hard times, until the two of them can watch peacefully their common history together, enjoying the fruits of their work, rejoicing with the children they welcomed to this world and brought up together. That kind of love life I never knew.

I believed, just as much as Aristotle did, that love is composed of a single soul inhabiting two bodies. That's what I was looking for. Having met my husband, at twenty-four, I believed I had found it. Like my parents, we got married quickly. We were in heaven, always together, a perfect match. We would finish each other's sentences, liked the same music and even preferred the same humor. I felt he was all that I needed, I forgot about my family and my projects, but I didn't mind. All I wanted was for him, for us, to be happy.

I did everything in my power to make it happen. I moved in to his place. I forgot about my exams and my dance troupe and, basically, my life. I fed his cat and I cleaned his apartment. It was our nest, as I believed at the time. I took care of my mother-in-law as she had a chronic disease, until she passed away. I helped him with his work project, then with another one, then a dozen more. I paid his debts. I cooked and cleaned and worked for hours and hours. I kissed and hugged.

Most of my married life was a Cinderella story. It was just missing the prince. My husband exploited, humiliated, and manipulated me. It was hard, but I still did what I knew was right. Day by day, I chose love, knowing that there must be a reason for the song in my heart.

Fairytales offer archetypes and all I knew was how to play those roles. However, what a mature relationship needs is much more than role playing. I was unconsciously drawing the picture of the happy family. It turned out it was only me who was growing, me showing up, forgiving and accepting. My husband was only pretending, although he was acting the part very well. For a while. And then the painful truth slowly revealed itself, in all its horror. I was cheated on, mistreated, financially depleted, ignored, and abandoned. It was painful and I tried to fight it, to get support, to cry for help, to make him understand, to heal, and to cope. Until one day I fell on my knees and weeped. I prayed, and cried, and prayed some more. I was granted strength, but couldn't change him. Never does the good Lord force us to change. Freedom is our ultimate gift. I started respecting his freedom, but I still hoped that love would enter his cold heart.

So what do I have to say on the subject of love? I know love in its origins. The love of God, visible in the perfection of nature, in gentleness and forgiveness, in peace and art. I know love of parents and children, between siblings, friends or an owner and his pet. In romantic love, all I know is the pain from waiting for it. I know patience from observing love. Although romantic love was never reflected back to me in my marriage, I felt in other ways.

For a decade, I went through the reverse process of falling in love… I tried to convince myself that I was happy… that my concerns about my husband weren't real. I wasn't ready to accept that I was angry, sad, and disappointed. Then I started to nag… then to demand… and then to beg. By the time I figured out he was never going to love me back, there was a rupture in my heart the size of a moon crater. That's when I gave up… became hopeless and helpless… I was at the bottom. Neglected, hungry for love, acceptance, and appreciation. I went day by day warming myself with God's love. I knew limitless love but somehow it didn't feel enough anymore.

So I entered the ugly duckling story, for I could not see myself as a swan anymore.

Who could love me, I wondered. Who could tolerate and embrace a broken woman, with no money, no self-esteem, no self-control, and no hope? And would I be able to love back?

I was active in my parish and participating in liturgic festivities when I met a handsome and refined man. From my despair and misery I considered him a brother, never having a clue that he liked me, all of ME. By that time I didn't think of myself as a full person... being a wife, yes, a mother, certainly, all the roles were clear, but my own person? As ME? I had already given up on myself. *This was my sleeping beauty phase.*

Sadly, for a very long time, I couldn't receive romantic love. Then, in my early forties, I discovered that a woman still lived in me. I found it through the need to be held and touched, the hunger I could no longer ignore. As I was relaxing one evening, there was a classic on, the one my American friends know too well, *Gone with the Wind*. A line in there hit me like a rock. "You should be kissed and often, and by someone who knows how." I realized that I knew how to nurture spiritual love, but I had ignored all the rest. God loved me, so why shouldn't I?

Then, in a beautiful park with my daughters on a sunny day, I was reunited with my original understanding of love. There was a smell of pine mixed with freshly cut grass. Childrens' laughter was coming from the playground and my distant thoughts glided in and out of fantasy. As I sit on a bench, observing people passing by, I notice I'm always holding my gaze for an instant longer on the couples, holding hands or whispering to one another. I cannot help but smile. My soul knows they are home and I feel happy for them. Let their love last as long as possible, I pray.

Then my seven-year-old's friend comes running toward me with a tender smile and places a drawing in my hand. There are two ladybugs, in wedding suits, smiling at each other. Her blue eyes look up at me and she says, "This is you marrying your new husband, Auntie Ana. I made it for you so you don't have to be as sad anymore." And at that moment I realized that limitless love *is* possible. I had stopped believing in it. How could this little girl have known that my marriage hadn't been true love and what real love really is? Looking at her drawing, I became certain about the love I deserve. I finally understood that all the tenderness and affection, all the respect and acceptance I wanted and needed was legitimate. What I desired wasn't a divorce or a new partner, a blessing from a priest or public acceptance. What I needed was my new updated version to love. *My own magic wand I would bestow upon myself.*

I gave myself time to heal, a time to rest, a time to love and nurture myself. It took a lot of patience, inner healing, tears, and in the words of Elsa from *Frozen*, I had to let it go. It took a lot of encouragement. I couldn't have made it without my daughters, my sister, and my friends. Along the way, I slowly started to believe in love again. By the end of this story I finally found courage to take my wedding ring off. And gave myself permission to love again.

Holding the idea of romantic love dear to my heart, I hoped for love, expected love, demanded love, and chased love of men. Not that it helped much. Then I tried to learn about it, write about it, to lecture and teach about it. Still there was no love in the way I hoped to receive it. Now, I have found love in loving. The eternal love that never changes, the universal love, the love of God. It's always present, everywhere. So I found love in the depths of my heart, in my own being. By giving and forgiving I kept connected to the Source and opened to immense inflow that never runs out.

I found my peace realizing that all the expressions of love are united. It's the same energy, coming from the same Source. I cannot thank all the beautiful souls enough who have loved me through this life. All the family members, all the friends, all the boys and men, acquaintances and colleagues. Limitless love turned out to be true: we are all children of God, we are all brothers and sisters and when we love, we flourish; when we care about one another, we feel the love within. We are here to remind one another of *limitless* love. We tend to forget it in the times of crisis. Then we need a close friend or a family member to remind us. There's a higher calling than any other, the one to be a human, to love and support yourself and others.

Now, I choose love and I choose it daily. I feel enormous grace each time I glance into a stranger's eye and our souls meet... even for a second. Within each and every person I find love and confirm that there is enough love in this world. Romantic love still remains a mystery to me. However, whether 'the right one' appears, reappears, or doesn't appear is of less importance now. The exciting part is that the story is yet to be revealed.

I have learned that we are the heros and heroines of our own lives. Nobody should tell us how to lead our love life; no one is responsible for how it develops but us. No other person is going to regret it as much as we will if we don't honor and nurture it. Furthermore, an 'unhealthy' choice is still a choice. Every choice teaches us something and has a gift within it. I can choose to be grateful and also forgive. I have learned that if I let others make the choices about my life, there's no way I can be blissfully happy about it. Never give your power away!

When we know who we are, what we need, and what we want, then the intention to have limitless love can be sent to the Universe and only then the prayer can be answered.

I sincerely hope your story is a happy one. In order to make it full of bliss, remember to choose love. There's enough love for all of humanity. Love never divides, it can only be multiplied. Otherwise it was never a love to begin with. Look in the mirror, tell yourself the nicest words. Say them although it seems silly, express them even if uncomfortable, speak them in spite of the fact it feels unfamiliar, yell them if you have to, until you trust them. I encourage you to claim your right to live *happily ever after* and live in limitless love.

IGNITE ACTION STEPS

1. Remember: you are loved, you carry all the love you need inside. *Blow a kiss to yourself every time you see yourself in the mirror.*

2. Reclaim: it's your birthright to love and be loved. *Sit in your carriage and wave all your stresses away.*

3. Refill: pray, meditate, connect with your core and with Universal love. *Ride your magic carpet and live in your Cave Of Wonders.*

4. Recognize your uniqueness: love yourself for who you are. *Be serendipitous, frolic in the rain, kiss a frog if you have to, and let your hair down.*

5. Receive and give, keep the balance of reciprocity in mind. *Do the 'Bare Necessities' and forget about your worries and your strife.*

Ana Cukrov – Croatia
Psychology Professor
anacukrov@gmail.com

Anita Adrain

"The Outer World is Connected to and Reflecting in the Inner World."

It is my intention that my story will empower you to see how you can 'not' work on your inner world without working on the outer world — your home. The place where we spend 30-50% of our lives. If you want to experience a loving intimate relationship, connections with family, and positive interactions, the 'energy' of your home must match the 'energy' of your heartfelt desires, goals, and wishes.

Feng Shui for Romance

We are conceived in the act or expression of making love. From the time we take our first breath and our last, love remains the theme of our lives as we seek to feel loved or be loved.

Growing up in a family with six brothers and four sisters, the ninth of eleven children, I did not always feel loved as it was easy to get lost in the crowd. I remember as a young child that I would often escape the hectic environment of our home to hang out in the sunshine with the birds and the trees. I was not aware at the time that I was intuitively practicing the ancient Chinese art of *Feng Shui*. Connecting to the soothing energies of the natural environment had a calming effect on my inner world, thoughts, and feelings.

I was in my early thirties when I was first introduced to the term Feng Shui; my official journey began. It became clear to me how the energetic influences of the seen and unseen had been a common thread interwoven in my entire life. Eager to add balance, harmony, and beauty to the spaces around me, my study began with the book *The Western Guide to Feng Shui* written by Terah Kathryn Collins. I resonated with each page, each chapter, and enthusiastically began to put the principles shared into practice. When I got to the end of the book there was an invitation to learn more by becoming a student at the Western School of Feng Shui. The seed was planted.

Three years later, ready for a change, the stars aligned. I left my parenting responsibilities and that of running a full-time brick and mortar business to attend the first module of practitioner training in San Diego, California. It was not an easy task. My husband was not supportive of my decision. I was spending thousands of dollars and leaving him and our three young sons in Canada for one week to take training on something no one in our circle of friends had even heard of; California was years ahead of where we lived.

Like many couples raising a young family, we were at that time in our marriage 'going through the motions' and having some challenges. Our intimate relationship suffered as the result of both of us working long hours (he, sometimes away from home) and juggling the responsibilities of everyday life. We were growing farther apart, neither one of us feeling secure in our relationship and uncertain what the future would hold.

I did not recognize then the courage that it took to take that training course and follow my heart with passion and purpose. It required a great deal of conviction and conscious determination to honor my inner feelings, disregarding what other people were saying, including my husband of fourteen years. I would later learn that the outer world spaces of our environment were mirroring our discontentment and, in fact, anchoring the energy in the depths of our subconscious. I am quite certain that had I not committed to studying Feng Shui, our commitment to each other would not have continued into what is now thirty-five years of marriage.

Igniting the flame of love or sparking a new romantic relationship begins with the awareness of the potential impact the intimate environment has in sustaining a healthy, loving partnership. When I learned to see my space with my husband as being energetically alive, with a new view through 'Feng Shui Eyes,' I discovered how powerful the practice of Feng Shui truly is.

It has been my observation in the last two decades or so, as an Essential Feng Shui practitioner, that what goes on behind the closed doors of the home reflects our core values, emotions, personal tastes, and life experiences. I have gleaned many insights simply by seeing the space of the home from an energetic perspective. Feng Shui is simply the 'study' of *energy*, the unseen and seen forces that permeate all things.

It has been an interesting journey in my own life and that of my clients to see how the relationship of the home's occupants is always being reflected in the intimate space of the bedroom. The sacred space where couples come together for rest, rejuvenation, and romance — what I refer to as the 3R's of the bedroom. We could also add another 'R' asking, "What *are* the current results?"

There are many energetic influences that may be contributing to achieving the 3R's. Prior to my training I had never considered the position of the bed and or the position of its occupants as a contributing factor for achieving optimum health and a healthy relationship.

I learned that when the bed is positioned under a window, the subconscious reads the cue as a source of potential danger. The nervous system then is on high alert for a possible night intruder activating the fight or flight response. Whatever is positioned behind and above the bed 'is' overhead or in the mind of the person. Just as a window might signal impending danger, so too does a heavy item placed above the bed as décor.

When I returned from my first trip to San Diego from my Feng Shui training, I had this new energetic view of our bedroom. Like many young mothers, I was sleeping in the position closest to the door for night-feeding convenience and toddler interruptions. I had assumed this position for many years while my husband slept soundly and deeply undisturbed. The resentment and frustration I felt in our relationship was partly due to our sleeping arrangement.

At my Feng Shui training, I learned that whoever sleeps with the view closest to the door is quite often taking on the attributes of the alpha male. It was no wonder I was not feeling fully supported as a wife and mother as I had assumed the role of protecting the entire family unit.

I was feeling the results of not having a supportive environment, eventually wearing on my mind, spirit, and body. Over time this repeated action caused imbalance and disharmony that ultimately affected all the fundamental aspects of my life.

Without explaining all the details, my husband agreed to switch the side of the bed he slept on. I can honestly say that within a short period of time I noticed that he was taking on a more dominant role in our family relationships, which instilled a deeper love connection between us. His primordial or Tarzan instinct to protect his Jane, his beloved family and territory, had been reactivated.

Assessing the intimate space of our bedroom from this 'energetic' awareness Ignited a new level of intimacy. My thoughts had been eliciting an emotion that was affecting my behavior (action) and, as a result, our intimate relationship had been suffering.

The acronym *T.E.A.R.* stands for your *thoughts* + your *emotions* + your *actions* = equal your *results*. This acronym has given me a deeper understanding of the powerful practice of Feng Shui. I'm not certain who should be given the credit for this concept as I found many teachers with similar versions. This mathematical and word equation has great relevance, in my opinion, in unraveling the complexities of Feng Shui presented by other authors. It has helped illustrate to me that how we show up as a partner, a lover, a parent, or friend is the result of our thoughts that determine our emotional state.

My husband and I realized that every possession residing in our bedroom was 'saying' a lot more than either one of us realized: from the pictures of family members, parents and kids, to the items that were chosen as décor. The subliminal messages received (thoughts) were activating an emotional response affecting the level of intimacy we shared (results). We had no idea our subconscious was receiving the signal or information that someone was watching our every move. — "Where the eye goes, energy flows; where energy flows, attention or intention goes."

I know clutter also influences the quality of rest, rejuvenation, and romantic relationships. I have seen office desks, filing cabinets, TVs, and work-out equipment to name a few that have also taken up residence in the sacred space of the bedroom: items that are constantly sending subliminal messages that there is work to do, keeping the mind active or, in many cases, overactive.

I went from practicing these concepts in my own life to sharing them with clients. I saw that all of the 'visual' stimulation and physical clutter (the outer world) equated to mental clutter that affects the inner world. I recognized how women equate a tidy home to self-love whereas men see clutter in the home as being lived-in — leaving dirty dishes in the sink is no big deal. Their garages or man caves may also be cluttered and elicit the same response. When a woman has repeatedly asked her significant other to please make room in the garage and her request has been ignored or dismissed, she interprets the message as 'he doesn't love me.' As soon as a woman feels she is not valued in a relationship, the intimate connection starts to deteriorate, leaving the man asking, "When will I be loved?" Neither partner is consciously aware that the behavior is affecting their sex life.

It has been said that, "We teach best what we most need to learn." When I started presenting Feng Shui for Romance workshops, I gained a new awareness and perception of the male/female dynamics. I reached a profound realization: women for the most part want to *feel* loved and men want to *be* loved. I see this orientation as the start of the relationship breakdown. This discernment helped me to empower my clients giving them the guidance to rebuild their romantic relationships.

At the end of one of my workshops, a participant shared with me that had he had this knowledge sooner he was certain that the love of his life would still be with him. One of his 'aha' moments came with the realization that a particular piece of furniture had been the center of many arguments. He described it as a large chaise lounge that consumed a significant part of his living room. It was one of *his* treasured possessions that he had brought into their shared living space. His partner repeatedly asked him to get rid of it as it was tattered, worn, and it did not match any of the décor. He loved his chair and didn't see it as a big deal. After a lengthy discussion, we were able to get to the root of his resistance. The chair represented a time in his life when he felt good about himself. That feeling was stored deep in the subconscious program of his mind and he wasn't consciously aware that his resistance to get rid of the chair was connected to a deep emotion. Over time, the repeated feeling of not being loved took its toll on his partner, until one day, she finally announced that she no longer wanted to be in the relationship.

> *"How you respect, care for, and value any possession is how you respect, care for, and value anything."*

Another attendee had a similar story. He also had a chair that took up residence in his bedroom that his new wife did not like, and he was resistant in moving it to another room. When he became consciously aware of the emotional value attached to the chair, it was a huge moment that brought him to tears. The chair had belonged to his late aunt, who had shown him more love and compassion in his life than his own mother. After our session he announced that the chair was going to be moved out of the bedroom as he realized the consequence of having his 'aunt' oversee the activities of the bedroom.

> *"Self-worth or self-love along with the feeling of being loved — the unseen energies — are always being reflected in the seen energy of the home."*

Following my second Feng Shui module training, I grasped with a deeper understanding the importance of sharing physical space with my husband in both the outer world and the inner world. The small closet in our bedroom contained my clothes, and his clothes had been placed in the spare bedroom closet. Over time this imbalance of spatial equality in the physical environment showed up as inequality in our relationship. With that realization, we went to work and installed a closet organizing system. It allowed us to use the full space with a his and hers side divided with a floor to ceiling shelving system. The result was an immediate shift in our personal energy that sparked a renewed appreciation for our partnership.

For many years, I have taught my clients and students to activate the positive emotions in the physical environment of their home. Just as my husband and I had, they also learned to activate more of the same in their inner world environment. This elevated state of awareness put them in a state of emotional excellence (higher frequency) which helped them to realize a greater existence of self.

> "Scientists at the HeartMath Institute in California have been studying the effects of the heart since the 1990s. *It is their belief that the next frontier of human awakening is about understanding how to better use the power of emotion to enhance the quality of our life experiences, improve health and ultimately find solutions to personal and societal problems.*"

HeartMath Institute www.heartmath.org

When I learned to sustain positive emotions and a happy-go-lucky attitude, my nervous system relaxed. I became at ease, and my heart became coherent, in harmony and in balance with all my other biological systems. A healthy heart, with feelings of love, gratitude, and appreciation are synonymous with a healthy person. This equates to a vibrant relationship. It is my goal to help others embark on the journey of mastering their own lives, starting in their own homes. When you match the energy in the physical space with your heartfelt desires, goals, and wishes, you will experience more of the same, as like attracts like. Your inner world, thoughts, and feelings are being reflected in your outer world, reflecting in all your sacred spaces. To create something different, or to have different results, the outer world energy *must* match the inner world's deepest desires and wishes.

Love holds the key to us co-existing on this planet, our first home. Love is the foundation where there is a deep connection of our physical body, our mind, innate spirit, and is the place we call our *inner* home. Love is the framework of the tangible home we build around us. All of these are interconnected and fused energetically. I encourage you to build your family fortress, create your castle of connection, and find your house of happiness. I encourage you to practice Feng Shui by living with what you love, and loving where you live, as "Home is where the heart lives."

Ignite Action Steps

Listen to your heart's desire and get ready to Ignite the flame of love when you take the first step in Feng Shui'ing any space. Declutter! The prime real estate in your bedroom should be home to possessions that you love, that you need, and that serve to make your life more enjoyable.

Whether you are wanting to share your life with a loving partner or are looking for a new romantic interest, you must be willing to share the space of your bedroom. Creating room in the physical world and having spatial equality sends the signal that there is room for each person to display their individuality without compromising their values. I recommend that women move on over and give their man at least one third of the closet space and one third or more of the bathroom space. In same-sex relationships the recommendations are to inhabit equally; whoever is currently dominating the space must be willing to share.

A single person will want to give the same consideration to their space when setting the intention for a new romantic partner, reinforcing the idea of dual occupancy. Take a good look through your energetic 'Feng Shui Eyes' to see if the room is being dominated by a singular energy. Are there two nightstands of equal height with two lamps? Is there space in the closet and the drawers in the bathroom for a roommate?

Ask yourself, what possessions are constantly sending signals of information to the subconscious that may be anchoring the energy of your current romantic relationship?

Recognizing the tangible things that take up residence in your bedroom should elicit powerful positive emotions that will ultimately bring you into a state of harmony and balance. Whatever makes you happy, whatever brings you joy, whatever makes your heart sing, do that!

Anita Adrain – Canada
Certified Essential Feng Shui Practitioner
www.fengshuisimplyput.com

KATRINA VAILLANCOURT

"What would Love do?"

My desire is to unleash the full potential of love from within your heart. May this story empower you to dissolve the barriers to love's 'free flow' so that you may thrive — creating harmony and fulfillment in *all* your relationships.

LOVE SHINES THROUGH

"Would you like to earn your first point?" I asked my nine-year-old son in hopes that the new emotional intelligence game I had created might reshape the way we were relating to each other. My hopes were that it might transition him from his tendency to yell at me into a new pattern that would serve us both.

It had only been six months since a Nonviolent Communication (NVC) mediated negotiation had successfully restored my joint custody arrangement. That alone had been an unforeseeable and seemingly miraculous victory. My son's father had previously determined that hiring a nanny was preferable to restoring my custody for any amount of time. In that three-hour mediation, however, I was relieved to have finally worked through our parental disagreements and my weekday custody was established once again. I had walked into the session with little hope of resolution, thinking I'd have to take him to court to regain my rightful place with my son, and I walked out feeling like a miracle had occurred.

After *five years* of only seeing my son one or two precious times a month, I thought that having him living with me again would heal my heartache, and life would simply get better. I was dismayed by the much darker reality of re-entry into each other's daily lives.

Our time apart had taken as much of a toll on my son as it had on me. Nearly every day he'd wrap himself around my leg and scream at the top of his voice for about a half hour, "I hate you! I hate you! I want to live with my dad!!" I often found myself in tears, physically shaking, struggling to pull myself together. Sometimes numbness would take over. It had been six months of agony. I had to find some way to change this painful and miserable pattern.

I had disavowed the tools for discipline which seemed to be common practice. I was determined to not raise my voice to match or outdo his. I would not threaten anything precious to him or warn him of any kind of consequence for his behavior and physical punishment such as spanking was entirely out of the question. I hold a firm belief in raising children without using any of these forms of power-over, domination-based authority. And yet nothing in my toolbox was working. Begging him to stop, trying to reason with him, asking my roommate for help, seeking advice from friends, breaking down crying myself… I tried all these things and more, to no avail.

Today was different. I had something new to try, and to my relief, my son said "yes" to my invitation to play his first 'card game' in exchange for a point. When he reached 100 points, I would buy him the video game of his choosing.

The idea for this game had come to me in a wave of inspiration — in answer to my prayer for help. The principles of NVC had made a world of difference in my custody mediation. If it could work there, perhaps it could work here.

The game I developed has four sets of cards. Three sets are based on the teachings of NVC. The first is called 'Universal Longings.' Each card shows a need, longing, value, or desire identified by Dr. Marshall Rosenberg, founder of the Center for Nonviolent Communication, as a primary driver for every choice we make in life. The second set is of the 'Emotions Connected to Fulfilled Longings.' This set contains the emotions we experience when our needs are well met. Then there are 'Emotions Connected to Unfulfilled Longings,' which are the emotions we feel when our needs are *not* met.

The fourth set are 'Character Strength' cards, which come from a spiritual teaching: We are here on earth to learn to love. These character strengths are like signposts for our potentiality, facets of love that can shine through our thoughts, words, and actions. Patience only grows when it is tested. The same can be said of forgiveness, kindness, generosity, humility, creativity, and all other character qualities.

When I look back on some of the hardest challenges I have surmounted in life, and I flip through these cards, I quickly see how many of my character strengths grew as a result of having worked through that challenge. This teaching has helped me remember that any challenge or tribulation that may arise in my life is also an opportunity to grow into the next best version of myself. This perspective has turned difficulties into adventures in personal growth. This form of empowerment, which has become popular in what is now termed 'Positive Psychology,' was yet another emotional intelligence skill set I sought to foster in myself and encourage in my son.

With my new set of cards in hand and my 'contract' in place with my son, I was ready to give this a go.

It was not long before the first opportunity presented itself. It was dinner time and I told my son's friends it was time for them to go home. Unhappy with this decision, my son argued for them to stay, telling me I was mean, unfair, and that he didn't like me. After his friends left, he walked toward me with that familiar look of frustration on his face. I knew what was to come — I imagined he was about to wrap himself around my leg and scream at me again.

"Would you like to earn your first point?" I asked him. "Ok!" he responded quickly, sitting down next to me.

Picking up the grey Emotions cards, I said, "For the first point, I'm going to go through these cards and guess what you are feeling. After I am done guessing, all you have to do is let me know if I guessed right or not."

I began laying my guesses face up: 'bored,' 'impatient,' 'sad,' 'lonely,' 'disappointed,' and 'frustrated.' I set the other cards aside. My son looked at the cards and said, "Yes. That is what I am feeling."

"Thank you," I said, feeling encouraged. "Would you like to earn another point?" He nodded and leaned into me, ready to hear what was next.

"For this next point, I am going to go through these cards," I said, picking up the green set, "and guess what you want. When I am done, please look at the cards I chose and let me know if I got it right or not."

I laid down the words 'fun,' 'play,' 'friendship,' 'connection,' 'choice,' and 'fairness.' He again affirmed my guesses were correct. "Would you like to earn another point?" I offered. He was up for more. Excitement was building in me. He was engaged and I began to feel cautiously hopeful.

For the next two points, I handed him the grey deck of emotions cards first, followed by the green set of needs and asked him to guess what I was feeling and then what I wanted.

I was not expecting him to have much accuracy on his first try. I sat behind him as he sorted through the cards. "Oh my God! It's working!" I exclaimed in the silence of my mind. I felt my heart break open as I watched him accurately identify my emotions: 'sad,' 'tired,' 'stressed,' 'uncomfortable,' and 'frustrated.' Next came my needs/longings cards: 'ease,' 'cooperation,' 'respect,' 'peace,' 'joy,' 'warmth,' 'rest,' and 'love.'

Silent tears wet my cheeks as his cards demonstrated his understanding of my reality, such a contrast to the screaming I had experienced in the days, weeks, and months previously. When my son completed his task, he turned to me to ask if his guesses were true for me. Seeing tears rolling down my face he asked, "Mama, are you ok?"

"Yes!!" I responded as the tears grew even stronger. Feeling the sweetness of our eye contact and heart connection, I expressed, "Thank you so much for understanding what I am going through."

"Mama, I love you!" His response was wholehearted as he wrapped his arms around me and gave me the longest, warmest hug I'd received from him in years.

To my surprise, those screaming fits stopped overnight. My son is now 22 years old and in college. I am delighted to share that we only had two conflicts between that time and now in which we needed to pull out the cards and work it through. We invented many 'games' that continued to develop our emotional intelligence, attitude of gratitude, and ability to resolve conflict, and that deepened the love bonds that we cherish so much.

This turning point rocked my world. A newbie at NVC, I was having overnight success with the help of a set of cards. And it didn't happen by diving into the nitty-gritty of the problem. There was no talk about 'right' and 'wrong,' 'appropriate' and 'inappropriate,' 'fair' or 'unfair,' 'respectful' or 'disrespectful.' Instead, we simply identified each other's feelings and needs, and each felt heard, understood, and loved. That was all that was needed.

The benefits of playing these card games were multifaceted. Not only did we experience greater gratitude and engagement, less conflict, and more love, but self-negating patterned ways of being were melting away and being replaced with new life-affirming practices. We both had come a long way.

Throughout my whole life, I had been a 'people-pleaser' who struggled to say 'no' to anyone and would put other people's desires ahead of my own. That pattern built up resentment that I eventually could not contain, exploding in bursts of anger that I could not control, followed by tears and thoughts of victimhood. Those episodes evaporated as I came to understand that I could reduce resentment by becoming aware of my own needs and caring for myself as I cared for others around me. I found my instinct to be critical of myself and others was replaced by a deeper and more compassionate understanding that we are ALL motivated by the same underlying needs. This newfound understanding provided me with a profound sense of relief! I had learned that when I felt critical of another person's choices, it was because their strategy didn't meet my own needs. But, if I could reach to understand the needs underlying their strategy, I could feel compassion for them and guide negotiations to find solutions that could work for both of us. As I replaced old critical and judgmental patterns of thought with these new practices, I increased my capacity to be compassionate, loving, and considerate while still caring for myself equally.

The successes I experienced inspired me to share this discovery with my community. I played the card game with friends who then asked me to make them sets of cards. I helped parents re-establish loving connections with their kids, and supported siblings to sort out conflict cooperatively. Lovers were drawn to the cards, as well as teachers, counselors, and therapists. Their enthusiasm led me to bring my game, *Love Smart Cards™*, to market. Since that time, we've sold almost two thousand card sets in the U.S., Canada, and Japan, and are currently translating them into Mandarin for use in China. This was definitely NOT in my original plan. Sometimes life has plans besides those we first imagine; it creates a lotus flower from the 'dark nights of the soul,' which is also the fertile foundation for something beautiful to come forth just as the phoenix rises from the ashes.

Since that challenging time, my experience of life has transformed and I feel like I'm living a series of miracles. My son and I have a loving relationship that is beyond anything I hoped was possible. His father and I have found harmony with each other, along with the clarity that we are very different people. All of my relationships have benefited as a result of applying the teachings of NVC and playing with the cards. I feel blessed by the opportunity to share this gift with others.

I have learned that being 'in love' is not enough. Love without skills hurts. It becomes a broken marriage, our best friendships turn sour, and parents and children disown each other. Wanting to be loving is not enough. We must learn the skills of thinking, speaking, and acting in alignment with love and compassion; we must learn how to love smart — to be empathic, to be able to understand the experience of another, their feelings and needs — as if we were walking in their shoes.

Having gone through this journey and discovered simplicity in the solution,

I know that anyone who has a sincere, heart-felt desire, backed by commitment and willingness to learn new habits, can create relationship breakthroughs in ANY of their relationships. As we open our perception to true compassionate understanding for ourselves and others, barriers to love dissolve. From this awakened state of perception, love flows. It is your underlying nature — to love and be loved.

You have the potential for unlimited love within you. In any given situation, ask yourself, "What would love do?" Speak your truth, but give equal urgency to your commitment to being empathic, compassionate, and being the love you wish to receive from others. This is what it takes to flex the muscle of love from within and create it as your experience of life in this world. The power is within you. This is your invitation to take it to the next level. Love Smart.

IGNITE ACTION STEPS

Cultivate self-awareness.

Listen to your body. Notice the sensations, emotions, and longings that arise in your body. It has so much wisdom for you. Learn to listen and find words to express your emotions and the underlying Universal Longings. Use the Love Smart Cards™ or words lists to support this practice.

Practice giving empathy – often!

Give yourself empathy by finding resonant words for your emotions and needs. Practice giving empathy to others by guessing what they might be feeling and needing.

Take time for gratitude and appreciation.

When you are caught in conflict with another person, take time to remember all that you appreciate about them. Appreciation supports a positive outcome for everyone. Notice your pleasant emotions and met needs in your relationships and in your life.

Make compassionate understanding a top goal in your relationships.

When two people fully understand a problem from each other's point of view, win/win solutions begin to arise.

Challenge yourself to create win/wins everywhere you go!

If you lose so others can win, over time you'll feel resentful which often leads to upset. If you are winning at a cost to others and they feel like they lose around you, the relationship will disintegrate over time. But when you can live in a way that meets your own needs while also caring for the needs of those around you, relationships thrive and life is so much more pleasant. It can take patience and commitment, but it is totally worth it!

Recognize habits that undermine connection and replace them with habits that serve connection.

Learn more about habits that create separation and habits that create connection by downloading "The 7 Adjustments" from www.LoveSmartCards. com and become familiar with character strengths in support of creating new life-serving habits.

Remember, the power to love is within you and every interaction you have is an opportunity to shine. Shine with love!

Katrina Vaillancourt – United States of America
Mother, Artist, NVC-Enthusiast
www.LoveSmartCards.com

ICO: The Incredibly Caring Organism/ Edward Fish

(they/them)

"As long as the people involved are consenting, it doesn't matter what anyone else thinks or feels about it."

I wish for you to be empowered to be honest with yourself about your wants, needs, and desires. Create the love life and relationships that work best for you, including a healthy relationship with yourself.

To Thine Own Self Be True

I have an amazing, loving, and supportive family. To be clear, I'm not talking about the biological family that I was born into. The people I live with today are my *chosen* family. They are a group of four individuals that I was blessed to attract into my life as a result of my journey of self-acceptance, and who also helped me to accept parts of myself that I had been previously afraid to embrace. It wasn't always like this.

This is what happened when I 'came out' to my biological family. One Christmas morning, I was at my grandmother's house in Illinois, United States, for winter break from college. My mom, dad, sister, and myself had just finished unwrapping our gifts. Both myself and my dad had received a fish-shaped carabiner. I asked my dad if I could have his. Both of my parents asked me why. They had no idea that I had expanded my beliefs of what was possible and allowable in my own love life. It was very different from the vanilla monogamous life that I had been taught and seen growing up. I was worried that being honest and authentic to who I'd been discovering myself to be might cost me my family's acceptance. I didn't want to have to pick between my family and love. I had a choice to make. I could either make up some lie or tell them the truth. I wanted to own who I really am, so I took a deep breath and said, "I want the other one because I'm in the 'kink' lifestyle. I want to have the pair to use with my handcuffs." Before my parents could even react, I decided to go for broke, "I'm also polyamorous. I have multiple relationships." As soon as the words left my mouth, I became afraid of how they would react.

My mother exclaimed, "Oh my God!" turned, and walked away from me. She wasn't willing to talk about it with me at all. My dad said, "Do you mean like that show 'Sister-wives'?" My chest collapsed and my heart sank. I lowered my head, shaking it. As I closed my eyes, I let out a heavy sigh and said, "No, Dad. Not quite like that."

My dad was willing to sit at the kitchen table with me and ask me questions, trying to wrap his mind around what he had just heard. At the end of the conversation my dad said, "It was nice knowing you." I was stunned. My body froze. Was my dad disowning me? Was I being thrown out of the house? On Christmas morning? I had been taught by one of my mentors to be less reactive and more curious. So, I took another deep breath and asked him, "What do you mean it was nice knowing me?"

Sitting as far across the table from me as he could, he said, "I think you're going to get some kind of disease like AIDS and die, so it was nice knowing you." That was the end of our conversation. I was in shock and felt devastated that my dad believed that how I chose to love others would literally kill me. A few weeks later, my dad called me and said, "I don't agree with your lifestyle and I still love you." That was the most acceptance and understanding I was to receive from my dad while he was still alive.

Most of my life I have felt that I was an outcast. I had a deep-seated belief that I didn't really belong. Any group or relationship that I joined, a part of me *knew* that it would come to an inevitable end at some point. I believed that no matter what, if I were to *really* show them my true self, I would be unacceptable to them. I held an idea that the world didn't want the whole me and couldn't handle everything that I am.

Starting at the end of third grade, my mother moved us around to a different city every one to two years. After divorcing my dad, my mom would change locations every time something big happened to her. I didn't know how to handle the changes and I was constantly the 'new kid.' I didn't make friends very easily. After the third time we moved, I developed a belief that I shouldn't even *try* to make friends nor even bother to unpack any more than what I absolutely needed. I knew that any effort that I put in would just be lost in two years or less. I had three constant companions: Garfield, my cat, the TV, and my Nintendo™ game consoles. My daily routine was getting up, going to school, coming directly back to my room, watching *The Disney Afternoon,* and playing Super Mario World. I spent fourteen years — from the age of seven to twenty-one — numb, completely disconnected from my emotions.

By the time I went to college, I still had *no* idea of how relationships with people worked or how to attract a lover. I turned to the one thing that I *knew* I was good at — studying! I started to delve into as many books and courses as I could get my hands on to learn about relationships, dating, and love. During the course of my exploration, I began to get an inkling for the first time in my life of what I actually wanted and needed in my own love life that would be fulfilling to me. I started to learn about relationship possibilities that resonated with my heart and soul.

In one of the first books that I invested in for my research, a concept stuck out to me. The idea was that there could be women that would be okay if I was interested in dating them, being their lover, and also wanting to date other people. This was my first introduction to the concept of ethical non-monogamy. I was excited and amazed that these kinds of relationships were possible.

As I started dating, I found that encounters that involved *just* physical sex without the heart and emotion in it were *horrible* for me — I felt disapointed, unfulfilled, and had difficulty maintaining an erection. These experiences helped me discover that it was very important to me that my romantic interests were centered around love and having a mental-emotional connection to my partners. I learned that the term for that is 'polyamory', which literally translates to 'many loves.'

A short time after that, I came across a personal ad on Craigslist. The heading of the ad said, "Prometheus was bound for all eternity." The body of the ad simply said, "This girl only wants to be tied up for a single hour." The picture attached to her ad was a black and white sketch depicting the scene of the Greek legend where Prometheus was bound to a rock as a punishment and having his liver being eaten by an eagle. I was intrigued.

I knew that this ad was written by a woman of intelligence and culture. If I wanted to capture her attention, I needed to show her that I was of equal caliber. Happily, I was already well acquainted with the Greek myth, so a response came easily to me. I replied, "I will bind you for your sins against humanity. You will writhe as I stoke the fires of your desires within you. By the end of the hour, you will be begging for release, however, not from your bonds."

I intrigued her enough to write back to me. After a few emails back and forth, she gave me her phone number. At this point, I was feeling pretty confident and more than a little bit cocky. When I called her, I went over the top with arrogance, nearly destroying her willingness to meet me in person. I was able to recover enough that she did eventually agree to meet with me.

I met Sunshine at a cafe downtown near the college campus. One of the things that struck me first about her were the fuzzy cowhide pajama bottoms. They were white with black spots, just like you would see on a cow out in the field in the Midwest.

The initial conversation was pretty benign, mostly filled with the usual kind of first date questions like, "Where are you from?" and "What are you into?" I was looking to take things slowly. I originally planned to build rapport, be laid back, possibly hold hands with her for a bit, and *maybe* if I was lucky I *might* be able to give her a hug and a kiss goodbye. I *certainly* didn't want to be seen as one of *those* kind of guys who are only looking to have sex and aren't interested in anything else. There was some connection between us, and I feared that if I showed her the real me that she would find me unacceptable and the relationship would end before it had even begun. Up until that point I had portrayed a confident persona in our emails and phone conversations.

Sunshine asked me to go on a walk with her outside. I agreed and we left the cafe. There was a walking path that ran through the woods nearby. It was a typical sunny California day with very few clouds in the sky and balmy weather in the low 70s. We walked hand in hand to a place in the woods that had a river running next to it and sat down facing each other.

As the conversation between us continued, I thought I would press my luck a little bit to move our budding relationship forward by lightly caressing her arm. With my heart racing, I reached out to touch her. This was the first time in a long time that I had even had a date with anyone. I was terrified that I was going to screw it up.

After a few seconds, she physically pulled away from me and looked me in the eyes. Hesitating, she said, "I'm sorry. This isn't really working for me." My whole body drooped. My shoulders pulled forward and in. My neck curved down and I could barely look her in the eyes as a frown formed on my face. Inside my head I was kicking myself, thinking that I had screwed things up and gone too far. I had enough presence of mind to ask the question, "What would work for you?"

What she said next blew my mind. I felt gleeful, and a mischievous grin sprawled across my face. I discovered my 'Dominant' side and boldly took action. After a few minutes of engaging in a brazen act of passion in public, I paused to check in with her. "Does that work better for you?" I said, with a smirk on my face. "Uh huh," she said, still a little breathless while shaking her head yes. "Wanna come back to my place?" she asked me with a huge smile on her face. That was more than my wildest dreams had hoped for! I gleefully proclaimed, "Yup!"

She led us back to her place, a private home, not too far from campus. We spent the rest of the afternoon in passionate love making. At the end of our time together, she printed out a single page and made it into a tri-fold, like a pamphlet. Handing it to me, she explained that it was a list of her sexual turn-ons, what she was curious to try, and what her hard limits were. She shared with me that a former Dominant of hers had ordered her to create that paper. Sunshine said it was one of the most difficult and most rewarding things that she had ever written.

I was amazed and impressed that someone had taken the time to discover and articulate their wants, needs, and desires. It was brilliant to know and realize that sexual desires, wants, and needs could be openly communicated. I finally felt that I was discovering a lifestyle that I truly belonged in.

I began to imagine how much simpler life could be in general if we were able to have a blatant and honest discussion about what it was that turned us on, what we were curious to try, and what to explicitly avoid, so we wouldn't even bother going there with our new partners and ruin the relationship. I began to imagine what our world would look like if we could have that level of vulnerability, transparency, and honesty in our most intimate relationships. I had a hope that this kind of world would be the world of true acceptance that I had always yearned for.

Through learning what is possible, I began to allow myself to access and examine my own wants, needs, and desires. I learned that I could have the exact kind of intimate relationships that my heart craved and my soul yearned for. My desires could actually be fulfilled with the consent of all others involved. I also learned that while not everyone else would like, nor approve, of what myself or my partners did, as long as those of us that were directly involved were consenting, my partners and I could still be completely fulfilled in my love life.

Through coming to terms with my own needs, wants, and desires and articulating them to others, I attracted my *chosen* family, who accept me for everything that I am. I have also made peace with my biological family. I accepted that while some people don't understand the lifestyles that are authentic and fulfilling to me, I can still have loving interactions with others that don't get me. As long as I am true to *myself* and own everything that I am and wish to be, I am in a healthy relationship with the one person who matters the most, the relationship with *me*.

It takes courage and vulnerability to honestly examine and accept the truth of what we really want and need in our most intimate relationships. You are the only one who can truly say what your needs are, and if your needs are being met or if you need something more or different. Only you can truly say if the relationships that you are currently in are working for you or if they are not. You are the final arbiter of your soul's truth. It is okay to get your needs and desires met with multiple partners, as long as you have the consent of everyone involved before you begin. Let the love *within you* be your guide.

Ignite Action Steps

Clarity: Get clear on what your needs and desires are. Use the NVC Needs Inventory to discover all of the Universal needs every person has and what needs are most important to you. Non-Violent Communication (NVC) is a speaking style that shifts how we speak to one another. It allows us to imagine what someone else's needs may be and understand what we are actually desiring in how we speak to someone else. It allows the conversation to proceed in a way that each need can be heard, understood, and respected. From the list, circle the top 10 needs that are most important to you. Rank those top ten needs from 1 to 10, with 1 being the most important to you. Then share your top 10 needs with your partner or partners.

Congruence: We can only love and accept others to the extent that we are able to love and accept ourselves. Being okay with who you are and what you want and need is critical. It is important for you to be okay with who you really are, what your heart craves, and what your soul desires. Reassuring yourself that it's okay to be true to yourself is very helpful. Here is a mantra that you can use to reassure yourself, that it's okay for you to be this new way : "This is safe. This is survivable. This is allowable if I choose it to be, and I choose it to be."

Communication: The best chance to experience your desires and get your needs met is to openly share with others what those needs, wants, and desires are. Ask people, "Would you be willing to create a win/win with me to help me get my needs met?" If you're afraid to state your needs and desires to others, try using Reid Mihalko's Difficult Conversation Formula. (see the references)

Care: Specifically Self-Care. You are the only one guaranteed to be with you for your entire life. Take the time to nourish the one relationship that will always be there — the relationship with yourself. If a relationship isn't working for you anymore, ask yourself, "Am I willing to change it or end it so I can be in a healthy relationship with myself?"

Compassion: Have compassion for yourself and others. You and they have done the best that you could up to this point. Delving into what your wants, needs, and desires are takes courage. You have everything that you need within you, to discover who you truly are.

Ico: the Incredibly Caring Organism/Edward Fish – United States of America
Sacred Sexuality Coach
www.EnlightenedConsent.net

Deborah Hunt Cook

"Surrendering the reality of humanity opens the door to your magnificence, creating miracles and magic in the awakening of your Truth."

I have been blessed with a spontaneous awakening to our Divine Truth. It is my desire that my story touches and empowers you to Ignite your Truth so you can soar to extraordinary heights of love, freedom, and joy. I invite you to engage in the practices from my story, allowing you to live more consciously and awaken to your Truth.

Your Divine Awakening

This is the first time that I have shared this story with the world.

At 19 years of age, I experienced something that remained a mystery for the next 39 years. Everything that I thought I knew about 'reality' was revealed to be nothing but an illusion.

It was 1978 in Vancouver, Canada. On any given night, you would find me on the dance floor, the loud music drumming through my body, a seemingly endless amount of energy propelling me in undulating circles. But the wild abandon on my face was covering an inner pain. A childhood full of abuse and neglect that carried into adolescence was beginning to show up in the form of drinking, drug use, and an eating disorder.

I knew that I was lost.

I felt completely alone in my pain and soothed it by surrounding myself with people who loved to party. I filled myself with artificial highs, binging on food and then punishing myself for my excesses, always throwing myself to extremes.

Feeling self-destructive and knowing something had to change, I was excited when I heard about a workshop called *Breakthrough*. It was about healing previous traumas and I knew that was something I desperately needed. I signed up immediately. I was so excited about it. I had never been to a workshop before. There, I was able to freely express and heal what was eating me up inside. After I completed it, I felt lighter and freer. I went on to the second level where I was introduced to meditation, which I had never even heard of. On day one, the facilitator guided us into a deep inner meditation. I felt a spaciousness, drifting in and out of an unknown state. It was different than anything I had ever known. While in this state, we were asked to do an exercise in groups of three.

Almost as soon as I sat down with my two partners, an energy rose up within. Words began spilling out of me uncontrollably, randomly, as if someone else was speaking through me. One of the women in my group began yelling, "She's a witch! She's a witch!" I was channelling her husband, speaking in his same sentiment. Words continued to pour out of me until I felt, from the top of my head, a surge of energy shooting down throughout my entire body. The message was completed and I began shaking uncontrollably. The workshop leader hurried over and hugged me, saying, "I can't believe how powerful you are!" Later, the woman told me that I had shared details about her husband, answering many of the missing pieces she had longed to figure out.

The workshop leader took me to a smaller empty room and told me to "Release it!" Intuitively, I dropped to the ground, rolled, and shook my body ferociously. After a few moments, an absolute peace came over me, as if a switch had flipped. It was miraculous, my life would never be the same. As I slowly stood up, I was emanating this expansive, divine loving energy as though I was formless. This extraordinary energy was beaming endlessly around me. I could not stop grinning. My smile was magical and captivating, radiating a divine loving presence. As I took my first step, it felt as though I was walking on clouds. My mind was spacious, there were no thoughts, nothing to say or do. I was simply *being* and *observing* through the eyes of God, knowing all humanity is Divine Love Consciousness, though unawakened to their Truth.

I was free of all fear, illusion, pain, suffering, and the sense of separateness.

Love filled me. Not a normal type of love, but something at the very center of my beingness. A kind of love that you can not label because it is simply an extraordinary state of *being*. My life was filled with magic, miracles, synchronicities, and healing. In that state of innate *knowing...* of *being* divine love... and *acceptance* of all... of what *is*... I stepped into the perfection of *all loving* knowingness.

I had no idea what had happened for me, or why. There was no need or desire to question it. There was a sense of flowing through life that was absolutely effortless. My entire existence had been shifted to something so much more spacious and expansive. During that miraculous awakening, everything in my life began to shift. I was walking around with a permanent grin on my face, feeling this enormous, euphoric high.

One day at my apartment, my roommate was laying on the couch, her foot on a pillow with a badly sprained ankle. At the same time, the leader from the *Breakthrough* workshop came by to visit me and see how I was doing. When he saw my roommate, he turned to me and said, "Heal her."

Once again I only had to hear it and my knowing guided me to place my hands on her ankle and pray for her healing. After a moment, I took my hands away and her ankle was completely healed. She leaped off the couch, jumped up and down excitedly.

During this whole time, I had a continuous image of an awakened man with a long beard sitting at the top of a mountain. I had an innate knowing that with him is where I belonged. Not with humanity, rather, sitting and just *being* beside him. My connection with him resonated powerfully within me and does to this day.

I was becoming used to being in this state and experiencing things that were beyond my understanding. In my openness to share Divine Love with others, I met a man who wasn't in alignment with my knowingness. He told me that I didn't understand what I was doing, that I could get hurt by absorbing the illnesses of others. His message planted a seed of fear inside my mind. That seed grew and began to wreak havoc with my state of being.

Having experienced this full awakening at 19 years of age without any previous spiritual teachings, I had no idea what had happened *for* me. During this time, there was no one I could share this with who could relate or who understood what I was experiencing. The God within was my only connection. Therefore, I chose not to openly share this sacred awakening. I knew it was divinely orchestrated through God and trusted that I would get my answers when it was time.

I maintained this state and served humanity in the most loving way I knew. Although, within a few years, I was back to living my life in what I now call the 'trapped box of illusion and fear.' The state where we live from a fear-based outward experience versus being what I call 'Divine Truth.'

After the experience I had at 19, I was awakened to the innate knowing that we are all loving, powerful beings. That inner knowingness assisted me during some of the most challenging times in my life. When I lived through a near fatal car accident in which I sustained a brain injury, I spent years in various therapies. Everyone around me was distraught and worried for me, but I knew that there was a purpose and remained calm and certain of my eventual recovery. In the end, I not only regained my active way of life, I also supported other individuals with brain injury.

I now see all of my lessons in life as blessings for which I am grateful. My journey has allowed me to experience profound lows as well as the extraordinary heights of full awakening. Each has served a very important role in my life. Having known deep suffering allows me to comfort others with compassion and understanding. My awakening allows me to be fully present, listening, unconditionally accepting, and loving of others without being attached to their pain and suffering, or even to my own. It also allows me to know that my injury doesn't exist when being in my state of Divine Truth.

Many years later, I was synchronistically led to do a course with Deepak Chopra, and the mystery of my awakening was finally revealed to me. I learned about the different states of consciousness and was able to understand intellectually what had happened. I began to spend a lot of time in presence and meditation. I listened to my Angelic Human reading and self recordings to remind myself of who I am. There was a sense of freedom and aliveness in it all. An expansion of energy as I danced on the beach, practiced Qi Gong, and walked in nature. As I surrendered fear, I became open and present. In that presence, I experienced miracles, magic, synchronicities, healings, joy, bliss, and an innate desire to serve humanity. In that freedom, I was powerful beyond the mind and enveloped by a sense of peacefulness, contentment, and a deep knowing that all *is* well.

For most of my adult life I struggled with knowing there was more, but being held captive by my attachments and patterns. Although the struggle is still real, I am finally able to be more consistently in a state of Divine Love. I have begun to receive the gift of messages and truths that I know I am meant to share. These are my perspectives and meditations that anyone can use to help break free from the 'human reality' and reconnect with their Truth.

One Truth was shown to me as *'Divine Truth' vs 'Reality of Humanity.'* The message is as follows:

'Divine Truth' encompasses Divine Love, Acceptance,
Trust, Compassion, Gratitude, Respect, Openness,
and Understanding for ourselves and others.

Knowingness of 'DivineTruth' opens the gateway to our Innate Wisdom. There is no right or wrong, good or bad, no hierarchy. We are all Divine Beings of Love! We are not our thoughts, stories, or emotions. We are not our points of view or our identities. We are all doing the best we can at every moment. Our emotional triggers are FOR us; they are opportunities of awareness, growth, healing, and awakening. Trusting everything is unfolding perfectly, no fear of our future or regrets from the past. Everything shows up for a reason and is seen as a blessing or tool for our awakening. In the state of Divine Truth, we have no expectations or attachments and accept everything and everyone as is. No longer seeking outside of self. All of our answers are within ourselves.

'Reality of Humanity' is being trapped in a box of illusion
and fear. It is an unconscious, Conditioned, Consumed,
and Controlled way of being.

I refer to this as the 3 C's: *Conditioned* because we are taught to believe in the illusion by our conditioning. *Consumed* because the illusion is very compelling and distracting, and it can consume all of our attention and energy. *Controlled* because we don't even realize how much we have submitted our autonomy and authentic choices to a paradigm that we are unable to discern. Humanity experiences this fear-based way of being in varying degrees, depending on its awareness and awakening to Divine Truth. This reality of humanity is pure insanity and causes our pain and suffering. Our fear-based thoughts, emotions, patterns, and beliefs create judgment, blame, criticism, and resentment. We feel alone, unsafe, and unloved as we continue the endless search outside of ourselves to fill that void within. This can leave us feeling depressed, addictive, abusive, controlling, and confused. When intensely threatened, it can create terrorism and war. We become attached and addicted to our pain and suffering. It's familiar and becomes our norm. This has existed since the beginning of time. We are all in this together; therefore, there is no one person at fault or to blame.

I invite you to be curious and interested in your 3 C's way of being. Not in the self-criticizing way with which we are most familiar, but instead by shining the light of Divine Truth onto them.

Awareness of the 3 C's allows you to have the power of choice. I call it shifting from the 3 C's to the 3 A's: Awareness, Acceptance, and Awakening. Awareness of what you are thinking, doing, and feeling, with presence, curiosity, and investigation. Acceptance of our human conditioning and embracing with all divine truth for our healing and challenges. Awakening to our wisdom and truth. When you view the 3 C's from the perspective of 'Divine Truth,' you can see through the illusion and release it.

Not too long ago, I had a triggering experience with a woman who brought up strong fear-based emotions for me. I went to my vehicle and said to my ego, "You need to get in the back seat; there's not enough room for the two of us in the front. I'm in charge now!' I brought in my Divine Connection and asked, "What is this about? What do I need to see, be aware of, or heal?" The part of me connected to Truth was in the front seat and was able to 'drive the car' of my soul. Free of the fear-based thoughts, I was open to receiving what needed to be released and what needed to be embraced to move through this. The immediate guidance I received was to put myself in the other woman's shoes. Within a few moments, I was sobbing with empathy for the person who had triggered me, flooded with feelings of love and compassion for her. I like to call this my 'Back Seat' Meditation.

Stepping into Divine Truth and Expressing Divine Love is something we can all manifest. Getting connected to presence, meditating, and going on your inner journey to shift your 3 C's to 3 A's, is the direct path to Divine Love. It's your doorway to freedom, joy, and true happiness, creating inner peace and contentment. The space in which it ALL exists! Presence is the Gateway to Awakening!

I invite you to delve into your inner truth each day, to awaken the powerful, unstoppable and Divine Loving Being that You truly are!

Ignite Action Steps

In presence meditation, ask yourself the following interchangeable questions about what is challenging you. Ask from a place of compassion, openness, love, and understanding. In a safe way, allow, accept, and release all emotions that come to you; they are part of the awakening process. Invite your Divine Connection to hold you in safety and love.

Ask yourself:

- Is this something I have control over? If yes, what action can I take? If not, how can I surrender the fear and trust the process?
- Is there someone to apologize to, including myself? Is there a conversation to be had with someone from a place of 'Divine Love'? What would I be able to see or become aware of if I were in another's shoes?
- What belief, perception, or point of view am I holding on to? Do I want to be right?
- Is there someone to forgive, including myself? What is there for me to see, become aware of, heal from, or awaken to?
- What am I not expressing? What fear is preventing me from speaking my Truth?
- Am I holding on to a regret from the past? What is there for me to let go of, free myself, to live in this present moment?
- What am I not accepting? How can I embrace what *is*?
- What am I avoiding and hiding from? What's the fear? How can I overcome this?
- How can I surrender my expectations and fill that void within myself?
- Where can I take responsibility?
- What am I passionate about that excites me to my core? How do I create this in my life?

I invite you to set an intention each morning to be more loving. Do a loving deed. It could be anything from acknowledging someone, smiling, opening a door, buying a person's coffee, listening to a homeless person's story with compassion, or bringing a flower and your understanding to an elder person in a nursing home. When we create an intention and are open to receiving, the Universe offers opportunities for us to contribute to one another. This allows us to open our hearts, reflecting our Divine Love.

Deborah Hunt Cook – Canada
A Divine Transcendence
universallaws7@gmail.com

JULIANNE McGOWAN

*"Claim your self worth and align yourself with
someone who is worthy of your love."*

**I share my story from my heart to your heart. I hope that it Ignites you
to unveil your beautiful self so you can create and attract love, freedom,
purpose, and a soulful partnership.**

WHO DO YOU SEE IN YOUR MIRROR?

I grew up in the 70s. I remember the time as one of carelessness, freedom,
independence, and few rules. Especially in Los Angeles. The days of free-spir-
ited 'Right on,' 'Groovy,' and 'Far Out'... those were the days of my childhood.

Some of my earliest memories are of sticking my head out of the back
window of our car. I loved the feeling of freedom on my face as we wound up
the mountainside on family trips. Some of my fondest memories were all us kids
piled into my parents' old blue station wagon with fake brown wood side panels.
At the cabin, we played endlessly in the snow, sliding down the mountain more
times than we could count. That would be followed by late night kids' dance
parties, our parents clustered around a large table in the kitchen socializing
with family friends while we boogied and laughed. Then, on the heels of each
carefree day, the inevitable would happen. I say inevitable because it always
happened: Dad would grab a can of Budweiser from the refrigerator in the
kitchen. With each fresh can, his voice got louder, more boisterous, more ani-
mated. His eyes would get smaller and his words would start to slur. Watching

the lovable and funny Dad I knew and adored vanish behind an uncomfortably loud man — that would start a tremor running through my body.

When my dad drank, everything around us and between us shifted. I felt like I was no longer seen or heard. Tip toe… tip toe… He disappeared from me, even though he was still there. I felt invisible. I was scared. I felt like I needed to hide. I often did hide, becoming as small as I could so I could fit into my toy chest, unseen and unheard. I felt unworthy and unloved in those times; if he really loved me, he would stop drinking, I thought, though I never once asked him to. During that time, maybe around 6 years old or maybe younger, my life programming and patterns began to be written.

As a child, I was shy and nervous. I lived in a self-preservation and self-protective mindset. I was uncomfortable with who I was and who my family was. I was safe in my secrets, in my own inner world of pretending and hiding. I did not want anyone to know the truth of what was going on behind our seemingly stable family and happy front door. I presented this facade that everything was normal and that whatever feelings I had could not be openly shared with anyone. Not with friends nor family. My feelings didn't matter after all, so why share them? So, I didn't.

While my dad drank his pain and suffering away, my mom, sisters, and I loved him regardless. The way we loved him, without measure or conditions, was the way I always wanted to be loved. But because of the chaos and the turbulence around me, I didn't feel that kind of love. I never felt loved enough. I never thought that my words, my feelings, or my innermost child's needs mattered. Feeling unconditionally loved was not part of my childhood experience. I was desperate to find *that* love, to know *that* love…

I reached for validation anywhere I could find it. Walking down the street, if I came across a stray dog, I would bring it home. If I passed by a shelter, I would ask Mom, "Can we go in and just take a look?" and we would always end up adopting yet another furry friend. Providing those dogs a home of stability, affection, and love was my way, as a child, to receive and give what I was seeking. To me, the dogs were nurturing and loving. They were my safe place. I loved them unconditionally and they loved me the same. I suppose it would be fitting that as an adult I opened up my own Pet Boutique and Dog Grooming business. The love they gave guided me to one of my passions.

Focusing on something outside myself allowed me to gratefully survive my childhood. My wisdom now tells me that we are all, almost always, doing the best we can from our levels of consciousness. I get that… and yet, it is in our childhoods, no matter the intentions, the circumstances, the life stories of our parents and care-givers, that the hard drives of our psyches begin to be written. That was what happened to me.

When I was 25, I lived in San Francisco, one of the most romantic cities in the world. I lived with three of the most memorable roommates I have ever had in a really cool apartment overlooking the Golden Gate Bridge. We were all single and quite social; our apartment was the gathering place for our friends, and all of us were looking for love. This was long before one would swipe right to find a next date; we were out in the world and meeting face-to-face to spark organic connections.

Just down the street from our apartment was a music lounge and we loved to hang out there. One night in particular, I was there listening to a band that a friend of mine played in. Between sets, my friend came over and he introduced me to this tall, blond, sparkly blue-eyed man with a great big smile. For the first time in my life, I had this unusual feeling of immediate comfort. I didn't have to try, it just came so naturally.

It was a typical *love at first sight* story. We had so much in common and talked the night away. We were both seeking the same things to fill the voids inside of us. Afterward, he walked me home and said, "Let's do this again."

After only a few dates, I felt butterflies in my heart. I was experiencing a new emotion in my life in a new way. Everything was just a little bit more sparkly and bright. I felt that he was the right person for me, and he thought I was right for him too. We moved quickly into marriage, the natural next step, as fairy tales go. For a while it was good, and then difficulties came, as they do in every relationship at some point or another. Neither of us had the tools, experience, or inner resources to navigate through turbulence. We were both so far from ready for marriage, having yet to work out our inner-child issues. We didn't know how to communicate with each other. We didn't know how to communicate with ourselves. We didn't know how to be vulnerable. We chose each other, unconsciously, as mirrors for where we were at that point in our lives, attracting each other in order to work these issues out. It was as if we were in Love School and the lessons were being fed to us mercilessly within all of our discomfort and difficulty.

The only person I hold responsible for the end of our marriage is myself. I was not living up to my own expectations and not truly being capable of revealing the unworthiness that I kept to myself. I recall moments when I felt an uneasy, uncomfortable reaction and my entire body would shake, but I did not have the words to accurately and lovingly express those feelings. What was my body wisdom telling me? Was this a trigger from my childhood that I was not ready to confront? I would let it go as usual, unaddressed, and appear happy and content with what was. Consequently, these 'feelings' or 'triggers' exacerbated over the years until finally I left my marriage. I ran from having to confront my deep discomfort. It was much easier to walk away.

It takes two evolved lovers who have learned to see their limiting beliefs and family patterns. It takes a commitment to heal together, to adapt to each other's needs, to accept and validate one another, and the awareness that the first step is looking within. I had none of these insights at the time. I had not learned those things. You see, I learned as a child, to not talk about Dad's drinking or how it made me feel. My belief was that if I talked about my feelings, it could turn into an argument and that I might have to feel that *I didn't matter.* That was the only model of love I'd known; being vulnerable was too risky, so again, I stayed quiet. Inside, I was still the little girl choosing to be muted, choosing to stay safe in my inner world.

For everything, over time, there is a silver lining. There are gifts to come if we are open to them. This first significant experience in love and relationship became the catalyst for my journey of true lifetime healing, healing that was necessary for me to unveil the beautiful parts of me, to be whole and to learn to love who *I* am.

Following divorce, I struggled with, "Who am I?" "What do I want?" "What did I do wrong?" I spent the next decade seeking guidance from therapists, spiritual advisors, and healers. I attended retreats and became a dedicated student of my evolution. Immersing myself in all that resonated with me, I came to better understand the root of my lack of self-worth and self-love. I made it my mission to *know* that I am a lovable person and worthy of love. And yet, after 10 years, this student and seeker was still single and still searching for love. What was I missing? What was eluding me?

One evening, as I was getting ready to go out for yet another date, I caught my image in the mirror as I was checking my lipstick one final time. What I saw there were my eyes looking back at me, saying, "What are you doing? Again?" I stayed within this moment, not just looking at myself but seeing myself looking back at me, asking me for something. "Stop hiding," my reflection said.

But what was I hiding from? Validation and self-love. I was seeking love and validation *from the outside,* one date at a time, and continued to attract the same 'emotionally unavailable' man over and over again. The man who was distant, not ready to be in a relationship, still working on his past and his own inner child. I suppose it was rather unconsciously convenient for me if they didn't ask too much from me. I wouldn't need to fail; they could be the ones failing me.

I cancelled my date, RSVPing to myself instead. I moved out to the deck with a glass of wine, my dog at my feet, and sat looking out at the early evening sky. I watched the boats cruise by, the sounds of traffic, and tourists excitedly exploring our magical town. "Ok. Ok, I'm here. No more hiding. I hear you. I'm here. It is all in here, not out there," I said to myself. I sat for hours. As daylight became darkness, I visited with my inner child. I connected with the many wisdoms I had learned and earned over the years. "It is not out there. It is all in here," I told my heart. I embraced the greatest peace I had ever felt in my entire life. A *knowing* rather than a seeking. The only thing I needed to do was to change the way I felt about myself. It was as if I was standing outside of my reality watching my own movie, quieting myself enough to truly see it. Stopping my unconscious movements long enough to pay attention. I saw my inner child from a different perspective. I identified with her story, embodied her beliefs, and I *knew* what was standing in her way. I began to feel moments of security and completeness all alone on that deck. My puzzle pieces became clear.

I had been exclusively focused on the lack of love from the outside rather than just loving myself. Rather than just *being* with myself. This required me to really look deep within and recognize all the wonderful qualities I love about myself. It required me to spend lots of time with myself and to love my company most of all. I was an archeologist digging within myself and finding all sorts of hidden treasures. This was not an easy nor immediate revelation; as with all things meaningful and sustainable, it took time. I encountered a few more, shall we say, 'lessons' and made a few more mistakes. But instead of beating myself up about them… I was attuned to the newly found wisdom from which I could not hide. I privately thanked those who engaged in the lessons with me and forgave myself for the moments of temporarily falling back to sleep. With each experience, it felt like my head was once again out the window of the car, loving the feeling of freedom and transformation on my face.

I believe the only way to heal from the past and learn how to be a better partner in the future is to take responsibility for self, and *only* self. To acknowledge our own patterns and to work from the inside out to be the best version of ourselves. That led to attracting and creating true love.

In March 2015, I met a man who loves me fiercely, challenges me, and accepts me wholeheartedly. He communicates what he wants in a relationship and invites me to do the same in the safest space imaginable. He is my greatest teacher and blessedly is my forever partner in life. At first resistant, I struggled with this depth of vulnerability. Although I was showing up so much differently, I was still most comfortable not being seen. He often reminded me how worthy and important I am. This was what I was longing for, yet I was not ready to believe that I deserved his love. I was unconsciously determined to challenge and test the relationship by going back to my old comfortable ways. How much did he really love me? Will he love me no matter what? Will he love me even if I am broken? Will he accept me and where I came from? I was looking for evidence that I could trust in his love, but no matter how I tested and tested, he stayed steady. In the face of his self-confidence, I had to take action before I was going to lose the man *who loved me unconditionally.*

It was time to *really* dig deep and work on myself. I had to accept that my father had a disease with alcohol, and what happened in my childhood, wasn't about me or who I am or how lovable I am. It was time to change my story. *I am loved and loveable.* Period. Always. No matter what. This is who I had been searching for. I know her now.

Those feelings were hidden deep down for so many years, but those old stories have transformed to a healthy understanding of who I am and where I came from. Now that I know who I'm looking at in the mirror, my life has opened up in so many beautiful ways. I appreciate my Dad for teaching me this lesson. My beliefs have been transformed, supporting healthy love and deep vulnerability. My dreams became my reality. My relationship with my husband is so pure, honest, vulnerable, safe, and loving. It is anchored in unconditionality in many ways. We are on this love journey together helping each other evolve into the people we are meant to be. Our joint purpose is nurturing our love. Disagreements are our friends, even if uncomfortable in the moment. When conflicts emerge, we lean into them knowing that on the other side will be the gifts of deepened mutual consciousness.

On March 18, 2019, my Father, who spent his last 22 years sober, peacefully passed in his sleep. He was a great man who was loved by many. In writing this story, I forgive, I accept, and I am healed from my childhood patterns; I love him, and I love myself, *unconditionally..*

I believe that each Being is on their own personal love journey and meets partners on their path to teach them. We are teachers and students to each other. Relationships are the *mirrors* that allow us to progressively open ourselves to confront our limiting beliefs, to shift our patterns, and heal our hearts.

My love journey was the inspiration for my life's work — becoming a certified Transformational Life and Love Coach. This is the space where I give back. This is the legacy of my father-daughter journey. It taught me to be capable of creating and participating in true, sustainable love, by healing my inner child. I facilitate this process for others like you. I show individuals how their passion and purpose can empower themselves. Guess what? You no longer need to keep seeking but can instead pause, see your movie, unravel the mysteries, and put the pieces of your puzzles together. Know that self-love attracts more love, and from there, all things are possible.

Ignite Action Steps

- **What do you want?** Write down specifically what/who you want in your life and how that makes you *feel*. Feel into that feeling for a while until you believe it. And then, believe first that you can give those things to yourself. From within.

- **Why?** What is your 'why' and what will having this do for you? This is an important step as it is your motivation to stay on path and reveal any blocks, obstacles, and patterns that are holding you back.

- **Tune into your inner-child** and what you longed for that you may not have had as a child. Revisit this time to heal from within, which will consequently impact how you show up, for yourself, first and foremost.

- **Appreciate your gifts**, where you came from, your lessons, and what you learned. Be thoughtful of any experience where you feel victimized and recognize this as a place to heal. No one can fill you. We fill ourselves.

- **Do something special for yourself**. Write in your journal, take a bath, eat your favorite food, self-honor, self-respect. Be in the present with yourself. The most important love story is the one you have with yourself.

Dedicated to my late Father who loved me unconditionally, supported my dreams, and taught me some love lessons. I love you.

Julianne McGowan – United States of America
Life & Love Coach, Matchmaker
www.pathtopurposelovecoach.com
julianne@pathtopurposelovecoach.com

ADRIANA MAIA
TROXLER

*"Love is a daily decision, it is a choice,
your choice — to love and to be loved."*

I invite you to consciously decide what *is* love and what *feels* loving. My deepest wish is that you learn to love who you are and to see the beauty in you! When you find a relationship, invest in your partner — make a conscious decision to love him or her and renew your love through daily actions. Be naked with your dreams and thoughts. Make your love amazing every day to create the very best story of your life.

INTENTIONAL LOVE

"Who wants to buy me a ticket to Switzerland so I can invest in my heart?" I asked my family at the Sunday dinner table. To my delight my father and brother both exclaimed, "I will!"

I have been raised in a family where I experienced and witnessed deep love throughout my life. My parents have been married for almost 50 years and I have seen true love in their actions toward one another. They are truly partners in crime. They do everything together and it is hard for them to spend one night apart. It's no wonder I absolutely wanted to find a love like theirs. I was so desperate that in high school I decided that I wanted to marry a boy I met on my exchange year from Brazil to the USA. The only issues were I was sixteen at the time and he didn't know that I had chosen him as my future husband. For seven years, I lived in a perfectly platonic relationship with him via email. That was a very good deal for me, because I felt safe that I had already found my soulmate at such an early age and I didn't have to keep searching.

My friends and family were concerned about my extreme decision to one day marry him and encouraged me, at 23, to make a brave move and visit my 'future husband' to share my desired feelings. My parents bought a ticket for me to visit him in another continent and explore if our platonic connection could become more. Upon my arrival, he told me that he couldn't meet me because his girlfriend would be uncomfortable with us meeting alone. Through a friend of mine, I communicated, in no uncertain terms, that I had traveled far and that he *needed* to pick me up. To my relief, he did. He didn't become my husband, nor my boyfriend, but he gave me an amazing gift. He took the time to talk to me and I started seeing things differently. I realized that it was okay not to have found the love of my life by 23. I was still hopeful that I would find him at the right time and until then I needed to live and experience life with more lightness.

My search continued to find the right man, but somehow I had ended up in a dysfunctional pattern; either finding guys who did not treat me well or acting as their therapist/mother/bank. None of the relationships felt balanced. Looking back, I was also not balanced. I was not confident with my body and with who I was. I remember crying non-stop one New Year's Eve at a party because I was so lonely and miserable.

I was living in Doha, Qatar, a very small Muslim country in the Arabian Penninsula. I was in my mid-twenties and one of my favorite activities was walking along the picturesque corniche, close to the sea. I had a good American friend who I would often walk with, talking about love and praying that we could find our life partners. Her prayers were shortly answered. She met a sweet guy from the United Kingdom. Their relationship was different than any other relationship I had seen before. They were going out and just talking a lot about who they are, what they want in life, and how they see their future. After several dates, my friend announced that they had decided to get married and that their first kiss would be at her wedding. I was shocked! I asked my friend, "How are you sure that this is going to work if you have not even kissed him before?" My friend answered, "Adriana, love is a daily decision."

That was an Ignite moment for me. My friend and her future husband had deliberately decided to get married and live a life together before being physical. Sexual chemistry didn't matter. She knew what mattered most was commitment from both partners to love, to take care of and to understand what makes one another happy. For them, the most important thing was that they both decided they wanted to be together and raise a family. The movies, soap operas, and TV series had taught me something very different about love. They told me that I will find my soulmate, fall in love romantically, and then live happily after ever. My friend chose to make her future husband her partner for life and fall in love with him daily through their actions.

I had heard before that love is a daily decision, but until that moment, I had not understood how much that decision needs to be mutual and rational. Now, I understand that a partnership/marriage has to go beyond the feelings and consider important questions like: Do we have the same vision for life? Do we share the same values? Do we want to commit to the same kind of relationship? Seeing the choices my friend made changed my approach to love and the ways I would view love going forward.

The first thing I did was practice the act of loving myself on a daily basis — accepting who I am with all my imperfections. That allowed me to let go and stop caring about my image. I became proud of who I was becoming and began to love *myself* daily.

Three years into the journey of learning to truly love myself, I met a Swiss guy at a conference in Warsaw. I remember talking passionately about micro-credits when I saw his big blue eyes looking at me with intense curiosity. He was different from any other guy I had met before. He was a pure soul which felt like a perfect match for my love story. We clicked and we started taking time to get to know each other. For the first time, I was not pretending to be someone else. I was myself and we were having a relationship with no games, no drama, no pretending. I was sure I had found someone truly special. He had broken my pattern! For the first time, I felt loved and balanced.

It seems perfect, right? Well, there was a small issue — he lived on another continent and I had just returned to Brazil, to my parents' home, with very little money and no job.

If I wanted to make it work, I needed to be creative and resourceful. I went to my family and asked who wanted to invest in my relationship and pay for my ticket to go to Switzerland. My brother and my father said yes to the investment and sponsored my potential 'love' future. I guess my family really wanted me to find my soulmate abroad — since they have always paid for my crazy trips of trying to find my partner for life. They were 'investing' in my heart. I knew if I wanted to make that relationship work, I needed to invest my efforts, determination, and my time as well.

I was amazingly creative in finding ways to meet my new love. Instead of asking for a raise, I petitioned my boss for a ticket to go to Switzerland. After some negotiation, we settled on an arrangement that had me traveling to Europe regularly and allowed my boyfriend to stay with me in various cities. These efforts led us to meet each other every three months and our encounters were always a honeymoon. In between our quarterly meetings, we would talk for hours on Skype; this long-distance relationship was perfect to get to know each other. Then, we aimed higher and looked for ways to live in the same country. He found a job in Brazil, near me, and lived there for one year after which we moved to Switzerland together, where I could study my MBA.

One year passed and I had just finalized my studies and felt it was time for us to get married. I had already invested four years and all my savings, and I desired a commitment for life. However, he didn't feel ready yet — he was a bit younger than me and he was still finalizing his professional accreditation. That was a really hard moment in our relationship. I had just finalized my MBA and had many opportunities in front of me. If he didn't want the same future, I could accept that. I would love him for everything he had done and for the beautiful story we had. I was full of love and gratitude for everything he did for me and for who I had become because of the relationship I had with him. But, I wanted him to set me free if he wasn't ready to make a commitment to getting married. I was certain that I would find another person to love — all the years of practicing *self-love* had given me this confidence. I was about to break up.

Eventually, we could not talk about this subject without crying and I realized that we needed to have a different kind of conversation in order to resolve our challenge. I had an idea to share our feelings in a notebook. In our notebook, we both wrote our thoughts, dreams for our lives together, and personal concerns. At that time we were living apart and we would meet only during the weekends. For one week, it was my turn to write in the notebook, and the next week, it was his turn. He would take the notebook, read what I had written down, respond to it, and then continue with his own reflections. This was such an important exercise. It helped us to tell our feelings and understand our reactions without the tears.

He didn't allow me to find another person and instead, he proposed to me. This whole process was not romantic like a movie; it was a careful decision based on what we wanted in our lives. It was thoughtful and at the same time full of emotions and love.

We got married, worked hard, and loved daily. Five years later, we were still a honeymoon couple. I was approaching 35 and my biological clock started ticking — it was time to have kids. I have always wanted to have children, a house, and the whole thing. That was part of my dream. But one thing made me somewhat scared to fulfill this dream. Many of my friends had their kids and then they grew apart from each other. I knew many people who had gotten divorced. I was astonished when I saw couples breaking up when they seemed to be perfect for each other. "What happened there?" I wondered. I had this amazing relationship with my husband and I did not want to lose that because I had a dream to have kids.

After talking to my husband for several months, we made an agreement and decided that our kids won't be our main priority, rather our first priority will continue being our relationship. If we take care of both of us, as a couple, our kids will be fine.

Overcoming the fear of children diminishing our relationship wasn't easy. It required vulnerability and open communication. My husband has been essential in helping me become truly vulnerable. In the past, I would cry by myself, now I cry with him. Before, I would spend days trying to figure out things on my own, now, I manage more readily to talk about what is bothering me and spend less time with my own crazy thoughts. Life is easier when we go together. With courage and hope, our love made two beautiful girls. Yes, having small kids does change the relationship and we definitely don't have the same energy and time to dedicate to each other. And that's why we need to be more creative in our efforts to spend it and remind ourselves daily that we made a commitment to love each other — every day of our lives.

Planning is key to making things happen. We needed to find a babysitter or a family member to take care of our kids so we could enjoy time *alone* together. If you are like me, sometimes it is quite hard to let yourself be helped. I don't like to be a burden to someone else — many thoughts come to me when I need to ask for external help. For example: what if my kid stays awake the whole night or cries like crazy? I don't want to bother someone else with a sleepless night so I can enjoy time with my husband. I had to learn that it is okay to ask for help — and actually believe the experience is positive for both sides: the person who helps us is actually having a good time and for us... well... let's agree that we really enjoy our alone time also.

Passion is scientifically proven to last only a few years. However, love can last an eternity — if you invest time, if you cultivate deeper connections, if you make efforts to satisfy your partner and show him or her that you care. In doing these things you will experience *daily* love. And you know what, I love my husband more every day — it is crazy, the tank of love just keeps filling more and more as we keep connecting. Yes, it requires effort for me to go to the tank station and fuel our love — I can do that easily either by just sitting on the sofa and talking about our day or paying attention to how he plays with our kids in a loving way. I have chosen him to be my soulmate and I will continue to make this choice daily.

The issues that sometimes come up in a long-term relationship can be very small household things that drive the other one crazy. I have learned the hard way that my husband and I see the state of the house in different ways. I see issues that are lower to the ground — maybe because of my height; I get crazy with a dirty floor. But, he sees all the objects that are lying on higher surfaces — papers on the table, glasses in the 'wrong' places. Realizing and understanding that we see things differently helps. However, only having an awareness of this is not enough, I need to make an effort to act in ways that he needs. My effort to do this for him makes him happier. His effort to support and participate in my household needs makes me feel special. Creating new habits to satisfy your partner is key — it is an act of love and appreciation. And a big plus in creating more admiration for one another.

For your sanity and for your partnership, let go of your thoughts of having to keep everything perfect and being perfect. Instead, agree with your partner about how you can grow and develop together and become a better team and human being every day. Take the time for talking to your partner beyond conversations about the kids — talk about your dreams and aims. Talk about the things that bother you, try to find solutions together, and be creative. Enjoy intimacy — not only of making love but also being naked with your thoughts and dreams.

Invest in your relationship by investing in yourself and your partner. Find the beauty in you and let this beauty shine around you. Find something you love doing that is meaningful to you. It is not the responsibility of your part-ner to make you happy. It is yours — your choice to love yourself. Love is a choice! A daily conscious choice of investing time and resources in *your* loved one and in *you*.

IGNITE ACTION STEPS

Here are some ideas to make your relationship last, by cultivating a few ingredients:

Cultivate Self-Awareness: Are you aware of your own emotions, habits, triggers, impulses, reactions, thoughts, and needs or are you living on autopilot?

I invite you to learn more about yourself. Find what you love, what makes you happy, and what bothers you. A coach can be a great guide for cultivating self-awareness. I have coached several people and noticed through a coaching relationship that a person can expand their awareness of themselves. As a result, there is a great positive change in how they act and how they interact with others.

Cultivate a Right Start and End to the Day: Make an agreement with your partner to start and end your days in a positive way. This helps to remind you of the *daily decision* to love each other. It is really helpful to try as much as possible to avoid going to bed without clarifying any issue — even if they are tiny. If you don't clarify them — they will become big issues. And there is a chance your partner won't have a clue of the magnitude of the issue, if you do not express it aloud.

Cultivate Gratitude: Be thankful and express your gratitude to your partner. Say thank you for every act — small and big. This shows you are observing your partner and appreciating what he or she does and giving clues of what you actually like. Say thank you for making the bed, for preparing a meal, for cleaning the bathroom and for giving some time for 'me time.' Gratitude has incredible potential for healing and making experiences beautiful. I invite you to give your partner a letter with everything you appreciate about him or her.

Cultivate and Practice Presence: Nowadays it is easy to get distracted by many things: phone, internet, work, kids, bills — the list is long. Therefore, you need to make a decision as a couple to assign time to each other when there are no distractions and it is only the two of you. My father always told me, it is not about quantity, but it is all about the quality. It can be a few minutes a day. But these 10-minutes count and it makes a big difference in your relationship.

Cultivate a Learning Mindset: As a couple, you are learning together. You are not perfect and you never will be. Allow time for learning and reflection. Try something new and, if it did not work, reflect with your partner on what you have learned and come up with something new. When we cultivate a relationship where we invite learning — then we grow together.

Adriana Maia Troxler – Switzerland
Leadership Development Manager & Coach
www.journeysland.com

Ivana Sošić Antunović

"Love is worth surrendering to. Let it shine through you."

I'd love to inspire you to open up your whole person — your body and soul, your mind and spirit, your past, present, and future — to Love! Love is either lived, or not. It's not meant to be lived half-heartedly. When you surrender to Love, you start really living! So let it envelop you, cure you, bless you, guide you, and spread its might all around you! I hope that through my story, you also experience the wholeness, the Oneness of Love. Love is about shining your light.

LET IT SHINE!

For me, Love is everyone, everywhere, always and forever. I discovered that Love requires me to totally surrender. I know I cannot love anyone truly and fully until I learn to accept and love myself, truly and fully. I had to learn many lessons before I was ready to let Love come into my life and stay. I had to grow, through all my experiences, the trust of an infant…. the courage of a warrior… the gentleness of a flower-petal… the patience of an hourglass… the curiosity of a child… the wisdom of a sage… the flexibility of a breeze… the endurance of an explorer… and the voice of a lion. I had to learn to accept. To forgive. To let go. To be. I had to learn all of that. I am still learning.

The moment that opened me up to Love was when I first realized that I am connected to God. It was through an illness and a miraculous healing that God decided to show Himself to me — a notorious atheist. I was a 25-year old psychology student, proud to have a scientific mind and vainly mocking all the spiritual people, convinced I was so much better than them, convinced my knowledge would be more than enough to help others heal. I wanted to support people; I truly felt that urge. It was a calling deep inside my core. That desire, as I understood at that point, was coming from my empathetic heart and my knowledgeable mind. Not knowing God then, what I didn't understand was how it was a true calling from the depths of my soul and its purpose. I still had much to learn about Love.

I was a perfectly healthy young lady, enjoying my youth. Then one day, I felt a breast lump. I tried to ignore it, but it was there. For weeks, the fear grew inside me. I tried to forget about it. But it stood there, like an ominous sign of my fragility.

And then, that crucial weekend came. I was all alone. No one was nearby to distract me or offer kind words. My fear built up and suddenly I was over-whelmed completely. I felt my breast lump. My heart raced like crazy. I felt utter panic. I was experiencing a huge existential fear of dying. For the first time in my life, I started praying. Really praying. I was openly crying to God, "Please, if You are out there, show yourself to me! I really need you now!"

He answered! In the next beautiful, blissful moment, I felt a beam of loving light shower me from above. I felt total peace. I felt complete Love. I felt bliss. Instantly, my heart, body, and soul just KNEW. I strongly and literally sensed, from my head to my toes, from my skin to my core, that I am a part of His Wholeness, that I am created by Him, loved by Him, and led by His hand and will. I felt completely safe and secure. My whole self believed. I was trans-formed. I remember thinking to myself, "How did I not see it before? Of course there IS God! Of course everything written in the Bible is true! Of course Jesus, His son, died for us and was resurrected! Of course our souls live forever!" I just knew. No doubt. No wondering. No suspicion. Just absolute belief.

I was ecstatic! I remember; it was about midnight and I was so happy I couldn't sleep. I searched for the copy of Gideon's New Testament I had put away somewhere. I only had it because of a peculiar incident. Months before, some people were giving the bibles away at the university and I was curiously checking one when my friend suggested, "Just take it, it can't hurt you." I took it because he was a good friend and I trusted him. His voice sounded authentic and true. Taking the bible also felt right, against my judgments. Years later, that same friend would become my best man on the day of my wedding. That is how important that moment was to me, to my newly discovered life.

The night I met God, I suddenly felt the urge to read it. I took the bible, opened it, and read it. I read all of it. From the first page to the last. I read for hours. I remember, while reading it, how I felt the rush, the joy, the bliss, the wonder… I soaked in every word. And I just knew that every word was true. The Holy Spirit was with me. It opened my mind, soul, body, and my whole self to *His* Word. That night, everything was clear, I understood every word. I literally felt like walking with Jesus and his disciples, hearing his message and witnessing his teachings. I passed through time, space and was beside him. I sensed it. I read it. I wept. I cried. I read. I wept. I cried. The dawn came. I fell asleep, soothed and calm like a newborn baby in a mother's arms.

The next morning, my twin sister Ana came home from her weekend out. We were always very close. We shared every secret. She knew about the lump and my fears. But she didn't know about my prayer and God's answer. The doorbell rang. She stood in the doorway, very excited and glowing, saying, "You won't believe it! I met a healer on the train today!" I was in awe. Back then, I didn't believe in any kind of alternative healing or anything non-scientific. But after the previous night, I curiously opened up to the new possibility. Trusting my sister, I followed it. She took me to this man. I remember my whole body was trembling with the mixture of fear, awe, worry, excitement, and hope. The healer performed energy treatment on me... he just moved his hand above my body… and I felt warmth and serenity... I felt the pain go away… I felt the fear melt away… and the bump literally disappeared. It was gone. I cried with joy and relief. When I asked how he did it, he simply said, "God gave me this gift to share. Praise the Lord!"

From that moment on, I did. I started exploring faith. It has been a long path, with lots of ups and downs... but the Lord has been faithful and patient, and revealed Himself to me slowly. I have searched for and discovered the treasures of spiritual life. My path has led me to find my place in the Catholic church, exploring the Holy Bible and learning how to live in community, practicing acceptance and forgiveness. I learned I am precious. I discovered I have dignity; I am a child of God. I learned it means I am worthy of Love, no matter how many mistakes I make. But I also learned about humility and about responsibility to share your gifts with others. I experienced the beauty of watching and rejoicing the miracles God puts in the lives of others, as well as in my life. I was able to accept the hardships and be grateful for all that comes. And above all, I *knew* that the Life that he gives is the biggest gift ever.

If it wasn't for that night, I would probably not still be married, and most definitely would not have given birth to five children. I wouldn't have received the insights of my own faults *and* accepted them, but I also wouldn't be aware of my qualities the way I am today. Through years of habitual praying, in deepening my faith by religious practices, I have also learned to accept other people much more in the wholeness of their own personality and experiences. I see the riches of the Earth with a grateful heart, and I feel all people are strongly interconnected. That does not mean I don't judge others. I'm no saint. And it doesn't mean I don't act selfish, get into fights, try to control others, or that I can't be really nasty as a wife, or a mother, a sister, a daughter, a friend, in a parish, or at a workplace. On the contrary. I remain flawed. But I also get to see my strengths and flaws more clearly. My connection to God helps me grow in my awareness about myself and about others, day by day. It helps me continue trying to be a better version of myself every day. I stumble. I fall. But I get up. I reach for His hand and rise, forgiven and cleansed, accepted and Loved. I get up, and go about my day, trying to give the same forgiveness, acceptance, and Love to other people I meet.

I would love to share with you all the ways I am blessed with Love in my life. I strongly believe these fruits would never have been mine without that night that changed my life.

God - Universal Love: Since the moment I became aware of God's presence and invited Him in my life, I started the experience of discovering the awesomeness of Him. He is the One who is always accepting and caring to me. He is the One always being near me. He never gets tired of me, never letting me down. He is the One always ready to forgive.

I overcame a lot of doubt and self-doubt, to develop my inner muscles of trusting God. Even so, I often have quarrels with Him. After all, isn't it something every loved child does? They question their loving parent and develop even more confidence, while leaning on the parent and learning from him at the same time. Day by day, bit by bit, I slowly and gradually deepen my confidence. He has immense quantities of patience and Love. As a loved child, how could I not love Him back and trust Him fully?

Self-Love: Even knowing I was loved by God and blessed with many blessings, I still had to learn how to accept and appreciate myself. Although, as a psychologist, I learned how to listen to others, support them, and help them evolve, I still had to learn how to listen to myself, support me, help my inner child evolve and grow up.

Can you imagine the hard task in front of me? Can you imagine being the second-born identical twin who has to accept the idea she is unique? Not easy. Can you imagine a girl, after her parents' ugly divorce at the age of eight, feeling wanted and precious to her parents? Can you imagine an ace student accepting she is free to make mistakes? Can you imagine a scientist needing to surrender to spirituality? Or an atheist needing to accept faith? Can you imagine a girl whose parents didn't talk to each other most of her life, striving to have a happy marriage? And can you imagine a young woman, afraid of making her mum's mistakes, hoping to be a great mother? That girl is me. That is my story. And I would never change it. It formed me to be exactly who I am today. And today — I finally love being me!

I probably wouldn't have come this far if it wasn't for my loving mirrors around me. My twin sister, my family, my community, my tribe. Looking at myself through their eyes, through their words and actions — was often painful, but revealing. It meant accepting that I too have to change if I want us all to grow. I learned I cannot truly love anyone until I get to know myself and love myself first. I realized, if God loves me exactly like I am, why shouldn't I? If I was born to this life with a unique purpose, why shouldn't I live it and enjoy it?

Yes, today I love being me. As for enjoying being me, I still need to practice. But it's a fun game. The game I invite you to play, also. To get up in the morning with wonder of new things you can achieve and discover. To be excited about learning new stuff, meeting new people, impacting new lives, leaving a mark on humanity.

Partner-love: I'm in love with my husband. It's been 26 years and 73 days since we first kissed and started dating, and I still love him. Oh, we have our ups and downs. We surely do. We fight and make up. We have our challenges to surpass and over the years there's been plenty of those. But the bond grows stronger and stronger. The spark is still on. Even when it somewhat vanishes, it always comes back. Even if sometimes I give up on myself or he gives up on himself, we never give up on the other. Even if at tough times we lose each other a bit. Even then, deep inside, I know our love is solid as a rock.

Waking up in his arms, starting a day together with a cup of coffee, discussing daily chores, or making plans (with five kids there is always a lot of planning and even more improvising). Returning from work, knowing we can share our daily stories, we rely on each other's support, have a few laughs or solve problems together, play a game together or watch a movie. And finish the day in each other's arms again. Priceless. Without relying on the love of

God, I wouldn't be able to accept our differences, to resist the temptations, to forgive, and to constantly change — all the prerequisites for a lasting marriage in my experience.

Parent-love: If ever I learned how deeply profound and gentle love can be, it was while holding my babies. The gentleness of their touch, heavenly smell of their skin, complete awe and devotion from them. To make it more incredible, I was blessed with twins. Twins twice! Many times I felt completely overwhelmed with love. Holding two perfect angels while breastfeeding them both, and witnessing their little hands close together in gentle touch. Seeing them love and support each other, play together, fight and get back together in a harmonious hug.

With more children, Love multiplies. They all grow up in abundance of joy and loving connections. They have a clear understanding of how different each person can be and yet, no matter how different, they freely accept and love fully. For me, having five children has been the perfect path. For me, motherhood is the infinite daily reminder of both practical Love and universal Love.

Sister-love: My first and strongest experience of love is being a twin. Having shared so many life experiences from womb on — it's impossible to describe the closeness and connection we have. It is both a blessing and a challenge. Having someone that close, supportive, honest, and interested in your well-being means you cannot escape the truth. Whether I liked it or not, my mirror has always been there — loving me and never giving up on me. What a chance to grow and glow!

Friend-love: I am grateful to have close, honest, kind friends. They impacted my life and supported my growth. For me, friends are people I can sit with and share my deepest fears and anxieties, and they listen. When I talk about my visions and dreams I feel their happiness for me. When I expose my faults, they still love me and accept me. And when in need, I can reach out and rely on them. I know I am not alone in the world, I am supported and through them I am connected to God, to all humanity.

Humanity-love: Feeling truly, deeply connected to all Life, I am calm and assured that my existence has a unique purpose and meaning. My path has gifted me with seeing other people as brothers and sisters. That is not always easy. It can be hard to feel connection and empathy to someone who goes against me.

When I remember that I am no better than anyone else and practice humility and forgiveness, getting to know someone before I judge them, the feeling of Oneness slowly becomes easier. In knowing Love and God, we start to learn to love ourselves, others, and the world. We learn how to put our gifts and capabilities in service to humanity. In the giving, we are receiving. In opening to Love, we let it cure us, bless us, guide us, spread around us.

I wish for you nothing less than what I have — for Love to touch you and cure you. By surrendering to Love, you will discover your own Divinity. By connecting to your core, you can become the best version of yourself. It leads to connecting to others on a new level — fully, bravely, proudly, honestly. Completely. For me, it started with being aware of myself as a small but crucial part of humanity. Open up to Love and let it shine!

IGNITE ACTION STEPS

- **Self-Love.** Fill your inner batteries with Love. Be it through prayer, meditation, nature, touch, sport, connection. Do things you love. Plan it and enjoy it!

- **Partner-Love.** Allow yourself to learn and grow from the insights you uncover. Forgive and be kind. Plan loving, bonding, nurturing moments and bask in them.

- **Parent-Love.** Get to know your children daily. Enjoy seeing them evolve and open up to being their true selves. Love them the way they want to be loved.

- **Universal-Love.** God is Love. We are all One, interconnected, brothers and sisters. See others as an extension of yourself, be kind to everyone you meet.

Ivana Sošić Antunović – Croatia
Educational Psychologist
 vanaDuplica

María Valentina Izarra

"Turn your dramas into your life fuel!"

May you let go of unnecessary baggage so you can step into *love*. May you surrender what you can't control so you can be *empowered* to move forward with what you can. May you be blessed with the gift of *forgiveness* and know *peace*.

For You, For Oneness, For Giving

So you want to manifest more *love* in your life? I have one word for you: *forgive*. *Forgiveness* leads to compassion, which leads to *humility*, which leads to *accountability*, which leads to *giving*, which leads to *oneness* (aka *love*).

Maybe that's where the word comes from: *for giving*. So if the word irks you, carries some bad connotations and has you rolling your eyes, perhaps change it to *for loving…* or *for oneness*.

Of course, I didn't always think this way. This way of reasoning didn't come overnight or as a fast fix. Transformation — whether physical, mental, or spiritual —requires discomfort and vulnerability. Just think of the caterpillar in the chrysalis while transforming into a butterfly, or the lobster undergoing ecdysis — shedding its shell in order to grow.

I grew up thinking life was simple. You mature, get married, have children, and then you die. I thought drama was for movies or was instigated purposefully by people in reality shows. I had little compassion for anyone who was living out their dramas — I imagined that they were getting what they deserved. I had a lot to learn.

My soap-opera drama started at 29. I was still breastfeeding my baby when I found out my husband was a serial cheater. Anger consumed the majority of my thoughts whether I was awake or asleep. I was furious at my ex-husband for entangling me in his web of lies and shattering my heart into a million tiny pieces.

I feel ashamed to admit it, but I would have dreams that I'd be punching and screaming at him mercilessly. The bloody fantasies never sufficed because somewhere inside I just knew that no matter how bad I could hurt him, he'd neither feel nor understand the pain he had caused me. To put this into context, you have to understand how foreign it was for me to have these types of thoughts — I'm a romantic at heart; I can't even watch trailers of horror movies. I literally switch the channels when they're on.

No need to get all riled up now; I never acted on my barbaric thoughts. I wasn't about to end up in prison. Yet, I couldn't help but daydream of him begging me for mercy during that time when I felt so powerless and miserable in real life.

Forgiveness... Ha! Are you kidding me?! When he was outright lying in the courtroom under oath, emptying my bank accounts, not paying child support or alimony all while driving around in a new cherry-red Ferrari and spending $3,000 on Father's Day at the strip club? I don't quite remember the name of the joint, just that it had the word gold in it. Yep, real golden experience it must have been. Seems quite comical now but back when, his behavior felt like a stab in the back.

He wasn't the only one on my poop list. His mother — whom I had loved dearly and treated like a second mother — was his main alibi. I learned she had even paid one of his lovers to keep her hush-hush and protect his illicit fornications. It was gut-wrenchingly painful finding out that my close entourage was filled with hypocrites who seemed to have no qualms in lying repeatedly to my face. It felt like the ultimate humiliation. Still, I was doing myself a disservice. All my attention was focused on them and how they did me wrong and how it wasn't fair. I came to learn that sometimes life isn't fair and shitty things happen.

In the middle of my drawn-out divorce, it hit me like a ton of bricks. The person I was beating up in my daydreams wasn't him... it was *me*. It was *me* I was really pissed-off at! Not him. It was me I couldn't forgive... for choosing him as a husband, for not seeing through his lies, and for being so utterly naïve. In all honesty, I had been quite the fool to the point that I had signed over a complete Power Of Attorney to him in my native country of Venezuela — you know, the POA judges grant at the request of adults whose elderly parents suffer from dementia or whose children are mentally incapacitated. Yeah, one of those.

That realization, the fact that the one person I had to work at forgiving was myself, changed my whole panorama. I was shocked, then I was horrified and then I was like, "Holy shit, the person I need to forgive is *me!*" I needed to find the courage within to forgive myself. I won't lie; it wasn't easy to forgive all my choices. It took time, immense compassion, faith, grit, and *love.*

I had made a consequential mistake by trusting my ex-husband and I had to reconcile with that reality. I had to own up to the fact that I had believed in someone who was untrustworthy. I had to forgive the 18-year-old me who had fallen madly and deeply in love with a con artist. I had to suck up the undeniable fact that I would inevitably be tied to him forever because of one person: our son, Luciano.

Admitting our faults can be so painstakingly difficult to swallow. On the flip side, pointing out someone else's shortcomings is so easy. Self-examination is not for sissies; that's why most people don't do it. Or they say, "I know what my faults are," brush them aside, and never gather enough gusto to actually work on their shit. Face it: anything worth pursuing is challenging and hard. We grow through struggle and hardship… through tears, sweat, and pain. I'm not saying all of life is a struggle but that dreams worth pursuing will take determination, persistence, and working through obstacles.

Love is worth pursuing. You know it! That's why you're here. Just know that your pursuit will require you to dig deep into your reservoir of self-compassion. Ironically, after I forgave myself, forgiving him was a piece of cake. You see, being at peace with myself miraculously allowed me to be at peace with others around me. I was still able to observe the flaws in others but I became so focused at bettering myself that I stopped taking the time to criticize anyone else. Perhaps my ex was a cheater; maybe I was more of a brat daughter than a wife.

Chances are you've left deep scars in someone's heart, even if you're unaware of it…Chances are you've also blurted out a hurtful comment, or two or 186,579,334…

Chances are you've failed to show up when either a friend or family member needed you… Oops! Chances are you've blown it more than once with your kid and now they're also scarred for life. Chances are if you knew all the things your BFF can't forgive herself for, you'd hug her, tell her you still love her, and tell her to let it go.

We grow up hearing stories of villains and heroes as if we are either one or the other. The truth is we are all both villains and heroes in one way or another.

When I arrived at this conclusion, I was finally able to open up my heart and experience a type of compassion that set me free. Blame is a double-edged sword. Whenever you point it at another, you are also directing it at yourself. Again let me be clear: this doesn't absolve us or anyone else of our wrong doings. It's up to every single one of us to clean our dirty laundry and atone — make things whole with the people we have wronged.

There's a lot of pain out there; there's no denying it. And some people are called to forgive 'bigger' things than others. I hear you; it's not fair. But who can judge what is fair and what pain is considered big or small? Pain is pain. I'm not saying put up with abuse or disrespect but I am saying surrender the past and release the pain. Let it go! It really is easier than you think. I find it truly amazing; some people are able to forgive their child's murderer but others can't even forgive a friend for forgetting their birthday.

Humans sure love a scapegoat — pointing fingers so they can blame all their mishaps and misfortunes on big corporations, the Republicans, and their mother-in-law (or taxes, the Democrats, and racial stereotypes). Fill in the blanks… anything will do. That's because it's easier to play the victim and never own up to anything; just like it's easier to relax on the sofa to binge watch replays with a soda in hand while you blame your diabetes on your genes or bad luck instead of getting your ass to the gym and swapping that third slice of double-cheese pizza for a bowl of broccoli and brown rice. It's much harder to put on our big boy pants or skirt (whatever you prefer) and develop real accountability and the rare ability to introspect and recognize where *we* blew it or where *we* didn't show up. Yet, that's why forgiveness is so powerful. As soon as we offer the gift of forgiveness, we are in essence forgiving ourselves too — forgiving ourselves for not having the discipline to replace the beer with water or for being such a bitch our spouse couldn't stand us.

In forgiveness, we are reconciling the fact that none of us are perfect and shedding the shame that keeps us hostage to an unseen yet powerful force of darkness. Anger, bitterness, and resentment worked like metal chains to keep me away from the possibility of love until I set myself free. Surprisingly this doesn't result in indifference — shrugging your shoulders and raising a white flag in defeat. Quite the contrary, it makes us lighter so we can think clearer, make empowered decisions, show up, and actually give enough of a damn to try something different.

I've learned that forgiveness is the only way to reconcile our imperfections and make things perfect. It says, "I'm imperfect, you're imperfect, and that's perfectly okay. I accept me, I accept you… now let's move on and live a purpose-filled life." Forgiveness is a verb not a noun. It's not something that you step into once and *Voila*! It's a moment-to-moment decision. Just like staying in love is a moment-to-moment decision, contrary to popular belief.

Forgiveness is a practice and a way of living. Interestingly enough, so is anger and resentment. Everyday I can choose to step into forgiveness or choose to step into the ugly bitter stuff. The only difference is, one will keep me stuck in the past forever and the other will wipe the slate clean… so I can step into possibility and love.

For many years, I saw the forgiveness of certain things as a weakness but I am no longer fooled by forgiveness' unappealing exterior. Now, I recognize it as a diamond in the rough. Forgiveness is powerful. It not only disarms the other individual, it makes you indestructible. With forgiveness as your ally, nothing can hurt you. You are at peace. The world is still and all is well. Forgiveness is not tolerance. Actually, forgiveness is a gateway to disassociating from that painful past experience so you can step into a new experience… as Princess Jasmine and Aladdin would say, "...a whole new world."

Which means you don't have to go back into business with the partner that screwed you but you do have to forgive them. You don't have to stay married to the woman who slept with your best friend, but you do have to forgive them. Well, technically you don't have to. You have free will of course, but you came here to manifest more love so I'm giving it to you straight, like a shot of cheap tequila with no lime or salt.

So here's what you need to know, straight up:

Forgive your enemies: those who have hurt you, betrayed you, abused you, beat you, embezzled you, cheated on you, criticized you, cursed you, and left deep scars in your heart.

Forgive your friends: for not always saying what you needed to hear, for not attending your wedding or baby shower (or for not inviting you to theirs), for saying those hurtful things you can't seem to shake off, for not being there in your time of need… perhaps that divorce or the burial of your brother.

Forgive your spouse: for not appreciating every meal you prepare or every paycheck you bring in, for not knowing how hard you have it sometimes, for not listening with intent to your every word, for changing less diapers than you or never picking up their dirty underwear from the floor, for not wanting to have sex sometimes, for not remembering your birthday, or for being your biggest critic.

Forgive your parents: for not believing in your talents or abilities, for only getting you hand-me-downs, for blowing their every attempt at a deep connection with you, for not realizing your someone was hurting you, for putting you up for adoption, or for not recognizing you as their child.

Forgive yourself: for getting divorced, for not being able to lose those extra 30 pounds, for being a bully in elementary school, for being promiscuous all those years (yes, this applies to men too), for making that really stupid decision that made the cops show up, for lying about the amount of porn you watch… you get the point. There's likely 186,579,334 things you need to forgive yourself for.

When you are denying forgiveness to someone, you are in essence denying yourself peace of mind and love. Love… the most sublime virtue and that feeling we spend our whole lives searching for. Remember the 'con-artist' at the beginning of my story? I now refer to him more appropriately as "the father of my first born." Even though it's not always a walk in the park, at the end of the day, I genuinely wish him and his mom well. Heck, this story has a happy ending because of *for-giveness*. Forgiveness allowed me to fall in love again… this time with a dynamo Italo-Canadian named Mark. It even gave my son Luciano his adorable baby brother Leonardo.

If only I could hand out forgiveness-like business cards. It's the keys to your kingdom. Oh wait, here you go: my gift to you.

HEAVEN ON EARTH

Phone: (800) FOR-GIVE
Fax: (800) ONE-NESS
333 Humility Drive
Compassion, FAITH 77777

Ignite Action Steps

Suggested steps for healing grudges, resentment, and anger you can't seem to shake:

1) Write an uncensored letter to the person(s) you can't forgive. Tell them off, cuss, and get the ugly stuff out... ALL of it. (You will not share this letter with anyone, rather this is an exercise to clean house). Don't worry if you're repetitive in your thoughts. The idea is to write until you have nothing left to say. Then, at the end of each letter write: God, I cannot carry this burden any longer. I hand this over to you. Thank you!

2) Have a little burning ceremony for the letters you wrote. For example, you can simply put them in a pot and set them ablaze (careful not to burn yourself). Remember to celebrate that night! Dance, pray, stay in gratitude. All those negative thoughts and feelings are now ashes and dust.

3) Pray for those you can't forgive. WTF?! You may be saying to yourself right now. That's right. I want you to pray for those you haven't yet forgiven. This exercise is the most difficult and yet the most miraculous and powerful. In the beginning, you may only be capable of asking God for the strength to forgive, but pray nevertheless. It can be a generic prayer dedicated to that person. The point is to get accustomed to sending good vibes their way. Disarm the wave of hatred you have built between this person and yourself. Eventually, build up enough humility and compassion to pray for the person's happiness, abundance, peace of mind, etc. Imagine they are you and start sending blessings their way. Remember, whatever you are wishing for them, you are in essence sending to yourself.

María Valentina Izarra – United States of America
Motivational Speaker, Life Coach, Content Creator, Actress and TV Host
www.mamasconganas.com

Piret Špitsmeister

"Sometimes our decisions hurt others, but will never harm them if made from love."

I hope that by reading my story you will be encouraged to embrace yourself in all of your colors both bright and dark. Too often we are wearing masks in our relationships, trying to be the person we think the other expects us to be. Trust that the soul of your partner has recognized your true nature and you are enough the way you are. By doing so, you may even find your perfect and loving soul mate.

Return To Love

I was 28 years old, and on the surface I had the perfect life. I was married with two wonderful children and lived in a brand new beautiful terrace house in an affluent suburb in Tallinn, Estonia. I even had my own little lifestyle company. What more could anyone wish for? Sadly, my reality was very different — I was deeply unhappy.

First, my company wasn't generating enough income for me to make a living. I loved what I did, however it also drained me. During the day, I looked after my children and worked at night. I barely slept and was permanently in a state of exhaustion. To compensate for all of this, I developed a horrible addiction to sugar: I was overweight. To say I was disconnected from my femininity was an understatement. I saw myself as a mother and defined my future through my children.

Second, my marriage felt like a trap I couldn't escape from. We had been together from the age of 17 and I still didn't know who my husband was. No matter how hard I tried, he didn't open up to me. I often felt expectations, judgments, and feelings of not being good enough. I tried to harmonize our relationship by shutting down my own voice and became someone I thought he wanted me to be, losing my own truth along the way.

One day, I discovered a business trainer named Eric Edmeades was holding a five-day seminar in Stockholm. I had a calling to go and one month later, after much perseverance, I found myself in a nice hotel in Sweden. I had hoped to sit quietly like a little grey mouse in the corner and take notes… how wrong I was.

The start of the seminar felt brutal to me. I remember my heart pounding and my eyes searching for the door to escape from when I heard about our first assignment — find yourself a team by convincing other team leaders what value you could offer. My plan to avoid conversations had failed rapidly.

Soon after its creation, our team decided to have lunch together. I sat down at the table looking at the menu when a man's voice whispered into my ear, "Come out of your shell."

What? What shell? I didn't understand. A man sitting opposite smiled at me. I was too shy to ask him any questions so I smiled back politely. For the rest of the conference I found myself near to him often, while consciously trying to avoid him.

On the last day of the event my team had lunch together. As I was queuing to pay for my meal, I realized the man wasn't there anymore. I asked my teammate, "Where is he?" "He left, he had to catch his flight back home." I was shocked that he had left without saying goodbye to me. "Maybe you can still catch him."

I ran, on my fancy high heels, through the whole restaurant, then I saw him on the other side of the corridor and shouted out loud, "Where do you think you're going?" He turned around and walked toward me. He apologized and told me that he wanted to take his luggage from his room and then to say goodbye to me. He gave me a hug and kissed me on the forehead. This was the only kiss we had.

I surprised myself by saying, "I am going to miss you so much." "I know. I'm going to miss you too," he answered. For the very first time, I felt like me. I found myself speaking words before I considered them. I had never felt that way before and it was unnerving and reassuring at the same time.

His taxi left. I watched him disappear and then I rushed to the ladies' room, heartbroken. I cried and cried like I had never cried before. It felt like a piece of me was being peeled away. I wondered if I was going crazy. I had only had a few conversations with him and most of the time did not understand him because English is not my primary language. "Why do I feel like this?" I wondered. My pain was real, almost physical and it took me an hour and a half to get myself back together. Fortunately, as I walked back to the seminar, there was an emotional closing exercise where most people were in tears already; I was relieved I didn't stand out.

I returned back home six kg lighter and feeling bouts of stress. I tried to go back to my life but couldn't. I kept thinking, "Have I dreamt this? Have I created my feelings or imagined this wonderful unspoken deep connection?" Then I got another wake up call. I realized, I was burned out. I couldn't work and spent my days doing nothing productive, sending my children to the kindergarten whilst laying in bed. I continued to interact with the man by messages. We both tried to convince ourselves that it was just a friendship. After a few weeks I admitted to myself I had feelings for him. I had tolerated a lot in my life. I had sacrificed myself and felt obliged to put others first. My husband was used to his and my children's needs coming first. It was an awakening to me when I finally saw my life the way it was. And I decided to change it. To change everything.

My Sweden experience gave me so much courage and faith in myself; I had experienced something new for the first time: unconditional acceptance. My team took me as I was; they didn't have any expectations of me, nor judgments. That gave me strength. Day after day, I started to speak my truth. Over time, I gained the courage to have 'that' (divorce) conversation with my husband.

I told him how deeply unhappy I was in our marriage and that something had to change otherwise we would need to go our separate ways. I will never forget the look in his eyes. He was amazed. He didn't see it coming; he was really, really surprised. At first, I saw anger, then there was fear. Don't get me wrong, I was afraid too because so many times I had wanted to leave him and never had the courage to do so. I was too afraid of his anger and feared I would be punished by having my children taken away from me.

"It seems to me that you have already decided," he said. I felt awful for hurting him and I gave him one last chance. We created a 'relationship rescue plan' using a calendar to book activities from gym sessions and dates to restaurants and movie nights. He really thought that it would help us; however, deep inside, I was already gone.

I continued to speak my truth daily. I had never seen this side of me before and was amazed by the depth of what I found. During that time, my husband

and I had a lot of deep conversations; however, in most of them, all I wanted was to end our relationship. But my husband is the most stubborn and devoted man I've ever met and he never let me go. He continually managed to convince me to stay a little longer. That process wasn't easy for either of us. Sometimes I barely could stand his touch and other times I wanted to make it work. I saw the pain I was inflicting on him, and I decided to clean up our messy past and be role models for our children. I wanted to co-create a relationship and be best friends again and show our kids what a real partnership looks like. Over time, we manifested the creation of a true companionship. Every day we took time to listen and tune into each other. The judgments slowly disappeared.

They say Venice is the city of love and that's where we found ourselves a year after the divorce conversation. We had a great time together without the children, spending our days walking on old streets, talking and laughing and enjoying one another. After a while it struck me; I was in love with my husband. Wow, what a big shift! One evening in Venice, we had been enjoying each other on the deepest level. I looked him in the eye and I took off my wedding ring, put it in his hands, and told him, "I don't want you to ever be afraid that I am staying with you only because we are married. What would you say if we let go of our rings to symbolize the freedom we are offering each other with the respect of two free souls? Every morning you wake up beside me, knowing that I have consciously chosen to be here, not just because we are married." I was afraid of saying these words. I was afraid of hurting him and I was fearful that he wouldn't understand that my words came from a place of love. I held my breath… then he took off his ring, gave it to me, and said, "That's the most beautiful thing anyone could ever say to me." I felt over the moon. We were finally on the same page and I hoped it would be the beginning of our happy ending.

Despite this amazing experience, I still struggled with guilt, so I went to see a therapist. She convinced me that it was not fair to keep two men on the hook. I had to make a decision and choose. But I couldn't — I loved them both. I made a decision and became clear on what love meant to me. I decided to break up with both of them.

Unfortunately, we were all about to leave on a family holiday and I had to wait until we got back. A week before returning home, we were in beautiful Slovenia's mountains, hiking and enjoying nature. However, every day felt like a burden, the weight of the delayed announcement was heavy on my heart. My husband kept talking about our future and new trips he wanted us to experience. One evening, I told him I was breaking up with him and the other man. It was not a decision against either of them but a matter of taking steps toward being whole with myself and growth. I needed to be alone.

He listened, with tears in his eyes. When I finished my monologue, he said, "Honey, yes but I believe you're pregnant."

He was right. My very next thought was, "Darn!" The pregnancy felt like a punishment for being selfish and wanting to love freely. I was so angry at life and behaved like a victim by telling myself how unfair it was. Again, I cried my eyes out. After pulling myself together, I chose to accept the pregnancy as a gift. I decided that from then on, I would be stronger and be the best mother to care for this new soul in my life. I truly believe that the best example for children is to live your life happily. Not from a place of selfishness but from a self-love point of view. My husband supported my choice, and that night we hugged and cried together.

In less than 24 hours after breaking up with my husband, I called the other man and told him the same thing. He was totally accepting of my choice. To my surprise I didn't feel relieved; I felt much sadness. At that moment, I was disappointed that he didn't put up a fight, but he had always accepted and understood my choices. After that call, I was heartbroken. Sitting in the woods of Slovenia, with fireflies and tears for company, I knew I couldn't go back on my decision.

The heaviness in my body stayed with me until we got back home. I tried to find an apartment to live in. Nothing interested me; the pregnancy and my emotions were tiring me out. A few weeks after breaking up with the two most important men in my life, I started a conversation with my husband about custody. I proposed to keep the house so that the children could be in a stable place at all times. We would each need to have an apartment and would come to the house every other week. In these conversations with my husband, I felt like I was hitting my head against the wall; he wasn't helping to crystalize a solution. He didn't make any decision other than to keep me beside him. He clearly stated his intention to play his role as a father in the new baby's life. I felt stuck like I was being held hostage in our marriage. I also felt guilty — what kind of mother wants to leave her husband and ruin her children's future? I didn't know what to do but I knew my self-sacrifice had to stop. There was no obvious nor right choice. It felt like I had to choose between ruining my family or sacrificing myself.

Then I thought, what would I say to my daughter in the same situation? What kind of advice would I give her? I knew the answer: Choose self-love. You are the most important person in your life. If you are happy, everyone else will be happy as well. It takes time but it will work out.

I stayed true to myself and magic happened. My husband put his ego aside. He couldn't stand seeing me in so much pain, so unhappy, so frustrated. He took my hands and said, "I understand you need both me and the other man in your life to feel complete. I know it and I accept it." He was asking me to open up my heart again to both of them. He was ready to welcome the other man in our lives. I couldn't believe it. I was amazed at how much love he found in his heart. How much selflessness one man could have. And then, I realized that even though our decisions hurt sometimes, you can never really harm anyone if you choose self love.

This was the missing piece I needed from my husband. By accepting my love for the other man, it showed me how much he loves me unconditionally. He accepted that the other man's love was a part of me. My heart opened again and I found so much love for both of them, my children, and myself.

A year later my heart and my marriage with my husband has transformed. We now have the strongest relationship I've ever witnessed and my dream of showing the perfect partnership to our children has come true. It's been a long hard journey which led us to a very deep understanding of each other that transcends words. We've explored the darkest corners of each other's souls and shone light on it. I know that we will be there for each other no matter what. I found my soulmate from the most unexpected love. Some relationships come to our lives to help us to heal. Some relationships come to teach us how to love. And some of them come to Ignite us to grow bigger than ourselves. Ignite yours and most importantly Ignite the love you feel for yourself.

IGNITE ACTION STEPS

When healing my relationship with my husband, I discovered that there were two important aspects holding me back from making peace with the past and moving on. These are the victim's mentality (blaming the other person) and blaming myself. I want to share a simple tool with you which helped me to release both:

1. Think about a relationship in your life you would like to heal. There's someone who has hurt you or who you have hurt in the past. Maybe both. Take some deep breaths and dive into the emotions related with that person. Is there disappointment? Blame? Sadness? What else is there? Take a piece of paper and write these emotions down. But hold

yourself back from going into details or blaming. *("He never understood me" etc)*. Focus *on your feelings only.*

2. Now take another piece of paper. Imagine yourself in that relationship. Try to look at yourself from new perspectives. What drove you to act the way you did? Take a look at your past self with love and kindness. Now it's time to forgive yourself. Write down everything you could imagine you would need forgiveness for. For example: *"Dear [name]! I forgive myself for not being kind. I forgive myself for not speaking my truth."*

Whatever it is in your case. Write it all down.

3. One of those papers describes your past. The other shows the forgiveness you need to give to yourself. Set them both on fire and release the past.

Then take out a clean piece of paper and start writing your new future.

Piret Špitsmeister – Estonia
Conscious Sexuality Therapist, Wellness Coach and Public Speaker
www.lumeliblikas.ee

Billie J. Williams

(they/them)

"Trust in the Universe can turn loneliness to love."

True partnership includes good boundaries, wonderful physical intimacy, equality, and a relationship in which each person's self-worth is strengthened. My desire is to show you although you may have experienced loneliness in your life, by trusting in the Universe and in yourself, love and true partnership are always possible.

From Loneliness to Love

I grew up on a large plot of land as an only child. I lived in a very small town where people's homes were few and far between. Friends were far away. I was left to my own devices most of the time and I was often feeling lonely, passing the time with my slew of imaginary friends. To alleviate my unwanted solitude, at around the age of 10 I began having crushes on boys in my class. I would imagine having many children with them. I searched for the perfect partner starting early and this continued throughout my life.

When I was fourteen, I went on a church bicycle trip for kids my age from Vermont to Maine. The days were arduous with bike riding, while the evenings consisted of typically fun times interacting with the other kids. One night, I slept on the carpeted yet hard floor next to an older, handsome boy on whom I had a huge crush. That night he sexually assaulted me, quietly, so as not to wake the others. I felt confused and scared. The next morning, one of the counselors commented that I was "*pure* as the driven snow." Hearing this made me feel especially dirty and ashamed of what that boy had done.

Watching my parents' relationship over the years had conditioned me to believe that men's needs always came before my own. Because of this, I continued to see that boy. My first time having sex was with him. We had been making out, and then he asked me to have sex. He held up a green condom in its wrapper and said, "You can't stop now. It would be like taking candy from a baby!" I felt trapped. I didn't want to have sex, but I was afraid if I said no he would reject me. I became promiscuous after those assaults, a behavior I have since learned is not uncommon for survivors of sexual assault. Alongside my promiscuity, I was still searching for 'the one.'

While participating in a summer theater institute when I was 17, I met a young woman there with whom I became very close. I felt comfortable with her; I felt like she was a kindred spirit. This relationship felt rich and loving. Even so, I continued to pursue boys. I didn't see at the time that my actual love was for this young woman who I had developed such a close relationship with.

College began a year later, and I had a few sexual liaisons. Each time I hoped the person would be the one. Spring of my first year, the man who would become my husband entered my life. My infatuation with this brooding young man who dressed all in black was intense. A few short months later, we were lying together in bed. My feet were relaxing against the wall, my toes pink with polish. I believed that our relationship was as good as it gets — my past experience had taught me to have low expectations. Leaning in, I proposed to him. My habit of sticking to my word didn't serve me well in that circumstance. Although my relationship with my fiancé started going badly while we were still in college, I stuck it out. We stayed in a four-year engagement, and I reluctantly moved to his home state after college, hoping that my love for him would return to what it was when we first met.

My dream since I was a child to become an actor led me to majoring in theater in college. For graduate school, I hoped to attend the excellent drama school at the state university in my fiancé's hometown. It was while on the phone with the head of the Drama Department that I learned my future would take a different turn. He told me that the program only accepted students with professional acting experience. I physically shook, feeling as if my stomach fell out of my body. "This cannot be happening," I thought. As my legs wobbled, I sat and gripped the phone tighter. "I am s-sorry to hear that," I stuttered. I was devastated.

Since I believed the man in my life was the priority, I stayed in my fiancé's hometown rather than applying to graduate schools elsewhere to pursue my dream of acting. Sadly, I threw away my childhood dream. Instead, I entered the library science program as it was the program my fiancé was attending.

We married at the end of school. After our wedding, we moved to Chicago. We both worked in libraries while he pursued his dream to attend graduate school for history. Deciding we didn't like the suburb where we lived, we moved to a small, isolated town in a nearby state. We worked in the same university library. It was there that his drinking moved from excessive to very extreme. We decided we didn't like small-town living so we moved to Seattle. I genuinely loved urban life. We had two beautiful red-headed children. They were practically the only sweetness in my marriage.

At about the 16-year mark in our marriage, my husband imprisoned me in our tiny laundry room and raged at me. He shoved his large, overweight body up against me and raged directly into my right ear. I automatically recoiled. Sheer terror filled me. I turned to look at his livid face. The look on it was deadly. "He hates me," I thought. In that moment, I saw my marriage crumble before my eyes. I had thought this man really loved me. It took me the night and the next morning to determine that I needed to leave to protect myself and my children because I was so afraid of what he might do if I said I was leaving. Despite my fear, I summoned my courage to leave. In the coming weeks, my husband took no responsibility for his abusive behavior. Not long after that I filed for divorce. That was the first time that I put *myself* first in any romantic relationship.

My LGBTQ journey began a mere year later, the inner exploration of my sexual orientation. Alone one night while my children were with their father, I sat polishing my fingernails. I was watching a movie in which two women were slowly, affectionately dancing, and it surprised me how much I was deeply moved. Tears filled my eyes. They spilled down my hot cheeks. It felt like that's what I wanted in my life. A big question popped into my head, "Am I gay?"

My beautiful, yet sometimes painful, sexual-orientation journey began on that night. I started at gay, then did more inner work and traveled through bisexual (attraction to both men and women) and landed at pansexual (attraction to all gender identities).

I did not date for the first two years after I left my husband because I was embroiled in a custody battle for my two kids. Finally, I decided to begin dating, not because the custody battle ended, but because I knew that I needed to start living my life. I met a woman at a business networking event who invited me to have coffee. We began dating. The honeymoon phase was exciting and fun, especially since it was my first time dating a woman. Being me, I asked myself, "Is she the one?" Unfortunately, she started exhibiting problematic drinking behavior, including a nastiness toward me that emerged when she was drunk. For the second time in my life, I decided I deserved better. I had dealt with an excessive drinker for two decades and was not willing to do it again.

My LGBTQ journey continued, but this time in the realm of gender orientation. During that month, I experienced one of the worst days of my life. On that day, it struck me that something was not 'normal' about my gender. "What the hell is going on?" I thought. I felt as though the building that was my life for 43 years pancaked in a bad earthquake. I was left broken, crying and alone under the rubble, unsure of my rescue. My terror focused around one question: How could I find the true partner I had yearned for my whole life when I hadn't figured out my gender?

The following month I participated in a weekend personal growth workshop. It was a wildly transformative experience. While I stood at the microphone on the first day of the workshop, I stated that my intention for the weekend was to decide whether to transition from female to male. The leader paused and looked me in the eye. She said, "I get that you have the community resources you need to transition. I don't think you see this, but I also get that you have the inner resources you need." I drew in a sharp breath. "Is she right?" I wondered. I stepped closer to the microphone. "You are right," I said, breathlessly. It was on that day that a new trust and love within myself began to grow.

Following that weekend came a series of classes intended to integrate the transformation and learning from the initial weekend. One of my intentions for the series was to find the partnership I deeply desired. I vowed to fall in love before the 10-week series was over, and I asked the Universe to help me.

The Universe was listening. I met Molly right around that time. It was a casual sort of get-together. We went out for food and drinks after a meeting of a weekly support group for transgender and gender non-conforming folks. We were with a group of people. I ended up sitting across the table from her. The majority of our attention was focused on one another. Molly was smart and funny, and her presence lit up the room. I felt really attracted to her as a person. I wanted to know more about her. I asked her, "What inspires you about electrical engineering?" as that was her profession. And her response blew me away.

"It's like a super power," she replied. It was the coolest thing I had ever heard. I had never thought about someone that way. I was so impressed and it intrigued me, suddenly I wanted to know even more about her! At the end of the gathering, I gave her my contact information hoping she would reach out.

We planned a coffee date in the LGBTQ neighborhood in town. Molly added ice cream onto the coffee idea which made the date all the more fun. I arrived at the coffee spot first and took a seat facing the door. I watched her enter, laden with what appeared to be large books. The sun was shining on her beautiful hourglass figure as she stood in the doorway. When she saw me, her face lit up, and she glided over to the table.

One of the things I loved about this coffee shop was its unique take on hot cocoa. I really wanted to share this with Molly, so I ordered the special, including whipped cream, chocolate syrup, and rainbow sprinkles. When it arrived, a smile spread across her lovely face, and I could tell she appreciated the festive presentation.

The books that she was carrying were actually photo albums. They were filled with her own photography. The close-ups of delicate flowers were as breathtaking as were her photos of the snowy Alaskan landscapes to which she traveled. We talked for a long time, and then we walked a few blocks to the ice cream shop where we stood in line and chatted comfortably. One of the things we talked about was the fact that we were both from the East Coast. We were each a little taste of home to the other.

It was stiflingly warm in the ice cream shop so we decided to walk around while we ate our treats. I was definitely interested in her — more than just as a person. The sun was out, but the air was chilly. We decided to wrap things up and returned to our cars. I had brought along a large collage that I had made about my transition from female to male. It was a snap-shot of my life at that time and included my political views as well as my love of fashion. I showed it to Molly as she already knew about my transition. She gazed intently at it, looking at the images. Despite making myself vulnerable by exposing this part of my life, I felt safe sharing. And I knew it was the right time for me to share it with her.

Spontaneously I leaned in to kiss her. Suddenly, I realized it was incumbent upon me, the man, to be a gentleman. I quickly leaned back and asked if it was all right if I kissed her. She said an immediate and enthusiastic, "Yes!" and I leaned back in. We kissed for a long time on the lips, and then my lips dipped down to kiss her neck. The look on Molly's face was one of revelation. "I've never felt this feeling before," she said and had to sit down due to her wobbly knees. I felt a mixture of joy and kindred emotion. Tears came to my eyes feeling as I had never made a woman feel that way. She had not been kissed on her neck since starting her own estrogen hormones. Molly too had been doing her own transition from male to female. I smiled at her, reaching down to take her hands. Having lived as a woman until that point, I knew exactly how wobbly knees felt. I said, "That's a girl thing." She laughed in appreciation. After that we parked in a quiet spot by the lake, making out like a pair of teenagers.

My Ignite moment came later that night holding her in my arms. Seen from the outside, it was subtle. From the inside, it was deeply moving. All was quiet in the car. Dim light filtered in from the street lights. Moonlight glinted off the lake. I held her pretty head against my shoulder. My heart felt full. I sighed contentedly. I stroked her dark, corkscrew-curly hair. "This feels right," I murmured.

"I feel the same way," she agreed. At that moment, the realization rushed in on me that love was possible.

Thus began my dating life with Molly. Sharing transition with her was a unique pleasure. We understood one another's gender intimately. One example came when Molly gave me the rundown on men's room etiquette. She explained that the cardinal rule of the men's room is to never talk to anyone else at the urinal. You should skip a urinal in between and not take too long.

One thing I appreciate about Molly is that she picks and chooses what to keep from tasks that are considered traditionally male and keeps on doing them out of enjoyment. She fixes her own car, does her own yard work, and adores her chosen profession of electrical engineering.

This picking and choosing has been an inspiration to me in my own gender experience. After I had transitioned to male for ten months, I realized I missed feminine things. I especially missed make-up and women's clothing. Molly encouraged me to try them back on. I did. That, together with Molly's total acceptance of me, led me to understand my gender in new terms. I now understand that I am not a transgender man but a *non-binary* human being. This means that I exist somewhere in the middle of the spectrum between female and male. My sexual orientation is about who I love, and my gender identity is about who I am. Loving and accepting my genuine self, including my pansexuality and non-binary gender identity, I find that I can authentically love others.

If you are looking for 'the one', look no further than yourself. You may have journeyed far on the outside, but the real journey of discovering love is on the inside. You may have struggled with loneliness, or perhaps yearned for a partner who respects you, your boundaries, and with whom you have passionate physical intimacy. Through trusting yourself and the Universe, you can experience true partnership that exceeds your wildest dreams and move through all things, into love.

IGNITE ACTION STEPS

A famous basketball player used to imagine the shot he would take before he took it. That helped him to actually make his shots. In the same way, you can imagine what you want to have happen in your life. Then you and the Universe can go about bringing you exactly what you dream of.

Record the following guided imagery, so that you can close your eyes and play it back to yourself:

Imagine you are walking alone along a forest path. You see sun-dappling on the trees as the light filters down from above. Shrubs with brightly colored berries line your path. You hear the wind in the tops of the trees. Birds chirp. A quiet sound comes from your feet treading along the path. You feel a breeze on your skin. A mixture of moss and pine needles make up the softness you feel under your feet. An earthy aroma fills the air. Your pace is comfortable. You begin climbing a gentle hill. After a few minutes, you hear a rustling. At first you assume it is an animal in the bushes. As you get closer and closer to the top of the hill, the rustling becomes louder until out from the bushes strides another person coming in your direction. Imagine this person is the partner, (or one of the partners), you have always wanted.

What does this person look like? What do they sound like? Perhaps they are humming or singing a song. As they get closer, you can smell a pleasant aroma coming from them. Maybe it is their perfume, cologne, or shampoo. Imagine this person with as much specificity as you can, right down to the textures of their hair. Imagine that a path goes off to the left, and that is the direction you planned to go. The other person turns in the same direction. The trail is wide enough for two. Suddenly, you are walking along with this person. You strike up a conversation. Envision what you talk about. Notice more about the person now that you are closer to them. The two of you plunk down on a bench. You sit in silence enjoying the forest and one another's presence.

Now slowly bring your awareness back to the room. You can return to the forest and meet up with this person as often as you like. They will be there for you to connect with.

Billie J. Williams (they/them) – United States of America
Librarian, Author

GORDANA HAY

"Love is the core of everything you do."

In sharing my LOVE story I can give you many reasons to weep. Instead I choose to give YOU reasons to celebrate! Love is the most powerful, most divine, most inspirational force I have ever known. I was made with LOVE, I was raised with LOVE, and everything I ever approached with LOVE gave me immense joy and immeasurable rewards. I hope my story inspires you to feel LOVE in you. That is my gift to you.

LOVE TAKES MANY FORMS

If I was to describe my love life, I would say it is like a flamenco dance. It is passionate storytelling, colorful, theatrical, magical, always evolving. It has a form, it has the mood, it definitely has an enormous energy, a grounding — intuition speaking with the earth through my feet. It is an ongoing work of ART fuelled by my own mother's love. My mother's love taught me to apply loving feelings as an essential tool to joyously connect with the abundant Mother Earth.

April 17, 2020 marks the 10th anniversary of my mother's soul's departure. Since the beginning of the year I have been secretly planning to arrange a surprise memorial service back in my home country of Serbia. Only, I cannot physically be with her, as all flights are suspended due to the COVID-19 outbreak. There is such an irony in all this: by not being able to physically reach her resting place, I am finally setting myself emotionally free! This physical blockade made me go back into my childhood, travel deep into my core being and into all the values that my mum embedded in me. She filled my heart with oceans of LOVE, enough to share with millions of people, and equipped me with the best virtue there is — LOVE — which I try to embody in everything I do. I am choosing to let go of the memories of indescribable physical pain my mum went through and let go of me feeling helpless while nursing her the last seven weeks before her departure. I am choosing to let go of buckets of guilty feelings during the sleepless nights prior to her death. I have to let those images go, as I know that she would not have wanted me to hold onto them; it is time to move on. I offer this story as a modest expression of the incredible loving legacy that she left in me and my sister.

The unity of my parents created an explosion of love. My father's name was Bogoljub. Bog means god and Ljubav is love in Serbian. My mother's name was Dušanka. Duša means soul, thus, the union of god's messenger and a beautiful soul could only result in an abundance of love. My father lost his father and the whole family fortune in World War II at the tender age of 7. My mother spent her early childhood in a small village and both her parents died in devastating ways. Despite these painful experiences, they were both humble and full of gratitude for what life had given them. There is the belief that our soul chooses our parents. I was undoubtedly lucky with my choice of parents and felt the power of love running in my baby veins.

When I was the age of 7, I asked my mother, "How come I am the only one with curly hair in our family?" My mother's beautiful deep hazelnut eyes lit up with amusement and she said, "When I was pregnant with you, I imagined you in every tiniest detail. I kept adding attributes that I thought were picture perfect." Looking at me with her amazing big eyes she continued, "I imagined a strong, noticeable girl with long sporty legs, thick curly hair, big happy eyes, Brigitte Bardot lips, my teeth, creative, musical, loving, kind, and curious." I felt very happy and very loved. These words have always lifted me, reminding me that I am special and cherished, whenever I feel lonely or down.

By socialist standards, back then in former Yugoslavia, our family of five didn't have much, yet as a child I never felt I was missing anything. Nana cooked the most delicious meals daily from then exclusively organic produce. Early in the morning she would go to the local market to buy fresh fruit and vegetables, whole milk and eggs, and sometimes meat would be delivered to our door from the local farmers, many of whom later become our friends. There was always the smell of freshly baked bread and ground Turkish coffee in our house. And lots of gorgeous plants.

Mum was working full time, a little avant-garde for Yugoslav women in the early sixties. There was a kind of natural rhythm in our household, and I was in tune with it all. Everyone had their own chores and everyone had 'me' time. That way I was raised with a sense of responsibility and independence. My whole childhood seemed like one long stretch of playtime — full of fun and discoveries.

Every Sunday was a joy. Mum would cook over the weekend and her meals were always a surprise. She loved experimenting and trying new healthy recipes. My parents introduced us to avant garde music and jazz and would play it in the background. Dad would cuddle with us on the couch, no one was worrying about housework, as the house cleaning was already done the day before. At around 2 PM Mum would call me to set the table. She would choose the linen tablecloth and I would lay the plates and the cutlery, glasses, freshly cut flowers from her garden and sometimes candles. Everyone had a particular location at the table. Mum was at the top, so she could be close to the kitchen and bring the dishes out. I was on the left hand side of Mum, close to her heart, and Grandma was on her right. Dad and Alex would rotate places, depending on the day's mood and if there was a movie to watch or not. We couldn't wait to be seated and start our long meal which was partially about enjoying food, but more importantly about our lively conversations about the events of the week that had passed. We had so much to share and sometimes would all talk together, laugh loudly and over each other. Those Sunday lunches were times I will treasure forever. All problems, no matter how small or big, were discussed and decisions made collectively with smiles and ease. It was in that environment that my *concept* of LOVE and my *expectation* of LOVE from others developed.

My parents loved traveling and took us on driving trips all over Yugoslavia and through Europe. Mum would make a picnic of mouthwatering chicken that my sister still makes today to welcome my arrival to Serbia, and we would fix our bikes or rollers onto the car and go. Sometimes we didn't even plan where, we just drove and when we saw a nice place to stop, it would be the beginning of a little adventure. We couldn't afford hotels, but we would camp in those early years. Before starting elementary school, we traveled to Italy, through Trieste and on to Venice and Rome. I will never forget my first ever stay in a hotel in Venice. A luxuriously decorated palace incorporating Gothic, Moorish, and Renaissance architectural styles. I will always remember the discovery of gold taps: the beginning of my love for richness in interiors and architecture and an appetite for the indulgent and extravagant.

After this wonderful childhood, nourished by delicious food and my family's support, I finished university and faced the challenge of finding a job and the diminishing stability of a country on the brink of civil war. I bought a three-month return ticket and imagined that summer would be the best time to learn a language in a new city. Little did I know that I would live in the United Kingdom for the next 19 years.

Even though I flew to London alone, not knowing anyone there and not having much money on me, one Latin phrase that I was raised with in my childhood gave me courage to leave my home country with confidence and excitement. My father always said...

"Omnia mea mecum porto" All that is mine I carry with me.
— Cicero (Bias of Priene)

When I left Yugoslavia back in 1988, I did not carry just a suitcase filled with 20 kg of clothes, shoes, accessories, and the essential 'Collins English Dictionary.' I carried my childhood-acquired traits in me. The treasure box full of hope, wonder, and curiosity — gifts my parents generously showered me with. I armed myself with Latin phrases, jazz music, my love for theatre, healthy food, sports, and espresso coffee — but most of all LOVE.

Whenever it was time to leave my parent's home at the end of each return visit in the years that followed, I would find endless reasons why I couldn't pack: I couldn't find my green polo turtleneck. My favourite jeans were not washed. How could I fit my favourite combinations with only one 20 kg bag? What about jewellery, shoes, bags, accessories...? I would typically find myself sitting in my father's armchair unwilling to leave and then sobbing. My sister, annoyed with my delay, would cause quarrels. My mother was always the expert at diffusing the ensuing tension amongst sisters, a typical reaction to a loved one leaving.

One particular evening however was different. My always-impeccable intuition was telling me that I HAVE to go back to London. If I'm in another country, I have an option to help my family if need be. Yugoslavia was on the brink of civil war! And I didn't want to part with my family but I felt I could help them better away from the war. The war lasted ten years and that kept me in London. I was constantly packed to go home, but it only happened for visits. And every trip back was celebrated with love and 20 kg of presents.

On a beautiful day in London, after just returning from celebrating my Grandma's 90th birthday, bursting with enthusiasm, overflowing with love, I was feeling happy and re-energized to return to my busy, hectic work life. Fiona, our receptionist and now my long-time friend, introduced me to a new colleague and our first chat is still going 18 years later.

My career was blossoming and while I was excelling at what I do, and being in love with my creative self, I found my soulmate at the tender age of 40. Learning and giving was the answer, pushing boundaries and curiosity, coupled with my love for people and all things beautiful. In my architecture career, I was leading teams and designing innovative healthcare facilities for which I and my team received three awards, two of which were presented by HRH Princess Anne.

While I was creating therapeutic environments for people needing care, in a cruel irony my mother's health had been severely deteriorating. Having been ill for years, she had managed to keep it secret from her daughters, not to place a burden on either of us. I was flying home probably four times per year during the busiest times in my career to see her and give her a tiny amount of love back. In the year leading up to her untimely death, the physical changes were marked. In my home country there was little that could be done for her; we reluctantly agreed to her being in hospital for full-time care.

Having despaired at how the hospitals in my home town were so ill equipped to help my beautiful 'Mama,' we decided to bring her home for her final days. I stayed with her during her last seven weeks, nursing her continuously. I would hear her moaning and stayed awake listening and wondering how this could have happened to my adoring, vibrant mother and how she of all people could have been treated the way she was.

Although it was awfully painful to watch her rapidly failing physical strength, coupled with excruciating and worsening pains, I will forever treasure our most beautiful, deep, and insightful talks, mixed with humour and the joy of being together. If the weather was nice, we would set the garden table outside, where we had peace and privacy and could be intimate. Mum, hardly able to walk, each day taking her closer to her deathbed, would prepare yet another delicious meal. I would set the table and we would repeat the memory of our treasured Sunday lunches laughing and exchanging stories. To this day I cannot understand how she could find the energy to move, let alone cook and even color her hair just to welcome me home in her way. My heart is filled with a mixed bag of deepest gratitude and love, but also the excruciating pain for what her warrior brave soul went through in the end.

That mixed bag of deepest gratitude and love has resurfaced during the turn of the world and COVID-19. My forever soulmate and I are in our Dubai apartment, in what they call 'stay at home' mandatory directions by the UAE government. We have nutritious food in the fridge, fresh flowers on the table, designery and a clean home, internet connection, his guitar and my piano and most importantly, one another. Yet something is brewing in my heart. I miss my mum badly.

If my mother was across the table from me now, her delicious food in front of us, Latin tunes playing in the background, this is what I would tell her: "What I am choosing to remember is your unmatched natural beauty, your dance moves in my first house in Cambridge when, on my return from work, I caught you and dad dancing in my living room to the tunes of Samba. And dad believed that he didn't know how to dance. I choose to remember you teaching me how to roll over back and forth when I was so little and thought it impossible. I am choosing to remember the boat cruise along the Thames on my 40th birthday and my male colleagues commenting on your beauty. I choose to remember you sending boxes with your delicious food to Belgrade when I was a student, just to make sure I was eating well. In those boxes I vividly remember always finding a different seasonal fruit, some nuts, healthy cakes, and somewhere in between the containers, your love note. Although you were not a woman of many words, your actions echoed LOVE. I choose to remember our laughter and storytelling while decorating the Christmas tree every year and planning what special cakes you would make us during that time.

I will try to let go of expecting LOVE, as all my life I thought that it was a norm that everyone should expect love. That is, after all, what you and dad taught me and my 'little sister' Alex so it had to be right. Instead, I am going to give even more of it and find more ways to build it into everything I do. Different life choices and a physical distance drew us physically apart, never in our hearts though. I know somewhere in the clouds your soul is watching us with a huge smile in those amazing brown eyes of yours. I know that your courageous sparkling soul is reunited with Dad and Nana in heaven. I also feel that you are patiently holding onto a thousand and one memories about us kids, our many beautiful adventures together, your wonderful grandchildren, and waiting for another opportunity for our souls to choose you as our family together. I intuitively know this is the only way."

My mother's love, her unconditional acceptance, and her warm embrace gave me my Ignite moment. Even though she is not here to hold me, her beauty lives in my heart. Her essence of love helps me feel love right now. You too can feel this love as there are many forms in which love is embedded in you. All of us have love in our souls, beauty in our lives, and the power to love ourselves, others, and the planet. Use this time to dig deep and find it!

As the wonderful ancient Sufi phrase:

"When the heart weeps for what it has lost, the spirit rejoices for what it has found."

Love Takes Many Forms

Ignite Action Steps

LOVE yourself the most, as you will need it to walk this life journey, to grow, help others, and lift yourself up when in the abyss. Loving is responsibility, establishing routine, and finding your best ways to express yourself. When you do that, love pours into you and becomes a magnet for all the joy there is in life.

BE CURIOUS. We are part of this amazing universe and everything has its purpose. Many life lessons are around us, in nature, in the streets, among the stars, and definitely in many books. Observe all there is around you and use your senses. Look, touch, smell, listen, taste, then take time to reflect.

APPLY YOURSELF fully in everything you do, but first master your inner strengths and boundaries. Stay focused on what truly matters, not the insignificant stuff.

RESTART when you get stuck, start again with tiny steps that help make you smile.

TRUST your unique beauty, as there is so much of it inside already.

DANCE DAILY. Music is soul to the ears and the movement is not only a great form of exercise but expresses your emotions, especially those of LOVE.

BE CREATIVE, with whatever touches your fancy: making food, writing, sketching, listening to new types of music, noticing details in nature, observing your immediate surroundings, learning a new skill, or expanding your ways of giving to others.

REMEMBER YOUR ANCESTORS. We are all born with certain values and certain lessons to learn. Dive deep into your thoughts, family roots, childhood; take an inward journey. Then note them down in your diary or use a daily journal.

TRY SOMETHING TOTALLY DIFFERENT, something that takes you into unfamiliar territory, out of your comfort zone. You may discover a new **LOVE**.

LOOK AT YOURSELF IN THE MIRROR. Look long and deep into your eyes and the LOVE will pour back toward you.

Gordana Hay – Belgrade, former Yugoslavia
Architect and Designer
gordana_bliss@hotmail.com
Gordana Hay
gordana.hay

Anne-Marie Charest, Ph.D.

"'Falling in love' will often result in someone getting hurt; to LOVE is the art of consciously 'becoming in love.'"

Many of us excel at cultivating our careers, dreams, bodies, and spirituality, yet few take the time and discipline to deeply practice the art of 'becoming in love.' My hope is that through my story you will be inspired to awaken to the simple yet profound tools and practices essential in re-Igniting your love life.

Beyond Falling in Love

Curled up in a twist on my bedroom floor, I was gasping for air, pieces of disbelief were striking my skin like meteors falling from the sky. I gripped my aching chest in a futile attempt to stop the shaking of my body and soothe my pain. Life, dreams, family, companionship, and what I thought to be love had been yanked from me with the dreaded reality that my husband of thirty years was not returning home. The truth is, he had 'fallen in love' with another woman. I knew this experience well, as years ago I too had been lured into the illusion of an affair, the seduction of novelty, the enchantment of passion, and the new sense of aliveness brought on by dormant hormones now flowing again. I wondered if our relationship had been an illusion.

Amidst the darkness, a sliver of light emerged from the distance as I began the inner journey to better understand my unconscious actions that had paved a path of pain and destruction in my own life. Fearful of what I would find, I knew it was time to sit still, self-reflect, embrace, and forgive. I wanted my life to be different as I longed for a deeper understanding of love. The veil of illusion opened up my knowing that this new journey and my beloved were utterly worth it. Eyes wide open, I began my inner dive.

As a child, I was taught that princes and princesses lived happily ever after. That love is something that emerges without effort when the right prince comes along. As a psychotherapist, I was well aware that, for many, unfortunately, this fairytale quickly turns into disenchantment with the challenges that relationships create along the way. I knew that 46% of marriages were predicted to end in divorce. I also remembered hearing my mother cry herself to sleep as she struggled through the pain of separation when I was a young teenager.

By the time I was ready to marry my own prince, both my parents and my fiancé's parents were divorced. That was not exactly the story nor the role models I had envisioned as a child. On my wedding day, I remember buttoning up my dress, eagerly preparing for the day ahead, yet also being completely flooded with awkward feelings and conflicting messages. It was as if I was standing at the edge of a cliff and about to embark on a new chapter of life without a compass. Here, I was asked to commit to "for better or for worse and to death do us part," while my elders expressed another reality. One part of me shouted, "YES YES YES I LOVE YOU! We can do this together," while another part of me stood questioning, "Why should I get married if it ends in this way?"

Despite the duality that lived within, I vividly remember the love that permeated as I gazed into my husband's eyes and spoke the words "I do." Every cell of my body illuminated with, "Yes, I am committed to making this work." We were both young, filled with dreams and vitality, and determined to not repeat our parents' story. I asked myself what had gone utterly wrong? Why did people have affairs? And how could such pain be prevented?

In the stillness of an empty home, I began reflecting into my distant past for answers. As chapters were brought to life, four distinct love phases emerged, each offering unique flavors of how love manifested itself toward my partner. I categorized these phases as: 1) Falling in Love, 2) Attachment, 3) Questioning, and 4) Becoming in Love.

The Falling in Love Phase is what meshes every great romance and love story. This phase was depicted by an insatiable attraction and thirst for my beloved, an irresistible longing, a flaring of excitement, restless nights dreaming of the next encounter, and an amalgam of swirling emotions. Love felt primal as my seductress archetype was in full expression in the hope of luring my ideal partner.

Unconscious of what was happening within me at the time, I navigated unconsciously the dance of lust, the desire to be seen, and the insatiable yearning to be loved. Today I understand that this love period is dictated by a flood of hormones that stems from an evolutionary need to reproduce. The cocktail of estrogen, testosterone, dopamine, norepinephrine, and serotine illuminate our bodies. During this phase, the world around me ceased to exist as thoughts of the other consumed every moment of my existence. It was in this early relationship phase that I remember a sense of giddiness, aliveness, and unmeasurable sexual attraction for my lover. My heart stopped when my partner would send me beautiful love letters, kissed me passionately, made love to me, talked with me for hours on end about life, or tended to my emotional needs. During this vivid emotional exploration, I also found myself having meaning by simply being with my beloved. My existential landscape shouted, "In your presence, I am." Being with my partner was enough and it gave me a great sense of purpose.

In retrospect, despite the passion of a great romance, I now understood this stage to be utilitarian in that it served the primal need to connect and reproduce. Although I absolutely adored the sensuous expression of the Falling in Love Phase, I soon discovered that it was short-lived.

Married with two beautiful sons, the illusion of love as I knew it had soon dissipated and transformed itself into something significantly more grounded and stable. We'd moved to the Attachment Phase.

Wild and hot kisses gave way to a gentle pressing of the lips; fiery caresses solidified into a deeper grounding and mutual reassurance of presence. Passionate sex and attraction tactics made way to a deeper connection. A long-term partnership and friendship took center stage as we developed love and intimacy through common activities, unified goals, family duties, cuddling, and lovemaking — all of which contributed to solidifying our union. That phase created a structure and level of commitment necessary for raising our children. I felt motherly, safe, and invincible.

During that period, two primary hormones dominated the landscape of the relationship: oxytocin and vasopressin. Today we know that oxytocin contributes to creating a healthy bond with our partner and children, while vasopressin is known to contribute to supporting monogamy. During those years, I realized that my partner complemented my qualities and that together we were greater than each of us alone. I found joy and meaning in raising our children and helping grow our respective careers and life visions. Our partnership stood solid in the purpose of doing a fantastic job of raising our children; and that we did!

Love felt very different during that phase. My seductress self had morphed into the mother archetype, as family duties took precedence. Being a Type-A personality, I dedicated myself to be a fabulous mom. Unfortunately, today I recognize that this was to the detriment of my partnership. During these years, many of the challenges in our relationship emerged. My husband wondered where his sensuous partner had gone? My acts of love felt like an extension of my motherly love as I gave profusely, yet all in the wrong ways. Exhaustion had become the norm as a full-time job and never-ending parenting duties took priority.

In hindsight, one of the biggest mistakes I've made in my life was to not honor and cultivate my inner goddess, the part of me that nurtured herself with self-love, self-care, and also embodied the sensuous. My upbringing had me believe that being a mother was the greatest gift of all and that mothers gave unconditionally, sacrificing themselves for the sake of their children. It was also during those years that lovemaking was seen as another chore rather than the expression of our mutual love. By choosing to be a giver, I had forgotten how to receive, leaving me longing to have my husband's arms around me and his hands caressing my skin; to have my heart rate slowed next to his steady calmness, enriched by his presence. Those times were accompanied by me rejecting many offers of intimacy, activating a shutdown response in my husband which mysteriously resulted in him forgetting the art of seducing. This led us into the unconscious downward spiral of our relationship.

Despite my exhaustion and overworked schedule, I longed for the fiery emotions that accompanied the Falling in Love Phase. Having no one to talk to, I began believing that something was desperately wrong with me. My libido had plummeted, my energy dropped, and my connection to my husband faded. I began to doubt and question my marriage. Why was all of this happening? Was something biologically wrong with me? How could I rekindle my inner flame for my partner? As I questioned my relationship, those times also offered contradictory experiences as a sense of aliveness emerged from men who attempted to court me at work. My longing for the feelings of passion and aliveness sucked me into the desire and trap of the Falling in Love Phase and caused greater disarray in my marriage. By then I was even more perplexed and lost. With parents who had failed at their own marriage, no friends who I felt I could turn to, and no healthy role models, I didn't know therapy was an option. Once again, I felt I was navigating blind.

As children grew and familiarity settled, so did the dissatisfaction I felt in my relationship. I sensed that something new wanted to emerge, but what?

We entered the Questioning Phase. For years, my partner and I were amazing providers, family makers, great friends, and powerful guides for each other. With children now out of college and mostly self-sufficient, I wondered what the purpose of our partnership was at this stage of our lives. I felt a heaviness; exhausted, an almost emotionless essence permeated my skin, leaving me restless and fidgety. All attempts to look outside of myself had failed. Unsatisfied, I turned inward to find myself and to better understand the dynamics at play that were causing so much havoc in my life.

Now that our relationship was in disarray and everything that we had worked so hard to build was dissolving, there was nowhere to go other than to sit in stillness. It was in this quiet space that I began to see clearly. I noticed that I knew very little about how to cultivate love. My life was dictated by a victim attitude where I believed that 'life happened to you' rather than stand in the knowing that 'life is working for you.' In the quiet space of my inner thoughts, I began compassionately reflecting on how my past behaviors had affected my relationship and how our unconscious actions were primal attempts to meet our needs for excitement, love, connection, and significance. This understanding morphed my pain into compassion and forgiveness.

The Becoming in Love Phase was marked by both choosing each other consciously. No longer bound by ephemeral hormonal influences or utilitarian purposes, a new sense of freedom emerged from consciously cultivating the art of becoming in love. My body was imbued with a deep sense of peace. It was a returning home. With the understanding of the elements crucial to becoming in love, I was no longer bound to an outcome. A transpersonal essence emerged in which mutual growth, deep honoring of the other, and the capacity to self-generate love from within was now the foundation of a new sense of purpose, meaning, and well-being. In that new playground, aliveness grew in our relationship along with a love that transcended previous relationship stages.

In that new dance together, we no longer blamed each other but rather engaged in a joint dialogue to explore and understand the dynamics that no longer served us. Choosing to love more consciously allowed us to be with each other authentically and vulnerably, leaving greater room for trust and intimacy. Hiding behind the veil of deceit no longer was acceptable nor an option. This was the foundation of our new existence.

At times, I did not like what I was hearing from my partner and found myself triggered and hurt, yet that became the platform for a deeper truth and understanding between us. I realized how I used to mold myself to please the people I loved for fear of being rejected. This included my husband. Love was no longer a destination but rather like a string of pearls that were cultivated through little gestures, patience, and a daily commitment to show up for each other.

Properly identifying, owning, and communicating one's needs took center stage. This tool and a new way of being together re-Ignited trust for each other. With greater awareness, we both realized how we had become deaf to each other's needs as we took the other for granted. Historical shaming and blaming made way for a deep understanding of each other and clear channels of communication. I learned to cultivate and value my partner's needs and wishes as highly as I valued my own.

Now cultivating a conscious relationship, I began understanding that I was 100% responsible for my own needs and no longer placed myself at center stage. My relationship grew into a luscious garden with nurturing, watering, and dedication on a daily basis. At times this manifested itself by sharing my appreciation, reflecting my husband's beauty, and honoring his uniqueness. As my consciousness grew and my understanding of the intricacies that created a loving relationship, I realized that it required commitment, discipline, and the courage to grow and change. My acts of kindness fueled reciprocity and mutual love between us. Cultivating the gifts of a conscious partnership, my love life was re-Ignited to new heights and realms I would have never imagined.

Today the only option that seems reasonable to me is radical honesty. This includes sharing parts of me that have been hard to share and allowing my partner to do the same. This approach leads to feeling seen, understood, and deeply loved. With this new way of relating, I am fiercely committed to being the embodiment of Love. Through my devotion and daily practice, love is a conscious choice. Giving is a deliberate act of unconditional love. Each act is tended to consciously and lovingly, knowing the joy it will bring to my partner. With greater consciousness, I no longer hold my partner responsible for my happiness. I am a master of my internal landscape.

Love, ultimately, is a practice we each can consciously choose. I encourage you to move from an unconscious relationship to a new conscious partnership. Let all phases of your relationship be filled with acceptance, forgiveness, and authenticity. It is when we are vulnerable that we are at our strongest. There is both richness and hope in BECOMING and BEING love.

IGNITE ACTION STEPS

If you are longing to re-Ignite your love life, you can step into the relationship of your dreams by consciously cultivating your actions. There are simple, easy steps you can start incorporating into your life today to fully Ignite your love life.

- Take 100% responsibility for your relationship. Know that you have the ability to take all matters into your own hands and make the change you want to see. Give yourself a daily hug.

- Go beyond a ME, Myself, and I attitude. Move past the 'self' and show up with acts of kindness and generosity toward your loved one. Take a pause out of your day to celebrate something about your partner you appreciate. Make them feel special.

- Own your baggage. Don't project onto your partner. Take a pause and look inside of you. Opening your heart will lead you to understand each other's challenges and truly move into forgiveness. Magic happens when we say sorry to ourselves and others.

- Take responsibility for your own needs. We all have needs. Allow yourself to understand your internal needs that live below your emotions. Then empower yourself by taking 100% responsibility for honoring and fulfilling them. You are your own gift.

- Plant seeds of kindness and gratitude, and water them daily. Tending to your relationship daily like a sacred garden brings it to life and opens hearts to a new understanding of what it means to truly love. Little gestures, from sending loving texts throughout the day, a shoulder rub, a scrumptious home-cooked meal, extending a moment of gratitude, or simply giving my partner a hug became my daily norm and soon turned into a generous wave of reciprocity.

Anne-Marie Charest, Ph.D. – United States of America
Licensed Marriage & Family Therapist, Mindfulness & Wellness Facilitator
www.heartfullyU.com

ALIDA DEL BIANCO

"Be You — Be Love"

I share my story to inspire you to always have faith in the highest principle of our Universe, in the energy that creates everything, and in the knowing that it is accessible in your heart. Life is your chance to experience and expand this energy, create magic and ecstasy. You choose how to use this opportunity, how to connect with your higher self, and what you create from this unified field of Love and Compassion.

ONLY LOVE CAN HEAL THE WORLD

When was the magical moment when I experienced that Love is the highest force in our Universe continuously creating life and fulfilling the existence of every atom and every star? Was this like religious epiphany, miraculous Divine Revelation that the saints and sages are describing? Or was this something very simple and warm, something so human that outgrows and magnifies our Spiritual Essence?

I have always adored the quote by fellow Croatian Nikola Tesla,

"If you wish to understand the Universe think
of energy, frequency and vibration."

I realized something that struck me as particularly profound and true. He said that "Energy... is God. God... is energy. All... is energy." He was the force that connected the different elements of my reality — what I see and what I perceive with my senses — with something that was beyond my perception. Reading his words was like a mini epiphany. Little did I know at the time that a bigger epiphany was about to come.

It was a very cold winter night, the howl of the northern wind was bringing the smell of snow from the mountains. I was gazing at the smoky reflection of my eyes on the frozen window and all I could see in them was despair. I was burnt out; I felt exhausted on all levels. I tried to comfort myself with some sleep and I lay down in my warm and cosy bed. But I could not warm up, my body was shivering as though it had a fever, my eyes wide open searching for meaning and significance in my life. "God, is this all there is?" was the only thought repeating in my head like a mantra, vibrating in every cell in my body.

For a long time, I could not move and I could not react. In this omnipresent anguish, I let go of living only to discover another awareness unfolding in front of me. "Oh my God, so *this* is my fate onward, *this* is my time?" In the blink of an eye, I saw the movie of my whole life in slow motion. Yet, all I could sense was the ending. From within a voice spoke up, both loving and confronting. A deep feeling of surrender was overflowing me and a sense of never-before-experienced peace was washing away the emptiness from my heart. "God, I surrender to you, take me to the Light!" I said.

"*No, dear One, you are just getting started, you are the doer!*" was the answer I heard. As there was no other thought in my mind, no other emotion in my body, I could hear clearly that voice and I knew God was talking to me, supporting me in that moment. "Thank you God, thank you, thank you…" I said. Repeating it over and over, I felt waves of gratitude overflowing me and melting my frozen heart.

I felt the entire surface of my skin infused with Divine energy that sank inwards, and God continued to talk to me. "*You are born to be a healer. Many people will come to you and you will know how to heal them.*"

"Me God? For sure not me, I am dying now!"

"*Yes, but only your old self is dying, and you have been through all of this to be reborn in your life's purpose.*"

"No thank you, God. How can I heal others when I am broken? All the pain and suffering of my life has broken my heart."

"*Dear Child,*" He said, His comforting fatherly voice a warming light that created a *knowing* in my heart, "*As you heal others, you will heal yourself. Your Soul is ready! We need you to be the Light in these days of transition that are in front of us.*"

Oh my God, what is going on? It must be the spirit molecule that is activated in my brain to make this passage easier. "*No, dear One. This is your calling. It is what you have been waiting for your whole Life. All your experiences have been preparing you to reach the maturity to let go of everything and surrender completely. Now you are ready and you are guided through your transition into a different understanding.*"

My body was melting in this Divine fragrance. I sensed the presence of Divine Energy all around me, in me, and I knew God was talking to me. I fell asleep and I slept for a very long time. When I woke up, I thought, "What a dream last night!" But I knew something was different. I felt joy in my heart after a very long time. God blessed me with an Ignite moment.

My Healing Journey

I visited my friend near the sea, a few streets away from my home, to get a relaxing massage. She showed me an article about meditation classes in the beautiful, aristocratic, and intellectual city of Zagreb, Croatia — a very proud city that is showing His magnificence at every step. And in a few days, we would both be driving from our hometown of Pula to Zagreb to attend the class.

We arrived at a modern glass-windowed hotel on the edge of the city, and I asked at the reception desk where the meditation class was. The receptionist directed me toward the sign that was in front of me... the only word I could see was HEALING.

My friend and I proceeded to the conference room where the class was being held. There were 60 people there, sitting in rows facing the teacher who was explaining what was to follow. It was a three-day class, and for me it was the deepest healing and opening to a complete new perception of my reality. During the days, I was absorbing the knowledge of how to direct energy and witness healing on all levels. During the nights, I would feel so nauseous, as if I had been purging with plant medicines. My digestive system was releasing literally all the traumas and limiting belief systems that have created so much pain in my heart.

The last day of the class, our teacher told me something that I will never forget, "Forgiveness in your heart is the Gate to Unconditional Love!" I realized how much my body had been paralyzed, locked in place by the heaviness of the resentment I had been holding in my heart. Intuitively, I started with myself and as I was seeing this resentment releasing, I could see why I created it and what I learned from it. I saw the positive side of my resentment and I found forgiveness for myself.

I knew that my depression served me to be reborn again. I knew that my mother was not showing me love to teach me how to love unconditionally. I knew that my husband had let me down to teach me how to stand up for myself. I knew that God abandoned me to teach me how to feel always connected with him. And I also knew that all of this was just created in my mind and it was emanating as my energy. It was a pattern repeating itself endlessly from generation to generation; energy imprinted on our genes. By shifting my perception, I was shifting my reality.

I came home to Pula after that weekend and I was myself again. I felt whole, healed, rejuvenated, and my thyroid gland was healed. My energy was radiating so vibrantly that all my family members and friends asked me to do a healing on them. Every person who came to me was mirroring on some level my experience, and I was shifting and transforming on a very deep level. My physical senses were magnified and my intuitive senses were growing exponentially. I could see, hear, and especially smell the hidden truth of every person who asked me to help them.

In that magical time, with Christmas bells ringing in our homes, I thought that the best Christmas present for my oldest daughter, Julie, would be the Healing Class. My youngest daughter, Lucy, was 15 and she asked, "And what about me?"

I said, "Let us go together!" And so we did. Each one of us experienced a profound healing on a personal level, and we felt healing in our relationships with each other as well. Our energy raised, our perception shifted, and we began to perceive life differently.

I clearly remember our trip back home. It was snowing; we were driving through the mountains covered with soft white snowflakes that were falling on the trees near the highway. Our car was driving on the untouched white cover illuminated by the full moon. All three of us were silent, our eyes wide open in awe and wonder. That night, another Ignite moment was unfolding in front of me.

All the missing pieces of the puzzle came together. The illusion of the physical reality has disappeared and the meaning of every decision, step, experience, and encounter was clearly visible to me. For the first time, I understood the Law of Karma and I recognized the interconnections, soul contracts, and manifestations of Karma in my life. I understood that I had fulfilled my soul contract with my husband, healing myself from victimhood and abuse, and forgiving him. Our Karma lesson was concluded. I saw our paths going in two different directions in the snow, and I knew the meaning of it.

After 20 years of marriage, the bond that I had felt was going to be eternal and the love that I felt should have lasted forever... was just fading away and transforming into something even more beautiful than our marriage.

God said, *"Do not be afraid. Your children are going to be fine and, in the unfolding of your lives, you will see that not everything is as it appears to be now."*

"Love is all that is, but before you realize that, you need to experience it in all physical manifestations here on earth."

"Love is our essence. We don't need to understand, we just need to be Love. We need to embody that vibration and simply be Love."

Deciding that it was time for me to leave our marriage and continue on my self discovery path was the hardest decision in my life, especially as it was a decision that impacted my children. But I had confidence that it was the right path. God's words had generated a warm, comforting truth inside of me that could not be denied. And yes, it was not easy, but all of us recovered and healed from the pain of separation, abandonment, disappointment, and from all the other attachments and projections of our egos. When I look at my three children now, and at my four-year-old grandson, a deep joy fills me with excitement and makes me want to dance with gratitude for who they are despite all that we have been through. Each one of us grew up to be very strong, independent, and focused individuals. The bond that is uniting us is our Love that has transcended all the earthly imposed limitations. We learned how to *be* Love!

Love is our essence. It is the essence of our Universe. When your heart is open and pure, you are connected with this magical power. Through self-discovery and commitment to your truth, you can rediscover your authentic self and, from that space of integrity, the highest vibrational force will embody in you.

In the depths of despair comes the hand of God. If we remain open and listen to our truth, the answer is always there. It is important to know that there are endless possibilities when we move out of our habitual perceptions. When we expand our understanding and let go, and let God — who is love — speak to us, we find the clear direction. There is always a good ending, even if we don't know it. Allowing the best of you to grow and shine is what God wants for you. My wish and my blessing to you is that you create your life from Love.

IGNITE ACTION STEPS

My story is unique, and yet it is not. It is the story of all of us. We are all called to live our life purpose. You may think something so spectacular like having extra sensorial perception and being able to heal yourself and others is rare, but I can assure you that this is our birth right and all of us can reach this state of consciousness.

Commit yourself to your truth. Dedicate yourself to the healing of your wounds, even those that sometimes we are not aware of. To discover truth and help your wisdom flow from your heart, you need to see *your own* truth and contemplate your life from a place of acceptance. You can transform everything. Here are some easy steps to help you on your own transformational journey.

Meditation is a state of consciousness when we disconnect from all distractions of the outside world and turn inwardly into our natural state of being. At the beginning of your practice, your mind will create all kinds of disturbances and distractions, but your only task is to observe and detach from all thoughts and projections of your mind, without holding anything. Especially if there is resistance to change, which is somehow embedded in our human Ego as instinctive survival mode.

It is essential to practice breath awareness. Sit in a comfortable meditative position with your spine straight and the palms of your hands facing upwards placed on your thighs.

You can join your thumb and index fingertip together, while holding other fingers straight in a gesture called *Gyan Mudra*, which will channel your energy flow to accept your own knowledge and wisdom. Inhale and exhale through your nose, going deeper with every breath, observing the sensations in your body and relaxing completely. When you reach your Inner Temple you will feel this state of Surrender, Peace and Forgiveness.

Forgiveness Meditation

We use resentment as our hidden power to cope with the pain caused by someone we may think, but it is only our deep pain reflected in the behaviour of others. It is an energy pattern which we are creating unconsciously and attracting even more pain in our life and completely closing our hearts.

Make a list of all your resentments and grudges; write down all the names and situations that caused you pain. Always remember to start from yourself and contemplate what happened, how this affected you and what positive you learned from it. Stay focused and be very specific. Continue with all the people and circumstances that have hurt you in your life and declare in your aligned state of consciousness,

> *" I am forgiving myself (or any other person) for... I am ready to let go of... and I am ready to move on in my life with all the lessons learned (find the concrete lesson, the virtue that you acquired!). With my heart full of gratitude for the lessons they taught me, I am releasing myself from this pattern on all levels of my existence."*

God is Grace and when your heart is open you are Igniting not only yourself but the whole Universe!

Alida Del Bianco – Croatia
Energy Healer, Ayurveda Therapist, Yoga and Meditation Teacher, Founder of Surya Soul Temple
www.surya.hr

ANNIE KALLIS

"Love starts with YOU."

Relationships are what matters to us human beings the most. So why do we struggle with them sometimes? Because we do not understand the most important one, the one with ourselves. And how do you do that, you ask? You do whatever it takes to figure this out. I did it and I encourage you to do the same. Love YOU first.

LOVING ME

As I was leaving Phoenix, to catch a flight back home to Melbourne, after a wonderful meeting with my conditioning coach, Mack Newton, he looked at me and said:

"Annie, I am going to tell you three words and nothing else after that. You will walk out that door, catch your plane home, and apply these words to your life…"

I hugged him and grabbed my bags. He looked me straight in the eyes and said,

"Commitment to Completion!"

These words changed the course of my life at the young age of forty-eight.

You see, I was a sad, empty, overweight, weak, overwhelmed woman. I was riddled by an anxiety that came from a very unfulfilled life. My stress was caused by an unhappy marriage, being estranged from my parents, disrespectful 'friends' who were not treating me well, a business that was dwindling down, and from a deep yearning for love and happiness that I wasn't feeling or getting. The foundations for what I needed to feel complete were missing.

Looking back, I realize that I was seeking love and happiness from my relationships with others. Relationships with my parents, siblings, lovers, friends, co-workers, and teammates. I was at a point where all I felt was rejection, abandonment, betrayal, criticism, and dislike. All I wanted was to be cherished, defended, protected, adored, and loved. The more I was searching for answers, the more I latched onto others and expected others to fulfill me.

What I realized that day when I left my coach and sat in the taxi on the way to the airport was that as much as I was seeking the love of others, the most important relationship that I must have is the one with ME. I had been looking for people to love and take care of me my whole life. In that taxi ride, I finally understood that I had the person who I needed and that it was me. I had been climbing the proverbial ladder and when I got to the top I realized it was leaning against the wrong wall. My wall was my temple and building it was up to me.

That trip started my journey of transformation from a life of despair to a life of contentment, joy, and happiness.

I was born in 1966 in Romania, a communist country where food, heating, and freedoms were scarce. I grew up in a very volatile family where some form of abuse was on the menu daily. It was a patriarchal culture where what I wanted to say or do didn't matter. My father was weak and let my stepmother rule the roost. All I ever heard from her was how I should learn to be a proper wife, stay a virgin until I got married, clean, cook, wash, iron, polish shoes, and shut up.

Even though there is nothing wrong with knowing how to cook or sew on a button, not being able to express myself was devastating. My big spirit was yearning to be seen and heard but there was no way for me to do this. Through my childhood years all the way to 20 years old, I lived in a world of fear from mental, emotional, and physical abuse.

In 1982, when I was 16, we immigrated to Australia and I found life difficult. I didn't have any friends, didn't speak the language, and was very awkward with permed hair and massive glasses that covered half my face. I would trip over my own feet and didn't know about body hair removal!! I was the joke of the school and got taunted every single day. I was relieved when I graduated high school because then I didn't have to see those people again. As much as the bullying hurt at the time, in hindsight I realize how strong I actually was and how relentless I have always been in moving forward no matter what.

I spent 26 years searching for some kind of fulfillment. Every job I had I loved. I enjoyed what I was doing; I appreciated the people I worked with. Interestingly though, there was always something that was never right. And after being let go by my last job when I was 37, I decided to work for myself and started a lingerie consultancy that I ran for 14 years. I loved it! Helping women feel beautiful in a good fitting bra and giving them opportunities to have their own financial choices was rewarding. However, toward the end, something was still missing. Although I was building *their* self-esteem, I knew I needed to help build people up in a different way.

I had married my prince in shining armor at 34. Most of our relationship felt distant to me. It was avoidant on his part and anxious on my part. Even though we really loved one other, we didn't know how to talk to each other; we argued and blamed the other a lot. We built a life together, holidayed every year, had the beautiful mansion, cars, and enjoyed the best restaurants. But we were lost in our connection. The birth of our son was an absolute joy and we bathed in the happiness of this little human being. All our love was directed toward him but we still couldn't connect. There was no emotional or physical intimacy in our relationship. I was wilting away.

The next thing I knew I was in an ambulance being overdosed with morphine and coming onto the handsome paramedic. I was being rushed to the hospital with a potential heart attack. I was in denial and asking myself how could this be happening to me? To my delight, there was nothing critically wrong. Instead I had had a massive anxiety attack. I was emotionally, physically, and mentally spent!

Despite the deterioration of my health and well-being, I stayed like that for another two years until that fateful day when my mentor, Mack, told me those words that hit me like a wrecking ball! I knew then that I had to get disciplined in all areas of my life, whether I liked it or not.

My journey in self-discovery had begun. I decided that I wanted to live and to be the best version of me for my son. I wanted to understand why I found myself in the life that I had created. What choices had I made along the way that led me to an anxiety attack and a hospital visit? Why did I feel so sad in my marriage all the time? Why did I feel so angry with my husband? Why was nothing going my way?

I needed answers. For months and months I met my sister every week in our favorite coffee shop to vent my worries and pain. She listened for hours and one day, as she got up to leave, she looked me square in the eyes and said, "Annie, when the student is ready, the teacher will come." Confused, I asked,

"What are you talking about?" She went on, "When you are ready to change your life, the right people will come into it and help you do that."

She was right!

Not long after that statement, I was invited to an achiever's congress that led me to my mentor, Blair Singer, who connected me to Mack Newton. Mack Newton brought me the wisdom "Commitment to completion." The rest is history.

I began to study with the best personal development trainers in the world, and traveled wherever I felt there was someone who could help me with physical improvement, mental clarity, or emotional and spiritual growth. I learned to listen to my voice, to get clarity on who I was and what I wanted out of life. Every time the pain of my past would show up, it would be so deep that I felt my whole being was on the verge of exploding. However, the breakthroughs were even more delicious and freeing.

At 50, I had realized that it would be best for me and my husband if we were no longer together. I left with a heavy heart, but I left. I was the healthiest — physically, mentally, and spiritually — that I had been in my entire life. Clearly, loving myself was exactly what I needed.

Now, at the young age of 54, I am healthy, fit, and energetic, I make time for me, spend quality time with friends and family, and am excited about life. I don't seek and depend on love and acceptance from others anymore because I have found it in myself. I am aware that people who chose to be in my life do it because they want to, not because they have to.

The BEST part is... I decided as part of my *commitment to completion*, I would become certified as a coach which enables me to now facilitate the growth of others as a...wait for it... Relationship Architect! As my life was turning around, I was loving how I was feeling and decided I wanted to empower others to feel the same way.

My mentor, Blair Singer, always says that we teach what we want to master.

I love relationships, every type, shape, or form and I am forever seeking to understand the depths of human behavior and personal freedom. So it is with sheer joy, happiness, fulfillment, and excitement that I get to do it every day as a profession.

"In order to love others, we have to love ourselves first. In order to give to others, we need to give to ourselves first."

This statement is so true for me. I bring all the tools that I relentlessly practice myself to empower couples to build the delicious lives they always dreamed of. I help them overcome resentment, fear, hurt, and anger leading them to discover their own brilliance and freedoms so they can bring passion and romance back into their lives.

I created my own AKRA (Annie Kallis Relationship Architect) methodology. It is based on the foundations that I built for myself. My goal with it is to arm my clients with tools that they can use for a lifetime.

I love being a relationship architect because I believe that the strength of a relationship lies in its foundations. Just like with a house or any building, the most important part is the foundation to uphold the structure when nature decides to create havoc. In a relationship, the most important part is the foundation also, so it can withhold the storms of life.

The foundations that I set for myself have come through understanding that everything that has happened in my life occurred in order to teach me to become the best version of myself. Now, I'm able to serve others, to support others, and to love others. Because, first and foremost, I love myself. Deep inside of me, I'm content.

This is what I want for you: for your eyes to sparkle and for you to laugh wholeheartedly. Dream big and live a fulfilled life, so when the time comes, there are no regrets, only brilliant memories of a life lived to the fullest. These are the gifts of loving yourself first.

IGNITE ACTION STEPS

Stay true to yourself.

When it feels right, it is right! Intuition is your best friend.

Continuously create action goals.

Goals give your life direction, boost your motivation, and increase your self-esteem.

Be disciplined with your goals.

Do what you should do, when you should do it, whether you like it or not. The most important part of this sentence is the middle: it emphasizes doing it NOW!

Never quit growing.

Be inquisitive about your life, keep on learning. As you do it to yourself, it will have a ripple effect and you will teach it to others, hence contributing to those around you.

Be responsible for your actions.

This means that you hold the power in your hands and you should not give it up by deflecting accountability. When you choose the actions, you also choose the consequences.

Practice forgiveness.

Start with forgiving yourself for the negative thoughts that you have and things that you've done. You are only human and we all make mistakes. Every mistake is a lesson, so forgive yourself and let go of the guilt. Once you are able to forgive yourself, you can forgive others.

Refuse to be manipulated by guilt.

Make a stand when others are trying to do it to you, never do it to others, and if you feel guilty, accept your actions and change the situation.

Celebrate all wins.

I said ALL wins no matter how small, as they change your state and anchor success into your body. And celebrate the wins of all around you, as it is a sign of acknowledgement and a sign that everyone is winning.

Celebrate failure.

Controversial, right? Failure is a very important part of life as that is when the biggest and best lessons are learned. When you debrief what you learned, you realize that perhaps the issue wasn't as bad as you thought and next time you'll do things differently. Big celebration here!

Love yourself

You have to love YOU first before you can love anyone else.

Annie Kallis – Australia
Relationship Architect
f *annie.kallis*

MARK JAMES BROWN

*The Bible says, "Give and it shall be given to you." I say, "Love
100 percent and it will come back to you like a boomerang."*

**I'm sharing with you the law of attraction and the power of vulnerability,
honesty, and being true to yourself. I want to encourage you to know what
you want in a partner, to become that yourself, and not to settle for less.**

IGNITE 100 PERCENT LOVE

My story is not your typical love story. It's the story of my transition from
an Amish-like community to polyamory.

> **Polyamory** *(from Greek πολύ poly, "many, several", and
> Latin amor, "love") is the practice of, or desire for, intimate
> relationships with more than one partner.*

I'm a very idealistic person. Not many people come from the outside and
join a church like the one I joined. I was looking for an authentic and deep
connection with others and I found it. We were set apart from the world and
in many ways I was happy, but I couldn't be my authentic self. The way I live
now — following my desires — would never have been allowed. They would
never accept me the way I am today. The journey has been very painful, but
now I feel it was worth everything I went through.

One of the lessons I learned in that church community was the power of crying together. There is cleansing and healing in tears. I lost a daughter in a freak accident when she was 10. She was a twin, with my middle son. It felt like my world had been shattered. I couldn't imagine ever having a normal life again. A couple of men in the church would hug me and cry with me every Sunday for an entire year. Wow! That was very transformative for me. I felt like they opened the door to their hearts and said, "Come on in." It was a great example of love and the power of being vulnerable.

I had a deep connection with those men, but I was longing for a deeper connection with my wife. We could never talk about sex. We went to see a counselor to help us have more intimacy. He asked me if I had ever cheated on my wife. I confessed that, six months before, I had had sex with a prostitute. That confession was the beginning of the end and my marriage ended several months later, then my church voted me out. I found an apartment a few miles outside of the community. Despite my close proximity, I was cut out and cut off from everyone who was near and dear to me. All my deep connections were with my family and my church. Those were hard times and I'd often roll up into a ball on the floor and cry my eyes out. I felt a loneliness that was so extreme it felt like panic. Many mornings, it took me forty minutes to talk myself out of bed. A church counselor advised I go into nature and meditate alone to work things out. For me, that would've been fatal.

I knew I needed a support group. I attended Sex and Love Addicts Anonymous meetings twice a week and started making new connections. I wanted to learn from my mistakes. I wanted to either get back with my wife or find a new partner and have a relationship; one based on trust and being able to talk about everything with no secrets. I didn't know what was in my future. I knew I had to focus on gratitude and building loving relationships with myself and a few close friends, or I wasn't going to make it.

My divorce changed my life in drastic ways… for the better. I went from being in a monogamous marriage of 29 years while living in an Amish-like community with nine children to living the life I desired. It took me seven years of deep personal exploration, but after serious soul searching and more counseling, retreats, and workshops, I made a decision that was best for me… polyamory. After a few years evolving on my own, getting counseling, attending workshops, reading books, doing inner child healing work, I started dating semi-regularly. After seven years, I found a beautiful woman named Joy; and yes, she brings me much joy. I'll tell you more about her later.

In writing this story, it dawned on me that it was my deep desire to be honest with my future partner. What I learned from my past caused me to choose to be vulnerable and tell women when they were not 'The One' for me. Each woman I told that to appreciated my honesty and told their own stories of men who had lied to them, making them think they were 'The One' only to find out there was another woman they were secretly intimate with. Every woman I dated had similar stories. I was tempted to lie sometimes because I wanted sex and being honest wasn't getting me any, but I didn't lie because I was committed to honesty.

Over the next few years, I moved several times, attending various churches and meeting women at dances and on dating sites. I started to explore sexuality and I came across Orgasmic Meditation. I saw it on the web and attended a class in Santa Monica to learn more. I guess my thinking was that if I can't find an intimate partner, at least I can enjoy stroking a woman intimately in the safe space that OM creates. Before I learned Orgasmic Meditation, I got excited just thinking about it; yet I felt scared at first and it took a while before I became comfortable and could enjoy it. Just after my fifty-sixth birthday, I attended a seven-month OM coaching program. Yep, that was quite a shift from my church days. I learned a lot about women. There was a group OM with 75 pairs, meeting every month. I spent time with probably 30 women there and many of them offered me insights into how to connect with women. I had loads of questions and it was great to get their feedback.

During the program, I had several men tell me, "You can't gush all over women. Love them too much and they will leave you. You have to push them down, not let them get too close." When I heard this, I knew right away that behavior wouldn't work for me. I didn't want to push women down — I wanted to tell them how much I loved them. I knew my nature and my desire was to have a relationship where we keep no secrets and love each other 100 percent... a relationship based on true honesty. I followed my heart and that led to connecting more with myself. I started to practice the law of attraction to find the right partner for me.

Allow me to share a story about the law of attraction. My Grandpa died of prostate cancer when he was 62 and my dad had his prostate removed at 65. For me, when I was 57 and faced with the decision of dealing with prostrate cancer or giving up my capacity to have sex forever, I struggled to make a choice. I decided I'd rather die than live without sex for the rest of my life. The church I'd been a part of believed that, since my wife asked me to leave our marriage, I was supposed to be celibate for as long as she was alive. You can guess that was a "Hell No!" for me.

I'll share another story about the Law of Attraction. I set my intention and focus on finding a woman who was a great match for me. The year before, I was at an Intentional Relating Games Meetup and there was a woman there who told everyone she wanted her husband to know how much she loved and appreciated him. I thought to myself, "I want that." Well, I got that. Her words led me to create that intention and I met Joy. I loved Joy first, 100 percent, gushing all over her with the admiration she deserved. I felt that 100 percent love coming back, boomeranging in return, so deep, so pure. I was living my dream. I had made a long list of qualities I wanted in a partner and Joy had them all, including polyamory.

A couple of years before I met Joy, I started telling the women who I was interested in dating that I wanted a girlfriend in each of the places I worked. I was in Santa Barbara one week of the month and back home in Northern California for the other weeks. None of the women I met were interested in that arrangement. But wanting it was my truth; it was my desire, and I waited for a relationship where polyamory would be possible.

It took a few years before my relationship dream was fully realized, but that is the life I now live. I love it. I realized I was following the principles I'm sharing here and how much it was helping me improve and maintain my relationship. It gave me the idea of writing this story.

It was seven years of searching before I met my wife Joy. Right away, I was so impressed with her. I felt she was totally worth pursuing and possibly 'The One.' We had so much in common. I was impressed with her commitment to her family. Her ability to connect with everyone. Her stable, loving, and giving nature. Her Christian background was similar to my Amish-like church. We share a love of music — both singing and playing guitar and piano. It was also important to me that we were on a similar life path — she was a coach and I wanted to become a coach. I could see a future with us working together helping others.

Within a week of meeting, Joy moved in and we spent every possible moment together. Now that I had found 'The One,' I was determined to live my relationship dream. I spoke words of affirmation to her at every opportunity. "I love you." "I adore you." "Thank you for sharing with me how you feel." "I'm so glad you enjoy sex with me." "Thank you for taking such good care of me." "I really enjoy sharing our meal times together." "You are so soft and beautiful." I massage Joy all over each morning after we make love. She enjoys this very much. I love her 100 percent and hold nothing back.

Of course she liked me loving her 100 percent. My belief is in the Law of Attraction where we attract what we focus on. I was focusing on totally loving her and it came back to me so powerfully. In time, her love deepened and she started loving me 100 percent.

Then one night, Joy called me and told me she was meeting with a man who had stood her up a few times, someone who had been dishonest with her. I was immediately triggered BIG TIME! I reminded myself that I can't control another person, that I needed to work on me. This started a few weeks of Poly-Agony.

Poly-Agony — *the hurt feelings of jealousy that sometimes arise in a poly relationship.*

I worked on changing my attitude and getting back to peace. After some time talking with a few others with more experience in polyamory, I was able to have the jealousy and discontent leave, replacing it with more love and trust in our relationship.

I wonder how many men think that the only option to *lay with* women is to *lie to* women; to deceive them by telling them they are the one and only. But I've found that there are women who respect a man being honest and saying his truth. "You can do that?" many men ask. "Yes, I can." I tell them happily.

When I called one of my daughters to invite her to our wedding, she said, "Dad, why are you getting married; I heard you were polyamorous?" I responded, "Because commitment is very important to us." I believe true love only happens when we feel safe, and commitment is the foundation to feel safe in our relationship. We have the same anniversary as her prior marriage with her husband, who died at 51. Others thought that was weird, but I thought it was a sign of good fortune that we had met on the same day as her anniversary, so we planned our wedding together to keep it.

Since we've been together I can say what I want, and my wife loves me even more, not less. Because I am being vulnerable and truthful with women, I am enjoying the life I now live. It took courage. And I'm so thankful for the courage to wait until I found the right woman for me.

With Joy, I can share my inner struggles; I can cry and she loves me all the more. When I went through my Poly-Agony stage, I could share with her that I was struggling. She shared with me that it set her free the way that I owned my own 'stuff.' Here's the key: I wasn't trying to change her or tell her what to do; I was just sharing my truth, how I felt.

Now that I've found my partner, I don't let my ego get in the way. When Joy shares things that trigger me, instead of reacting, I thank her. This builds trust in her.

I've told Joy that even if I find a younger beautiful woman, I'm not leaving her, because then my commitment doesn't mean anything. I trust in her commitment to me. I choose to be committed to her. Since we've been together, yes, there have been some struggles and hurt feelings. I think that our trust in our commitment creates the safety to really experience 100 percent love.

Before I met Joy, I created four important principles of connection to help people connect with others on a deeper level. These are the steps that Joy and I use every day.

Safety first — create a safe place for your partner to be able to talk, and thank them for everything they share. When I'm triggered, my first thought is to create a safe place for her. This has helped me to avoid so many times where I could have reacted and made things much worse.

Law of Attraction — we get more of what we focus on, so focus on the positive. Find blessing by blessing your partner.

Compassionate Communication — share your feelings and needs without trying to blame or change. It's best to listen first, to be curious, and really try to understand. And if you get triggered, go back to step one.

Celebration — tell your partner, every day, things that you appreciate about them. Appreciation is a power tool in a relationship.

Practicing this helps us avoid fights. After three years, we're still enjoying our relationship because we're so conscious of these principles. In the last few months I've been practicing these principles with a new polyamous girlfriend and it is working great with her too. She has other lovers also, but none of them give her the positive words and encouragement like I do, and she loves it.

It seems so obvious to me that we don't learn about something by avoiding it. In my church days, sex was never talked about. My new life allows for curiosity and exploration. I've learned so much about sex and pleasing and it allows me to fulfill my deepest desires — to please my partner and live my truths. I have a richer life, being able to explore with Joy our love, adoration, passion, and sexuality. We feel more deeply connected and trust in each other as a result.

Trust is the foundation of love. The purest way to build trust is to be authentic, to know what you want in a partner. Make a long list of traits you desire in your partner and wait for the one that lines up with your list. Hold out for the partner who accepts you as you really are. Your authentic self. Anything else is basing a relationship on a non-authentic caricature, an imitation.

Be authentic and let your partner be authentic also. In other words, treat your partner with the respect and safety that you would want. To find 100 Percent Love, you must give it. I want that for you.

IGNITE ACTION STEPS

- Learn to love your inner child. I worked with a retired Unity minister once a week for six months on inner child healing — to realize that I am the only one who is always with me! You can do your own work by looking at a picture of you as a child and imagining throwing that child up in the air, catching them, laughing, smiling, and being together in happiness.

- Be the person who you want to attract — have integrity, be patient, thoughtful, generous, authentic, working on yourself while accepting others. You can do this by writing out a long list of qualities, ideals, attitudes, hobbies, body features, sexual chemistry, spiritual understanding, and all that matters deeply to you. (Note: you can only be polyamorous with people who want to be polyamorous. Don't try to convert anyone.)

Mark Brown – United States of America
Life Coach
www.ultimate-life.live

MADALINA PETRESCU (M)
& CRIS AGAFI (C)

*"Authentic love and connection are possible when you boldly
face the inner barriers holding you back from love."*

**Our desire is to inspire you to create a relationship with your partner based
on true love and authentic connection by first cultivating that relationship
with yourself. Once you have the courage to look within and discover your
unconscious patterns, beliefs, and unprocessed past hurts, then you can
see what has been blocking you from receiving love. Only then can you
show up consciously, with an open heart, not to seek love but to *be* love.**

LOVE AND CONNECTION STARTS WITH YOU

PREFACE

*We decided to write this story together; to pass the microphone to one
another and have our independent voices heard, sometimes speaking together
with one voice. When we started, we were curious about what was to come
from opening the pages of our story to the world. When we met, we thought it
was enough to fall crazy in love and have the epic love story of our lives. We
discovered that it wasn't... there was so much more to love than we had ever
imagined.*

(C) "Wow, she is beautiful! Wait, what's this I'm feeling in my chest? Oh crap, I'm getting nervous. 'You're gonna mess it up, Cris.'" That was my experience as Madalina walked toward me, pulling her heavy luggage behind her, messy after a 13-hour flight from the United States. But all I saw was her radiant smile and her long hair bouncing in slow motion with each step. "I think I'm in love."

I was twenty-three at the time and living in Romania, the country of my birth. Madalina had come for the wedding of her cousin, who was a friend of mine. I had offered to pick up some of the guests at the airport, always happy to help. In the car with Madalina, I was so nervous that I kept on babbling whatever came to mind. Historically, babbling never had a good outcome for me, but this time was different. I felt very connected to her and could sense that she was feeling the same. It seemed that I was saying all the right things.

At the wedding, we danced and talked all night, deeply bonding. I was intoxicated by her beauty and her personality. She was funny, smart, real, grounded. When I was asked to film the bouquet throwing, I took the opportunity to ask her if she was going to catch it, secretly trying to figure out if she was seeing anyone. She confessed that she had just ended a long-term relationship and was looking forward to some time for herself. My balloon of hope was punctured and fast deflating.

Madalina retreated to the back of the giggling ladies so as to not steal the opportunity of another hopeful bride-to-be. I raised the camera and looked through the screen to the sea of joyful bouncing heads, every woman attaching her hope of marriage to a superstition. As the flower bouquet flew through the air, I noticed some of the heads in the middle of the crowd go down and not come back up. It looked like whatever force was affecting them was fast moving toward the front of the group. A moment later Madalina materialized from behind the women in the front line, magically leaping and catching the bouquet. My balloon was instantly repaired and rapidly inflating.

We became inseparable for the rest of her trip. It felt like we were living in an alternate Universe, floating in the gravity of our connection. In her eyes I could see the life I'd always dreamed of, filled with magic and adventure. In her touch I could get lost for eternity, every cell vibrating with unimagined life force. In her breath I found life, her words carrying me to new heights of undreamed possibility. On her lips the fire of passion burned with every kiss. My body pulsated with every heartbeat, hers and mine in a synchronized dance. Together we waltzed to our music, in a crowded ballroom where only she and I existed.

What followed after she returned to Boston was a rollercoaster of confused emotions. I craved to be with her, to feel her touch, her presence, to stare into her eyes and listen to the music of her voice, but there was a part of me that didn't believe that would ever be possible. The ocean between our two continents seemed to drown our dream of being in each other's arms, making our long-distance relationship an unbearable voyage to our ultimate desire — to dance together till the end of time.

Through an alchemy of fortunate events that fall in the category of 'when you want something, all the Universe conspires in helping you to achieve it', I found a way to go to the US, thus turning the page to one of the most beautiful and also most challenging chapters of my life.

(M) I am awakened from a nap by the flight attendant's overhead announcement. We are about to land in Bucharest, Romania. It's been nearly a decade since I set foot in my home country. I had reluctantly agreed to join my parents on this trip, mostly at the plea of my mom, to attend my cousin's wedding. Although excited to reconnect with my family, truthfully, this trip was the last thing I wanted. In the US, I was finishing up internal medicine training and applying for a cardiology fellowship. It was a very competitive program where women were rarely accepted. I was intensely ambitious and career driven. Nothing mattered more.

After a tearful and joyful reunion with my extended family, my cousin introduced me to the friend he brought along to drive us home. As he pointed to a handsome man with sparkling eyes, I glanced up and he smiled. Our gazes locked. To my surprise, I felt my heartbeat quicken. I was flooded with a rush of energy that left me dizzy and flushed. "What is going on with me?!"

"Yes!" I muttered to myself as Cris introduced himself and loaded my bag in his car. "I'm going with him!" I thought with excitement. There were other people in the car, but I barely noticed them. Cris was handsome, also incredibly funny, witty, and authentic. His sincere character was like a breath of fresh air, inviting my heart to open. The drive to the apartment in Bucharest was filled with laughter and surprisingly deep connection.

The days that followed melded into one exquisite moment that felt like eternity. Time stood still. There was a powerful force in my heart pulling me to be with him; it was impossible not to surrender. We shared our life stories and dreams, got lost in deep philosophical discussions. We stared into each other's eyes, letting our feelings speak more than words could ever say. Every touch sparked intense vibrations in my body. I felt overcome with profound joy and aliveness that grew with every moment we spent together. He seemed to accept all of me: the wild, adventurous, intense, and vulnerable parts of me that usually intimidated others, which I kept hidden. Being with *him* became the only thing that mattered.

The closer we moved toward each other, the further away the rest of the world faded. We had ascended into a new dimension where the only reality was the love we shared. Our magnetic connection awakened a new life purpose for me: to be with him, forever.

However, when I returned to the US, all we could see were the hurdles to living and being together. There were so many obstacles — from the vast geographic distance separating us to my demanding cardiology fellowship in Boston and Cris' professional commitment to diplomacy in Romania. I now know that the heart always wins over the mind when it's stirred powerfully enough. No mountain nor ocean can stand in the way of two lovers' desires. The heart always finds a way out of a no-way situation, and so... passionately driven to be together, our burning love melted all doubt, logic, reasons, and impediments standing between us and our destiny.

A few months later Cris received an opportunity in Boston and surprised me with a visit. Reunited, we determined that we never wanted to be apart again, no matter the obstacles. We turned the page and started writing the new chapter of our life together.

(C) The honeymoon felt like a cosmic heartbeat; in reality it was no longer than a blink. Before long, the endless eye gazing turned into critical gazing. Unconditional love was replaced by conditioned patterns. The lover masks came off, replaced by righteous ones. Our party was just starting and the masquerade was in full swing.

Madalina was in the middle of her cardiology fellowship — a men's club where the price of admittance for a woman was double — work, effort — everything. I watched the toll that the stress of proving herself worthy was taking. It became clear to me that cardiology was a field *for* the heart but not *of* the heart. During the same time, newly arrived in the

US and with my own crushed dream of following a career in diplomacy, I went job hunting. I finally found a sales job going door to door selling office supplies. I walked with a spring in my step, knowing it was the ticket to my ultimate dream of starting a life with Madalina.

As both of us became increasingly stressed, overwhelmed, and over-worked, romance fell off our radar. Sensuality was replaced by familiarity. Her cardiology career was a powerful presence in our life and I slipped hand-in-glove into a support role. I was the faithful shoulder she could count on. This identity became a very comfortable cloak and, as long as I was shrouded in it, I didn't feel responsibility for much else. I felt like I was doing everything for her. Every deed was a sacrifice on her altar. While her constant pestering angered me, we both avoided conflict, which led to many unsaid words and harbored resentment. Soon enough, my lack of action in other parts of my life began to frustrate her.

Eventually her suppressed emotions had to be released. When the vol-cano erupted, it spewed the hottest words, burning my ego. My thoughts became clouded; I felt suffocated. As her yelling got louder, I became quieter. My last resort was to bunker in place and wait for the winds to change. I felt that anything I said only made things worse. Shutting down inside was my place of refuge. I felt weak and powerless — a victim. In my suffering, I did the only thing I could to relieve my pain — blame her for it.

My actions became guided by the desire to avoid conflict at all cost. When Madalina suggested something, like working out together, I would occasionally go along with it (even though I hated running) simply to avoid her criticizing my motivation and pledges. I made sure my pain was visible and my sacrifice evident — moaning over any small runner's cramp as we ran. I felt life was unfair when she got mad because I didn't buy the right cereal, but I couldn't express my frustration when she would leave a messy kitchen. Her actions were justified by her scarcity of free time and she expected me to understand that. This became our 'normal' and somehow we became comfortable with it.

I was certain our relationship would improve with the arrival of our first child. A second daughter later, it was clear I had miscalculated — our marriage was under even more strain and it didn't feel like we could bear the weight. Everything started to change though when Madalina became seriously injured. She was forced to look inward for healing, as all medical experts only provided bandaids. That marked the beginning of her spiritual journey. She tried to light up my path so I could follow, but I experienced her efforts as attempts to control me. Every book she gave me on personal growth collected dust on the shelves. Every meditation was an opportunity to ruminate over my resentment for having to sit still. I felt as if Madalina had discovered fire and was enjoying all its benefits while I saw her offer of fire as a threat that could burn down everything that was familiar to me. A part of me knew the ashes were necessary for my rebirth, but I resisted. I saw her as a threat and was ready for battle. With life at its lowest, I realized we were at a crossroads. We could either make a drastic change or walk on separate paths. The status quo was not an option.

(M) Our honeymoon phase was fading as problems started trickling in. It started with small nuisances, such as Cris refusing to join me on my runs, even though he'd spoken about his desire to get in shape. I could feel his irritation when I left a mess in the house. I felt frequently frustrated when I thought his actions weren't matching his words. However, any arising issue was diluted by the intensity of my demanding cardiology fellowship. The heavy burden of sleepless nights on-call exhausted me and I had little time and energy for much outside of work. The pressure of life and death situations and the accelerated learning was enormous. As a woman surrounded by men, I pushed myself to work harder than anyone to prove myself and validate my worth. My career became the primary focus of my attention and Cris rose swiftly to be my support system. Our romantic connection took a backseat. In our minimal free time, the last thing we wanted was to fight, so we avoided conflict. This approach worked until the cauldron of resentments boiled over into dramatic arguments, with both of us yelling and one of us often storming out of the house. Cracks started to appear in the connection that we valued so much and a rift was inevitable.

Two kids later, my unhealthy work/life balance, aggravated by my perfectionism, culminated in the most severe back pain of my life. I was barely able to walk. My tireless quest for the physical cure proved futile. This left me feeling extremely unhappy with myself, my life, and my situation. I didn't know at that time that I had depended on running to numb my painful emotions. I sunk into a depression that lasted a year. Unable to find answers outside, I turned inside. For the first time, I saw that my misery was a product of my patterns — patterns that I had developed over my whole life. That realization opened my eyes to the deeper truths of my life choices — I saw that they had been driven by unconscious patterns and beliefs. My whole life I had defined my entire self worth by external attachments. This understanding Ignited a spiritual existential crisis, leaving me confused about the meaning of life and my purpose in it. I no longer knew who I was. I became hungry to understand my deeper consciousness and find the authentic me.

My crisis served as the last straw unveiling the truths Cris and I had hidden from ourselves. It rattled us and brought to the surface what we had buried, what we denied and avoided facing. I desired, even expected, him to join me on this spiritual journey, which became the most important thing in my life. I would excitedly come up with a palette of ideas for our shared inner growth, only to encounter reluctance and even rejection from him. He met my passion with retreat and this infuriated me. The more I insisted, the more he resisted. He told me my invitations were pushy and controlling. I was disappointed by what I saw as his lack of willingness to look within and take responsibility for his personal growth. When he did not follow through on his commitments to do the self-work, I felt discouraged believing that his lack of action was evidence of him not loving me enough to do the work. I was not aware at the time that I, myself, was not meeting him halfway, assuming our relationship was a one-way street — toward me.

It became impossible to have any conversations together. The smallest dis-agreement would provoke a reactionary war zone, degenerating into 'you vs me' finger pointing. Each of us felt righteous, convinced the other was wrong. Feeling unseen and rejected, I would react explosively, loud with emotions. He would push away and shut down, becoming a stone wall. I felt angry and betrayed when I saw his aloof unemotional response; it felt callous, like he was abandoning his commitment to us. I felt I was losing his love, which was unbearable. Blinded by desperation, I boxed him up in my projections and judgments. I criticized him left and right without the capacity to see anything positive in him. I was not aware then that my lost faith in him was sucking the life out of both him and our relationship. I held him completely responsible for our failing marriage. I blamed him for my hurt and unhappiness. "If I could not have his unconditional love, I would rather not have him at all," I thought. As I closed my heart to him, hope evaporated.

We had reached the very bottom. Our once arduous love that used to ground us became extinct. The joy and romance that used to light up our lives faded into ghost memories of the past. We were unhappy and unfulfilled. Lifeless. Our interaction was toxic with negativity, spreading to every aspect of our lives, including our daughters. We could not see it at the time, but the girls were sounding the alarm through increasing emotional outbursts. We were all trying to survive in a quicksand of heartache, reaching out for each other and only sinking deeper.

(C) Buddha said, "When the student is ready the teacher will appear." One of our first teachers was Valentina Simon, a conscious systemic couples and family psychotherapist practicing in Romania. For this reason, the sessions were through Skype. We both needed the kindness and tough love that she exuded. The problem for me was that she spoke 'Klingon.' She talked about foreign concepts such as personal responsibility, boundaries, patterns, shadows, and unresolved childhood wounds, and I did not have a clue what she meant. I was a responsible adult, I knew my boundaries, I definitely didn't have any patterns, and the only shadow I had was the one I cast on a sunny day. She pointed out my patterns like victimization, giving my power away, and man-pouting. None of what she said resonated with me — I was fine!

Ever diligent, I had recorded some of the calls so I could go back and take notes. On the first one I reviewed, I watched myself talk, I witnessed my body language, I really *saw* myself. And what I saw wasn't easy to look at. "Is that me?!" I thought. I cringed at how I came across as a powerless victim. That was not who I wanted to be. Everything Valentina and Madalina had said about me was true — I just hadn't seen it. The wall I had put up to protect myself from others had also prevented me from seeing myself. I felt my ego contorting in pain from the sight of its own reflection. That unbearable rock bottom became my change catalyst, my Ignite moment. I had faced the most unappealing truths about myself and I refused for them to define me going forward. Although uncomfortable, I accepted Valentina's words as truths that had been hiding in my blind spots. I resolved to look deep within so I could truly understand myself, unmasked and ready to face the world.

Soon enough, Valentina discovered a very simple problem in our relationship — that we truly did not know how to argue. She suggested that for one week, instead of avoiding arguments, we pick a fight with each other every day. I felt trepidation and worried, whereas Madalina picked a fight with me as soon as the session ended. There were rules we had to follow: we could not raise our voices, we could not interrupt, and, probably the hardest of all, we had to *see* the other's perspective. This exercise alone upgraded our relationship tremendously. It took time to build courage; but eventually I did truly see Madalina and I felt seen by her. My wall crumbled under the weight of mutual trust. There was finally a safe space where we could create a new possibility for our connection where we allowed each other to be authentic without fear of judgment.

I saw the arc of our relationship become illuminated by our rising awareness. I could now see how when we first met, although adults, inside we were like two little children, wounded by our past and looking to the other for healing and to be made whole. Familial patterns ran our subconscious, forcing us to relive the lives of our parents, experiencing the same emotional reactions. I could see how we were just the latest link in a tangled ancestral chain.

"Cris, you know, I am not your mother; I'm your wife!" Madalina told me lovingly during a profound argument as she held up the mirror to show me how I was not taking personal responsibility. This truth left me speechless. The tears rolling down my cheeks were those of a blind man seeing for the first time. I realized in that moment how every time I felt controlled by her, it was nothing more than a projection of my past experiences, unhealed childhood traumas replaying themselves in an endless loop. For the first time, I could see that I had been hearing her like she was my mother — pestering me, trying to control me — but she was my wife, behaving lovingly and supporting my empowerment.

When I stopped perceiving Madalina as trying to control me, I freed myself from reactivity. I took my first steps on the path of personal growth, following the trail of breadcrumbs she had left for me, slowly walking inward toward myself. The trek was challenging. The growing self-awareness constantly brought me face-to-face with my patterns and shadows. At times I felt in awareness hell, locked in battle with my demons. My energy was low, I was short-tempered with my kids, and I felt triggered so much of the time. I strongly wanted to capitulate and go back to my blissful ignorance. However, Madalina was an awakened woman and gave me no place to hide; no exit to escape through. She exposed my actions as patterns, showing me my responsibility and my power. Our relationship became a house of mirrors, reflecting back our truths, and the only option was to take a good look at our own reflection.

I had a persistent belief that I could not change. This was the same illusion the circus elephant believes — that because it had been tied to a stick since it was young, it can never break free. This belief chained me to the victim mentality, and a victim doesn't have to take any responsibility for himself. It's up to others to see their pain, to tend to it, to somehow make them whole.

When I was willing to create a new reality, I learned that only I can make myself whole. The journey to wholeness is through acts of integrity — doing what I say I will do. I learned how to use the feelings of guilt, shame, and anxiety as a barometer to realign with my values. That became my compass, guiding me back to the person I wanted to be, a person who shows up powerfully to the world. The only way to do that is to upgrade my mindset *and* heartset. How can I truly love Madalina if I don't love myself first?

I used to believe that in order to be powerful I had to first feel powerful. I know now that feeling powerful comes from powerful action. This takes courage. I have had to look inward, to accept and love every part of me just the way I am. I don't avoid situations that trigger me anymore. Triggers are painful and hard to accept but I welcome them now because they reflect what I need to work on. It's an ever-evolving process. I realize that happiness is not found at the illusive destination called perfection. It is found in the journey toward the best version of ourselves.

(M) We felt stuck in a life we no longer enjoyed together. We discussed divorce but deep inside we wanted to make it work. It was at this stage we met the person who brought rays of hope into the darkness of our gloom. Valentina, a conscious psychotherapist in Romania, came highly recommended by our close friends so we decided to give it a shot. I felt relieved to have an expert work with Cris and get *him* to change. Valentina's character was a unique blend of compassion and tough candidness. She specified that the success of our relationship depended on our willingness to look inward and make personal changes.

I conceptualized that with my mind, but it was during one of our sessions when I truly understood what Valentina was telling us. I was describing the details of an argument I had with Cris when she stopped me. Looking straight into my eyes, she said, "Take the focus away from Cris and bring it to *you*. What feelings and beliefs are coming up for *you*? How are *you* reacting? Are you willing to get honest with yourself?"

"Whaaatt?!" Her words pierced through me like an arrow and reached inside, hurting me deeply. I forced a smile to appear composed but inside I felt uprooted by an emotional storm. A battle was ensuing. The headstrong part of me (my ego) rose to defend my position as the blameless party in our conflicts. Simultaneously, a larger conscious part of me was inviting me to lean into a bigger truth. This part washed over me as warmth, connecting me with great feelings of courage and love.

On my battlefield, I had to choose which side I stood for. I felt ready to open into seeing the truth of my part. With calm conviction, I redirected the blaming finger pointing at Cris and aimed it toward myself. My ego was furiously rebelling but I was ready to take personal responsibility. This decision Ignited an inner shift that powerfully changed the trajectory of my life. I was done being hypnotized by the allure of victimization and ready to create the total alignment I desired.

The reflective sessions with Valentina led me to a shocking and humbling discovery. *I* had been the common source of *my* unfulfillment. My sole focus on blaming Cris was my ego's mechanism to divert my attention from my role in our conflicts. I also realized how my life had been guided by unconscious programming — stories and patterns that I had collected throughout my journey, which were distorting my world view and sabotaging my actions. I recognized that my only key to inner freedom was conscious awareness. This Ignited in me a burning desire to journey within and explore my shadows. I didn't have to travel far as our relationship served as my greatest mirror. Once I looked at my own reflection, I saw why my ego was trying to protect me from seeing the truth — it was far from pretty and terribly painful to accept.

I realized how unfair and selfish I had been. I had expected Cris to fit into *my* definition of the 'right way to be', not allowing him to be his natural self, telling him all of the time he was wrong for being the way that he was. I learned that *my relationship with Cris was a projection of my relationship with myself*. The patterns I followed with him reflected those I was using with myself. I realized that when I was hard on him, it was a reflection of how hard I was on myself. I saw that while I wanted him to see and love me for how I am, I had not been willing to do the same for him. I held him responsible for making me happy. When he didn't meet my needs, I blamed him for not being loving. All of these were hard truths for me to swallow.

I recognized that my endless need for love and attention from him meant I was not generating these for myself. I had been seeking outside to fill what

I was lacking inside. That's why what Cris offered was never enough. My thirst for love brought me face-to-face with the truth. I first had to believe I was worthy of love before I could receive it. Where was the roadblock in me?

The answer was hiding in plain sight, in the most painful moments of our relationship — our fights, which I found to serve as powerful reflectors of our shadows. Each time we got upset, we blamed the other for the hurt within, unwilling to take personal responsibility for our part. On an emotional level, we were like two young children having some version of a tantrum. I discovered the reason we reacted so explosively was because we were each triggering emotional childhood wounds that had remained unrecognized and unhealed. By blaming the other for the hurt we felt inside, we were literally dumping past unprocessed baggage on the other through projection. These times brought to the surface the unconscious limiting beliefs I harbored: that I was not enough and unworthy of love. These false beliefs had blocked my capacity to connect to my own love for myself and to authentically receive love from him.

(M&C) It was no wonder that before we worked with Valentina we could not meet each other with unconditional love. Our unconscious beliefs, false stories, and unhealed wounds had formed impenetrable walls to our authentic connection. We had been trapped in automatic patterns running our lives. We were interacting like two emotionally hungry and reactive children, desperately seeking in the other the love and wholeness we lacked within. Every time we angrily blamed the other for the triggered pain, we denied ourselves the opportunity to grow up. The process of maturing requires taking responsibility to heal the emotional inner child.

Our relationship had become the grand stage where we played out the drama of our old childhood hurts, each playing the victim and casting the role of villain on the other. The inevitable result of this drama was the deterioration of our marriage. We realized that if we divorced, we would just end up casting the next partner in these same roles. An unconscious relationship is a theatrical production often ending in tragedy, sometimes a comedy, a farce, nonetheless.

(**M&C**) We both realized the key to a truly happy, loving, and fulfilling relationship is to meet each other at the heart level, rather than blindly wandering through an entangled forest of fear-based patterns and pain projections — which is what we had been doing for years. Gaining true heart-to-heart connections means shifting from *Love Seeking* to *Love Being*. This could only occur once we each took steps to connect with self and cultivate an internal culture of love and wholeness. The journey back to our hearts can only be through the barriers we unconsciously built against love, as Rumi pointed out. This meant we each had to do our part and courageously face the difficult task of doing the inner work — to become present to our patterns and beliefs and to be willing to process unresolved emotions that were living in our subconscious. We understood that without this work, we would never achieve the authentic connection we desired. The inevitable alternative would be continuing to project our unconscious patterns onto each other.

This work was challenging and we recognized that in order to truly transcend the old version of self and align with the truth of our *conscious love,* we had to go outside of our familiar constructs and break free. As Einstein said, "No problem can be solved from the same level of consciousness that created it." With passion for change and an attitude of doing 'whatever it takes', we engaged in immersive experiences for inner work. We attended the Hoffman Process™ designed to shine light on our patterns and beliefs and connect with Higher Self. We worked with Dr. Heike and Jonathan Hudson and dove deep into somatic work involving the release of old emotions trapped in the body and unhealthy belief systems based on negative past experiences. These were standing in the way of true connection with ourselves and with each other. Their program gave us the ability to heighten our authentic reconnection to an elevated vibrational level through sexual, energetic, and spiritual work that powerfully up-shifted the paradigm of our relationship. We attended Landmark Forum, which emphasizes developing awareness of personal responsibility so as to create new possibilities in life rather than continuing to be driven from unconscious stories. We immersed ourselves in energetic work with Venant Wong, an energy transmission master and spiritual teacher, to awaken our Kundalini; our Life Force energy. This exploration helped us to align with our conscious selves and deepened our compassion, awareness and sense of inner freedom, bringing us closer and deepening our connection at the heart level. All of these experiences helped us discover our blind spots; release and heal the unprocessed emotional wounds; and discover unconditional self love.

Everyday we choose ourselves first so we can fully choose the other. It's a conscious process of giving ourselves love first so we can love the other from an overflowing tank, to vibrate at the frequency of our higher self so we can recognize the higher self of the other because we notice what we already have inside of us.

This process of connecting with our heart requires us to first release what doesn't serve us — the internal voices that sabotage our internal state. We tried suppressing them and meditating our way to a higher vibration. That's called spiritual bypass. We found the best way to release the voices is to let them be heard and fully felt. We give the microphone to the voices of fear and worry and let them speak freely until they have nothing more to say. In these moments, we embody the emotions in order to feel their rawness and intensity. Then we pass the microphone to the higher self and always let it have the last word. This is only but one of the many release practices we have in our toolbox.

As artists of our life, we are free to create anything we envision. Every dream starts with an intentional brush stroke that brings it into reality. Our expression of love has many colors. When one of us walks in the room, we give them our undivided attention because they truly are the most important person in our life. When they speak we hold space so they can be witnessed. When we feel triggered by the other, we receive it with gratitude because we know we have just been shown a wound that asks to be healed. We bring poetry in our life by opening our hearts each morning — sometimes with a cacao ceremony, sometimes by hiding love notes in each other's lunch bags, other times by sharing what we're grateful for, what we desire, and what we recognize in the other, by planning date nights and adventures where only the two of us exist.

We hope our story inspires you to realize that to experience loving connection with your partner, you must first cultivate a loving relationship with yourself. The depth of your love for another is a reflection of your capacity to love yourself. To deepen this capacity you must boldly face the unconscious anchors holding you back from connection. Once you recognize, process, and heal your limiting beliefs and childhood hurts, you become free to connect with your partner at the level of the heart. Abundant with love, you will be able to accept and enjoy each other authentically and commit to a heart-conscious and growth-filled life together, no longer *seeking* and finally *being* Love.

Ignite Action Steps

Look inward

It all starts with you. To have an epic relationship with your partner you must first nurture a healthy and loving relationship with yourself. Make it a regular habit to take time and space for self and build self awareness by becoming your own observer. Journal your reflections daily.

Practice personal responsibility

You are the only one responsible for your life and your happiness. Your current reality is the result of choices you made in the past. Love yourself, you did your best. Start now, consulting with your heart to make the next conscious choice.

Never waste a good trigger!

When you get triggered by your partner, resist the urge to react with blame. Instead, direct your focus back to you. What feelings and beliefs are coming up for you? These are clues to unresolved emotional wounds needing to be processed. As emotions come up, allow yourself to feel and express them through release exercises such as crying, screaming (in a pillow), journaling, talking, or going for a run. Once you've released, listen to what message your heart (higher self) has for you.

Create poetry

Create poetry by bringing rituals to your life to enhance connection, such as going on a new adventure together, and keeping things spicy by taking turns weekly surprising each other with romantic gestures.

Plan

Plan your date night and connection time. In the busy-ness of today's life, if it doesn't go on the calendar, it's not happening. Don't assume things will just happen naturally. You make them happen!

Epilogue

We were very excited about the prospect of sharing our story of conscious love, but we had no idea how powerful it would be to actually come together and write it as we recounted to reflected on our journey, we received the gift of re-living the memories, processing emotional experiences, and deepening our growth and wisdom through the lessons we experienced. We wanted to each take turn sharing our own personal perspectives... the phases of our journey as we each fell in love. The difficulties we encountered nearly separated us; however, we each emerged from the trap of unconscious chains to the freedom of conscious love through commitment and personal responsibility to inner growth. The experience of writing was transformational in itself; it literally took what was inside us and brought it to the outside, expressed through words and forever giving life to our journey. Writing this chapter helped us to transform and grow more deeply than we ever imagined. We are grateful for our love story and for the opportunity to share it with you.

Madalina Petrescu & Cris Agafi – United States of America
Founders of HeartQ
www.heartq.com

HOW DO YOU CHOOSE LOVE?

As Nicole Gibson so eloquently stated in the foreword of this book, love is not only a verb, it's a choice we make daily. On the following pages, you'll find a wealth of inspiration, practical suggestions, and useful tools to help you choose love every day. From positive affirmations that help us shower ourselves with love to romantic date nights and love letters to the Universe, these tools will help you feel that joy and bliss that come from knowing how very loved you are.

SELF-LOVE PROMPTS

Schedule time in your calendar to do an activity you love doing but never find time to do.

Make an appointment for a hair cut, a manicure, or a massage.

Take a look at your To Do list. Move something you love to do and keep putting off to the top of the list.

Who makes you feel loved every time you talk to them? Call them right now.

Show your body some love with a yoga class or gym workout.

Buy yourself flowers. Or jewelry. You don't need a reason to feel special. You ARE special!

So much of our identity gets tangled up in our work. Write a list of all the reasons you love your career.

Stand naked in front of the mirror and smile at yourself. Accept everything you see without judgment. Look deep into your own eyes and let your knowledge of how amazing and unique and wonderful you are shine through and warm you.

Clear your schedule for an afternoon and devote some time to the projects you most want to work on.

Have an imaginary conversation with someone you admire. Tell them all the things about yourself that they would find inspiring.

Put on some great music and get sweaty! Move your body joyfully, secure in the knowledge that your joy is beautiful.

Have a bubble bath with your new bath products.

Spend a day at the spa.

Go to the sex shop and buy the latest toys.

You get to choose your favorite game today. Which is it?

Kiss extra long.

Hug extra tight.

I will prepare a picnic for us to enjoy together; just pick the date.

DATE NIGHT SUGGESTIONS

I just want to cuddle and make out.

I want to do nothing with you without our phones.

I want to adore and love some part of your body. You choose.

I want to lovingly cook your favorite dish. What is it?

What can I do for you to make this day even brighter?

Day Date: Go shopping to your favorite store(s).

Stay in and cuddle while you watch a movie.

Make dinner together.

Day Date: Go on a picnic. Remember to bring a few romantic touches like flowers or a pretty tablecloth.

Stay in bed ALL DAY.

Fix a romantic candlelit dinner, put rose petals up the stairs and on the bed, and send the kids somewhere else for the night.

Have a date night in the city in a luxurious hotel.

Buy tickets to a show that you know your partner would love.

Cuddle beneath the stars while making wishes for our future.

Spend some quiet time together discussing three things we are grateful for.

Spend some quiet time together discussing three things we desire in our relationship.

Take a partner dancing class together.

Date Night - Your Way! Take turns supporting your partner to take you on a date night adventure that is perfect for them. Get curious as to why? Discover something new about the person you love from the inside out.

Got the tickets to the game, wear the scarf!

Swan Lake is in town, wear your LBT, I'll pick you up at 6:00 pm for preshow dinner.

"I AM" AFFIRMATIONS

I am worthy, beautiful, enough, courageous, powerful, abundant, loved,
deserving, brave, confident, capable, radiant...

I am present, resourceful, loving, caring, resilient, compassionate,
daring, collaborative, conscious, connected, deep, infinite, abundant,
spiritual, grounded, peaceful, forgiving...

I am awesome, great, cool, loved, strong, courageous, brave,
legendary, free, clear, happy, successful, a brilliant mum,
prosperous, responsible, open, receptive, an influencer,
an inspirationalist, a great leader, love, potential.

I am deserving of love.

LOVE TICKETS

In a romantic relationship, even the smallest loving gestures can fill us with so much joy. Be a source of happiness for your partner and raise the vibration in your relationship by surprising them with one of the loving thoughts on these Love Tickets. You can tuck one in their lunch box, slide one into their wallet, tuck one into the book they're reading, or tape one to the bathroom mirror so it's the first thing they see after they get up. For a little extra magic, carry the Love Ticket around with you for a few hours first to infuse it with your unique loving energy. Many of these Love Tickets are great for giving to kids, too.

♥ YOU ♥
LIGHT UP
MY LIFE

YOU ARE THE
.... ♥ ....
Love of my Life

YOU MAKE MY HEART GO
PITTER PATTER

KEEP BEING YOU.
YOU ARE
Magnificent.

7 BILLION SMILES,
········· AND ·········
YOURS IS MY
FAVORITE

EVERY LOVE STORY
IS BEAUTIFUL
········· ♥ ·········
BUT OURS IS
MY FAVORITE

WHEN I WAKE UP IN
THE MORNING,
·····················
♥ I THINK OF ♥
YOUR SMILE

♥ My heart ♥
MELTS AT KNOWING
YOU ARE BY MY SIDE.

YOU ARE MY
♥ DREAM ♥
♥ MAKER ♥

YOU MAKE OUR
LOVE STRONGER.
Thank you

LET'S GO

I JUST WANT
YOU TO KNOW.
········· ♥ ·········
OUR LOVE IS
SO DELICIOUS.

YOU ARE THE
BEST THING
THAT HAPPENED
TO ME ♥ ♥ ♥

Have a great day at work!
CAN'T WAIT TO BE WITH
YOU AGAIN IN THE EVENING

I FALL FOR YOUR SMILE
♥
Every single time

I WANTED
TO SHARE
WITH YOU...

LOVE YOU FOR THE
WAY YOU NOTICE
**THE SMALL
THINGS**

I LOVE YOU BECAUSE
**YOU MAKE ME
DREAM**

Let's Talk
I WANT TO BRING
US CLOSER

YOU ARE THE
*Sunshine and
Moonlight*
OF MY LIFE

I LOVE YOU BECAUSE
YOU'RE ALL KINDS OF
WONDERFUL

YOU ARE THE REASON
FOR MY ♥ ♥ ♥
HAPPINESS

LIFE IS AN
ADVENTURE.
LET'S KEEP
EXPLORING.

I FELL IN LOVE
WITH YOU
TODAY
WHEN...

LOVE COUPONS

There's nothing quite like the feeling we get when someone drops everything to devote their full attention to meeting our most deeply-held needs. On the following pages, you'll find Love Coupons you can use to help someone feel absolutely treasured by you.

WATCH A MOVIE/SHOW YOUR PARTNER MOST ENJOYS.

ONE MASSAGE... ON ANY BODY PART YOU'D LIKE.

I WILL TAKE CARE OF THE KIDS FOR ONE HOUR AND GIVE YOU SOME ME-TIME

I WILL DISCONNECT FROM ALL DEVICES AND SPEND TIME WITH YOU WHEN YOU PRESENT THIS COUPON.

I WILL PLAY IN YOUR
SANDBOX ALL DAY.

I WILL PLAY A GAME WITH
YOU OF YOUR CHOICE

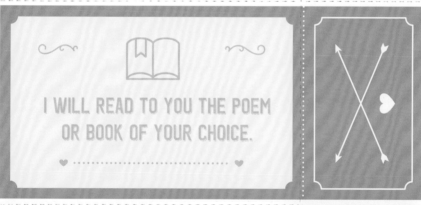

I WILL READ TO YOU THE POEM
OR BOOK OF YOUR CHOICE.

I'LL BE WAITING IN THE BUBBLE
BATH WITH YOUR FAVOURITE DRINK

LOVE LETTERS TO THE UNIVERSE

When we think of love letters, often the first thing that comes to mind is the glorious missives of the great romantic writers of decades past. This is closely followed by memories of the angsty expressions of hormonal attraction our teenage selves scribbled down in journals and notebooks while simultaneously hoping our crush would never actually read these letters and that they would, upon receipt of them, immediately pledge their undying love. But love letters can be so much more than that.

In our romantic relationships, love letters can be the most treasured expressions of caring we ever receive from someone.

Among friends, they can let us know how much we are seen and treasured and valued by the people who are important to us.

At work, they can show us how much we are valued for our skills and contributions to the greater purpose.

Written to the universe, they can be powerful tools to help us manifest our most deeply held needs and desires.

And when they come from ourselves, they can be a powerful reminder of the importance of loving ourselves first, best, and always.

Who are you going to write your love letters to?

I AM SO GRATEFUL FOR YOU BECAUSE...

MY WILDEST DREAM ABOUT YOU IS...

I LOVE YOU BECAUSE...

♥

WHEN I THINK OF YOU, I...

A FAVORITE MEMORY I HAVE OF YOU...

I LOVE YOU FOR TEACHING ME...

♥

YOU STOOD APART FROM THE
REST BECAUSE...

♥

Thank you

A tremendous thank you goes to those who are working in the background editing, supporting, and encouraging the authors. They are some of the most genuine and heart-centered people I know. Their devotion to the vision of IGNITE, their integrity, and the message they aspire to convey is of the highest possible caliber. They all want you to find your IGNITE moment and flourish. They each believe in you and that's what makes them so outstanding. Their dream is for your dreams to come true.

Editing Team: Alex Blake, Andrea Drajewicz, Jock Mackenzie, Nicole Arnold, and Chloe Holewinski

Production Team: Dania Zafar, Peter Giesin & JB Owen

A special thanks and gratitude to the project leaders, Alex Jarvis, Katarina Amadora and Tara Lehman, for their support behind the scenes and for going 'above and beyond' to make this a wonderful experience by ensuring everything ran smoothly and with elegance.

A deep appreciation goes to each and every author who made Ignite Love possible — with all your beautiful stories embracing this powerful idea of the modern goddess found within each and every one of us.

To all our readers, we thank you for reading and loving the stories; for opening your hearts and minds to the idea of Igniting your own lives. We welcome you to share your story and become a new author in one of our upcoming books. Your message and your Ignite moment may be exactly what someone needs to hear.

Join us on this magical Ignite journey!

Alex Jarvis
- https://lonerwolf.com/different-types-of-love/
- https://en.wikipedia.org/wiki/Greek_words_for_love
- https://www.thelovefoundation.com/

Ana Cukrov
- 1 Corinthians 13, New Testament
- The Five Love Languages by Gary Chapman
- Mother Theresa's Sayings

Annie Kallis
- How To Create or Rebuild a Passionate and Intimate Relationship ...Without the Fear of Being Rejected, Criticised or Controlled
- Get my 21 Tips for a Passionate & Intimate Relationship. It is completely FREE and if you'll tell me where to send it, I'll email it to you straight away. http://bit.ly/_21Tips

Anita Adrain
- www.theheartoffengshuisimplyput.com

Deborah Hunt Cook
- Toni Petrinovich Sacred Spaces
- Landmark Worldwide
- Deepak Chopra
- Ren Xue

Capt. Dionysis Drakogiannopoulos
- https://www.instagram.com/CaptainDennyDiary/

Frederic Lafleur-Parfaite

- https://amourkit.com/

Gordana Hay

- Roman philosophy: Marcus Tullius Cicero - considered one of Rome's greatest orators and prose stylists.
- Sufism, the mystical branch of Islam, emphasizes universal love, peace, acceptance of various spiritual paths and a mystical union with the divine.

Ico: The Incredibly Caring Organism/Edward Fish

- NVC (Non-Violent Communication) Needs Inventory: https://www.cnvc.org/training/resource/needs-inventory
- Printable 200 Question BDSM Checklist, created by the Colombia Erotic Power Exchange: http://archive.is/rHcFL
- Difficult Conversations Formula created by Reid Mihalko: http://reidaboutsex.com/difficult-conversation-formula/

Ivana Sošić Antunović

- Holy Bible
- The Art of Loving by Erich Fromm
- Dying to be Me by Anita Moorjani

Madalina Petrescu and Cris Agafi
- Valentintina Simon, Systemic Couples and Family Psychotherapist, www.simoninstitute.ro
- Hoffman Process-, www.hoffmaninstitute.org
- Dr. Heike and Jonathan Hudson, Revolutionary Somatic Bodyworkers, www.sextraordinaryliving.com
- Landmark Forum, www.landmarkworldwide.com
- Venant Wong, Founder of KAP - Kundalini Activation Process, www.venantwong.com

Natalie Syrmopoulos
- Balancing Act, by Raising Humanity
- The Four Agreements by Don Miguel Ruiz
- Connected Parenting by Jennifer Kolari

Toma Molerov
- Mindvalley - mindvalley.com
- Evercoach - evercoach.com

PHOTO CREDITS

Adriana Maia Troxler - *Martin Häusler*
Alex Jarvis - *John McRae*
Annie Kallis - *Kosta Iatrou from Ikon Images*
Capt. Dionysis Drakogiannopoulos - *Melia*
Gordana Hay - *Vladan Milisavljević. Belgrade*
Ivana Sošić Antunović - *Marie Kinkela*
JB Owen & Peter Giesin - *Kersti Niglas*
Julianne McGowan - *Stephanie Mohan*
Natalie Syrmopoulos - *Kanellos*
Piret Špitsmeister - *Kersti Niglas*
Toma Molerov - *Alberto Rossini*
Tracy Finkel - *Doug Ellis*

Leading the industry in Empowerment Publishing,
IGNITE transforms individuals into
INTERNATIONAL BESTSELLING AUTHORS.

WRITE YOUR STORY IN AN IGNITE BOOK!!

With over 400 amazing individuals to date writing their stories and sharing their Ignite moments, we are positively impacting the planet and raising the vibration of HUMANITY. Our stories inspire and empower others and we want to add your story to one of our upcoming books!

If you have a story of perseverance, determination, growth, awakening and change... and you've felt the power of your Ignite moment, we'd love to hear from you.

Go to our website, click How To Get Started and share a bit of your Ignite transformation.

We are always looking for motivating stories that will make a difference in someone's life. Our fun, enjoyable, four-month writing process is like no other — and the best thing about Ignite is the community of outstanding, like-minded individuals dedicated to helping others.

Our road to sharing your message and becoming a bestselling author begins right here.

YOU CAN IGNITE ANOTHER SO JOIN US TO
IGNITE A BILLION LIVES WITH A BILLION WORDS.

Apply at: www.igniteyou.life
Inquire at: info@igniteyou.life

Find out more at: www.igniteyou.life